Children of Drug Abusers

Children of Drug Abusers

by

by

Stephen Jay Levy

and

Eileen Rutter

LEXINGTON BOOKS
An Imprint of Macmillan, Inc.
NEW YORK
Maxwell Macmillan Canada
TORONTO
Maxwell Macmillan International
NEW YORK   OXFORD   SINGAPORE   SYDNEY

Library of Congress Cataloging-in-Publication Data

Levy, Stephen J.
    Children of drug abusers / Stephen J. Levy, Eileen Rutter.
      p. cm.
    Includes bibliographical references and index.
    ISBN 0-669-27332-5 (alk. paper,
     1. Children of narcotic addicts—United States. 2. Narcotic
addicts—United States—Family relationships. 3. Children of
narcotic addicts—Health and hygiene. I. Rutter, Eileen.
II. Title.
HV5824.C45L48 1991
362.29'13—dc20   91-3704
                                            CIP

Lexington Books
An Imprint of Macmillan, Inc.
866 Third Avenue, New York, N. Y. 10022

Macmillan, Inc. is part of the Maxwell Communication
Group of Companies.

Printed in the United States of America

printing number
1 2 3 4 5 6 7 8 9 10

Contents

4 Healing the Children: A Call for a New Advocacy
   System   127

5 Treating the Children of Drug Abusers   167

Preface

"Once upon a time . . ." clinicians had the opportunity of working in all kinds of social agencies, where they performed most of their work with families who were free from the ravages of drug abuse. If, upon completion of intake and assessment, the family appeared to have problems with drug abuse or addiction, they were referred out!

Few practitioners sought out clinical assignments with families and children caught in the web of addictive behavior. After all, "clean" patients were plentiful and they showed up for appointments, were highly motivated for treatment, and offered little therapeutic resistance. Clinicians were suspicious and frightened of clients troubled by drug abuse and thus preferred to let the drug-abuse treatment community "handle" their problems. But the times they are a changing!

American society is threatened by the use of horribly destructive drugs whose users come from all class and economic backgrounds. All of us, regardless of social station, are threatened by the ravages of the crime, family disorganization, and declining human productivity that is a result of drug abuse. Entire clinical treatment communities, wearing blinders, have walked along the safe and narrow path of traditional clinical practice for too long. Their blinders allowed them to separate thinking from feeling, thus widening the gap between a growing social/health problem and the availability of trained professionals to combat it.

As our nation geared up to fight the "War on Drugs," our clinicians remained anonymous managers, not leaders. They languished on the sidelines as the law enforcement community and the "Just Say No" crowd took over. The latter's first act in the war on drug abuse was to deeply slash the budgets of the National Institute on Drug Abuse, the National Institute on Alcoholism and Alcohol Abuse, and the National Institute on Mental Health!

The children of drug abusers had already begun a course of unprecedented suffering. They were the very "silent minority" while the children of the drug-free led relatively carefree lives. When the children of the drug-free run into difficulties they reap the rich rewards of an eager, professionally trained helping community. A group of helpers who were never better trained and who have spent their professional lives mending children and families awaits the privileged child. They stand ready, fully committed to working with the middle class and the wealthy, those with the right insurance coverage, and the "clean"!

The authors hope that this book will be more than just another book. It is intended as a manifesto for a change of policy, a change of attitude, and a change of heart—one that we hope will be felt as well as understood. The children you are about to read about need our help, and they need it now!

Children of Drug Abusers was written out of our love for babies, children, and teenagers.

Happiness is probably the easiest emotion to feel, the most elusive to create, and the most difficult to define. Its absence, ironically, is all too readily registered and observed.

"Happily ever after" should not be an ending reserved solely for the lucky and the strong!

Acknowledgments

Many have contributed to the thinking that led us to write this book.

Our clients must remain anonymous, but it is their voices that are heard throughout this book.

We would like to thank our colleagues, the foster care and administrative staff of the Saint Agatha's Home of the New York Foundling Hospital, to whom we are indebted for their unstinting exchange of theoretical ideas. We would also like to thank Mr. George R. Doering, Jr., Executive Director of Youth Counseling Services, Town of Ramapo (Rockland County, New York) for enabling the authors to initially work together and for his encouragement of excellence in the treatment and prevention of drug abuse. We also thank Dr. Sherry Deren of the Narcotic and Drug Research, Inc. in New York City for sharing with us her knowledge of the research literature on the children.

1

The Children of Heroin

Mother Is Charged in Assault on Baby. . . . A woman is accused of giving her 3-month-old daughter a bottle of methadone to make her stop crying. . . . The baby's father awoke to find the infant rigid and barely breathing. . . . the mother said she gave the baby the methadone to make her sleep. . . . the baby is listed in critical condition. . . . mother is charged with first and second degree assault, reckless endangerment and endangering the welfare of a child. . . . she is being held in $2,500 bail. . . . her 11-year-old son and the infant are now in the custody of the city's Special Services for Children.

—*New York Times,* 6 August 1989

"My kids are part of me. When you look at kids, you know, like kids are helpless. . . . like, when I look at my kids I see myself because I'm helpless too. . . . When you become addicted, usin' stuff. . . . is as much a part of you as bein' a husband, a father, provider or whatever. It's an integral part of you."

—Icepick, a male heroin addict (from *Life with Heroin*)

"At first I hid my percodan addiction. I would score from the pharmacist at the hospital where I was a nurse. It was a trade-off . . . a little sex for a few pills. I knew I was in trouble when, one night, I fell asleep at home with a lit cigarette in my hand. One of my two kids received third-degree burns trying to put out the fire. I was so stoned I slept until the fire department got there."

—An addict named Marie

"A lot of conflict came in with my family 'cause I'm not working. The kids need this, you need that. . . . I don't have it to give them, sometimes. . . . I only have enough to take care of me and there's not even enough to do that."

—Slim, a male heroin addict (from *Life with Heroin*)

"I want to live with my parents. I don't care if they are drug addicts. The court makes me live with people I don't know. I want my mommy and daddy back. Please help me!"

—Luz, age six, child of heroin addicts, currently living in foster care

"When we came to pick up John and his sister we found the children were living in squalor. There was no food in the refrigerator, the apartment was filthy, there was no toilet paper. The place was littered with empty glacine envelopes, dirty works, and broken needles. There were no toys. When we arrived John was reading a sexually explicit pamphlet on AIDS prevention to his sister that had been provided to his mother by an outreach worker from the needle exchange program. How can parents do this to their kids? My god, these two are only seven and two!

—Social worker from the Bureau of Child Welfare

"I lost my father twice. First, he became a junkie and I saw less and less of him. Then he got AIDS—he was real sick before he died. Like I said, I lost him twice."

—Bernard, age sixteen, son of a deceased addict

The children of heroin addicts have existed for many years but they have never commanded the same degree of public and media attention as the children of cocaine—crack cocaine in particular. Heroin addicts usually commit crimes against property, not crimes against persons. Cocaine addicts commit crimes against both property and people. They often carry guns and terrorize entire neighborhoods. Heroin addicts by contrast were "invisible." So were their children! Cocaine addiction probably represents the first true drug "epidemic" in American society: hundreds of thousands of addicts have come into being in just under five years (1985–90). While U.S. society has made a comparatively great noise about heroin addiction as a social problem, the public's imagination has never been ignited by the plight of these addicts or the plight of their children. Indeed, no one seemed to mind very much as long as heroin was confined to the slums of America. But when white kids started getting strung out on drugs in the late sixties and early seventies (some during their military service in Southeast Asia) a hue and cry went up and funds started to flow. Unfortunately, while treatment services for adult addicts proliferated, programs for suffering families and children failed to materialize. Except for extraordinary efforts by people like "Mother" Clara Hale in Harlem taking in very young children, nothing much was happening for the children of heroin.

Major efforts to help heroin addicts began in the late 1950s with the advent of Synanon on the West Coast. Synanon was the first of the drug-free therapeutic community programs founded on the principles of strict abstinence within an extended tribal family (Yablonsky, 1965; Deleon, 1984). Synanon was followed by Daytop, Phoenix House, Marathon House, Guadenzia House, and others too numerous to mention here. All operate on the premise that the addict is developmentally blocked and character-disordered. To end his/her addiction, the addict must learn to drop his/her character distortions and street "games" and live a more value-based functional existence in the community, after residing in the therapeutic community for twelve to eighteen months.

The mid-1960s saw the formalization of early experiments with methadone, a synthetic narcotic, into a formal treatment regimen (Dole & Nyswander, 1965, 1976). By the late 1980s some 35,000 men and women were being maintained on methadone in the State of New York alone. Methadone blocks the opiate euphoria induced by heroin when taken at appropriate dose levels and when the client does not purposely overwhelm the blockade effect with additional self-administered opiates. Methadone has no significant clinical action with other drugs such as alcohol or cocaine or marijuana in terms of blocking their effects. Although methadone treatment has generated a great deal of sociopolitical debate, sometimes heated and rancorous, outcome studies for this type of treatment indicate that significant numbers of heroin addicts do get off the addiction merry-go-round. When addicts cease intravenous drug use, they reduce their risk of contracting AIDS, ARC, HIV contamination, endocarditis, abscesses, sores, and venereal disease, and they give up the criminal practices so often characteristic of the addictive life-style. Many go to work and school and become homemakers.

What about the children of these addicts? As the heroin treatment system grew by leaps and bounds thanks to large infusions of federal monies beginning in the early 1970s, what was happening to the children of addicts? In 1980 Dr. Barbara Sowder and Marvin Burt reviewed the literature on the children of heroin and concluded, "The literature, in summary, told us very little about children of addicts. The research that had been conducted up to 1976 was focused largely on young children born to addicted women. There was little information about older children of addicts or about children who live with addicted parents but who were not necessarily exposed to heroin in utero" (Sowder & Burt, 1980, p. xxv).

Dr. Sherry Deren reviewed the literature on children of heroin whom she named "children of substance abusers," or COSAs, in 1986. While a convenient shorthand, we do not use this or any other acronym to describe the children of drug abusers. We believe that this detracts from consideration of each child as a unique individual. It is important to note that Deren's review focused on studies of children of heroin addicts. Neither she nor anyone else foresaw the impact that cocaine—particularly crack—would have on the drug scene, the family, and children. In 1988 it was estimated that there were almost one-half million COSAs in New York State alone. The number of babies born to cocaine-addicted mothers had caught up to the number of babies born to heroin-addicted mothers by 1986 (Deren, 1988). Deren's seminal survey article covers studies dating from the mid-1970s to the mid-1980s. Dr. Deren, like Dr. Sowder, observed that most of this work concentrated on examing the effects of maternal heroin or methadone use on the neonate.

As both methadone-maintenance and drug-free programs proliferated, several important facts began to emerge.

The Impact of Drug Abuse on Women and Children

The proportion of women entering treatment for heroin addiction was growing. Prior to the advent of crack addiction most heroin treatment programs reported ratios of three to four men for every one woman in treatment. Demographic surveys were never clear about the actual ratio of males to females in the heroin-using population. According to the federal Client Oriented Data Acquisition Project (CODAP), statistics maintained by the National Institute on Drug Abuse (NIDA) in their Report of Drug Abuse Treatment and Rehabilitation Services in December of 1973, 20 percent of clients across the nation were women. By 1981 the figure had risen to 30 percent.

The vast majority of these women were of childbearing age (sixteen to forty). During his many years with the Addiction Branch of the National Institute of Mental Health and later with the Services Research Branch of the National Institute on Drug Abuse, George Beschner promoted important, seminal research. Beschner and Thompson (1981), in reviewing earlier studies, found that 67–73 percent of the women entering drug-abuse treatment were mothers. Colten (1980) reported that 58 percent of women in treatment for heroin addiction had some or all of their children living with them when they first entered treatment. The Division of Substance Abuse of the Albert Einstein College of Medicine in New York City operates a methadone-maintenance program serving 3,200 patients in eight clinics. They report that approximately 75 percent of the patients are parents. Eighty percent of the 5,000 children of these patients are in parental custody and another 20 percent are in foster care.

Despite a rapidly expanding literature on the children of alcoholics (Woititz, 1983; Russell, Henderson, & Blume, 1984), very little is known about the children of substance abusers. Estimates of the number of heroin addicts in New York State have remained relatively stable since the early 1970s at 250,000. National estimates for heroin addiction run around 500,000. In contrast, national estimates for alcoholism indicate 10,000,000 alcoholics and another 7,000,000 alcohol abusers. The children-of-alcoholics movement is primarily a white, middle-class phenomena. The children of heroin and cocaine addicts are primarily nonwhite, minority members who live in poverty. They have no national movement. They do not write books and make the rounds of the talk shows. In New York State alone, the estimated number of children of substance abusers is 467,000—or approximately one out of ten children in the State. Of 24,000 babies born to drug-abusing women in New York State in

1986, 2,600 births were attributed to narcotics-abusing women (Deren, 1988).

Virtually nothing has been published concerning the role of male heroin addicts as fathers. Slim and Icepick—the addicts quoted at the beginning of this chapter—epitomize the childlike, irresponsible, selfish, and chauvinistic behavior of many males. Heroin addiction has contributed greatly to the breakup of families, particularly in the slums of America. Researchers have noted again and again that female clients who enter treatment are far more likely than male clients to have responsibility for dependent children (Beschner, Reed, & Mondanaro, 1981).

Treatment programs for heroin addicts are uniquely male-oriented and male-dominated, a situation that reflects the fact that most addicts are male, but that also mirrors the sexual politics of the drug scene and the larger society. Female addicts were not being given equal opportunities for personal growth in treatment (Levy & Doyle, 1974; Levy, 1975; Levy & Broudy, 1975; Beschner & Brotman, 1976; Levy and Doyle, 1976). As we have already documented, mothers are the primary caretakers of dependent children. When treatment fails to serve women properly, the family suffers as a direct consequence of this failure.

Nationally fewer than 1 percent of treatment programs for heroin addicts provide directly for the needs of clients as parents. As a consequence of this poor policy, very few children have been served by these programs during the past twenty years. Programs that directly serve addicts as parents and bring the family together for treatment only began to appear in the mid-to-late 1980s (Beschner, Reed, & Mondanaro, 1981).

The child welfare and child mental health fields were having no direct impact on the heroin addiction treatment field. Addiction workers had to begin helping the children more directly (Juliana et al., 1989). The child mental health field did not see the children of heroin addicts as a clear priority and as a target population for their services. The child welfare system was acting to divert some addicts into treatment and many of their children into foster care. Sadly, neither these two systems nor the addiction treatment field were directly serving the multiple needs of the children and the addicted parent(s).

Dr. M. Duncan Stanton reviewed the treatment literature (1985) and conducted his own studies on how addicted families differ from other dysfunctional families. He offers the following impressions:

- An addict's family exhibits a higher frequency of multigenerational chemical dependency—particularly for alcohol among males—plus a propensity for other addictionlike behaviors such as gambling. (Such practices provide modeling for children and also can develop into family traditions.)
- The addict's family appears to be characterized by more primitive and direct expressions of conflict, with quite explicit (versus covert) alliances, for example, between the addict and the overinvolved parent.
- Addictive parents' behavior is "conspicuously unschizophrenic."
- Addicts may have a peer group or subculture to which they (briefly) retreat following family conflict—but the illusion of independence is greater than its reality.
- Mothers of addicts display "symbiotic" childrearing practices further into the life of the child, and show greater symbiotic needs, than mothers of schizophrenics or normals.
- An addicts family exhibits a preponderance of death themes and premature, unexpected, or untimely deaths within the family.
- The symptom of addiction provides a form of "pseudoindividuation" (false independence) at several levels, extending from the individual-pharmacological level to that of the drug subculture.
- The rate of addiction among offspring of immigrants is greater than might be expected, suggesting the importance of acculturation and parent-child cultural disparity in addiction.

Sexism in Drug-Abuse Treatment Programs

Against this backdrop of addicted family life we can pose the question How well do addiction treatment programs meet the needs of women as clients? The answer, unfortunately, is not very well, which bodes poorly for these women and for their children. During his tenure as director of the Division of Drug Abuse at the New Jersey College of Medicine and Dentistry in the mid-1970s, Dr. Levy and his coauthors conducted several studies and published several papers concerning sexist attitudes and policies in both a large therapeutic community and a major urban methadone-maintenance clinic in New Jersey. The major findings are reported below (Levy & Doyle, 1974; Levy, 1975; Levy & Broudy, 1975; Levy & Doyle, 1976; and Levy, 1981). The information reported here will help the reader to understand why during the past several decades the needs of heroin-dependent women (and, as a consequence, their children) were not met by most treatment agencies. The implications for the children of heroin addicts are staggering when one stops to think the best we had to offer women in mainstream addiction programs failed to such a significant extent.

The Therapeutic Community Study

• Male staff predominate in administrative and clinical decision-making positions. This ratio prevails despite the fact that all staff stressed the importance of same-sex-staff and peer-level-residents to client retention in the program, particularly in the first four weeks.

• Female residents were viewed as more emotional, more sensitive, limited by their biology, needing to please men, and implicitly "sicker" than men. Women are also seen as having poor relationships with the opposite sex, difficulty being a parent, bad feelings about their bodies, and as being childish and dependent. Men, in contrast, are viewed as lacking job training, being passive, and having no desire to improve themselves. Greater emphasis is placed on interpersonal relationships (i.e., "having a man") for women and on competence and striving for men.

• A comparison of client's stated problems with staff perceptions of their problems revealed a lack of awareness and sensitivity and sensitivity to client problems overall and women's problems in particular. Residents reported significantly more concern over lack of job training, poor family relationships, poor relationships with the opposite sex, childishness, lack of education, suicide attempts, dependency, bad feelings about body, prejudice, and not feeling smart. Significant discrepancies for women appeared on these dimensions, the most important of which were bad feelings about body, suicide attempts, and not feeling smart. There is a tendency to perceive all clients as "dope fiends" and a failure to attend to individual and sex differences (Levy, 1973).

- The Attitudes toward Women scale (Spence & Helmreich, 1973) revealed that staff members hold only somewhat liberal attitudes regarding the rights and roles of women in society and that the women who work in therapeutic communities (T.C.'s) must meet some implicit criteria that makes them similar to males in their orientation toward female clients.
- While staff agreed that all residents should share all work therapy functions in the T.C., an analysis of actual job assignments revealed a profound difference between men and women.
- When queried about sex, crime, and life on the street, the answers revealed a consistently conservative strain of sexist thinking that mirrors views of the society at large more than the unique addict subculture.
- No unique programs for families such as couples therapy, parent skills workshops, or family therapy were made available to male or female clients. The program made no provisions for child care while parents were in treatment.

The Methadone-Maintenance (MMTP) Study

- Employed female clients earn significantly less for comparable work than males. Over half the men were employed while only 20 percent of the women were employed.
- Considerably more male clients than women clients perceived being in a methadone-maintenance program as improving their lives. Men stressed material gains while women stressed personal gains.
- Most clients felt hampered by a lack of education and a lack of job training, and believed that they were looked down on by society because they are addicts. Women reported these feelings more intensely than men and also felt burdened by bad feelings about their bodies and poor relationships with the opposite sex. More women than men stated that they were troubled by poor physical health and problems in expressing their feelings.
- Staff more readily failed to perceive the problems reported by female clients than those reported by male clients despite the fact that the majority of staff were women. Once again, staff failed to perceive the extent to which women are troubled by lack of a job and money to support themselves and their families.

• Staff perceived the lower ratio of women in treatment as the fault of the program and a failure to reach out to and offer needed services to women (and their children).

• Methadone clinics failed to offer services such as parent skills workshops, couples therapy, or family therapy. No day care or baby-sitting services were available to help families make clinic appointments without disruption of family life.

We have now seen that the emerging treatment systems of the 1970s and 1980s failed to create a solid foundation of knowledge or understanding in three basic areas:

1. Children of substance abusers
2. Meeting and defining needs of women in treatment
3. Treating male addicts as fathers

A study done for the U.S. Office for Civil Rights on the extent of sex discrimination in health and human development services (Naierman et al., 1979) found that drug and alcohol services were generally most deficient in (1) their availability to women; (2) types and quality of support services needed by women; and (3) adequacy of their referral and follow-up procedures for women. With things in such dismal shape for women, was it any wonder that programs for children also failed to develop or thrive?

Joanie's Story

"I've been on the streets for years. My old man used to beat me and my mother up regularly. I started using heroin at age fifteen and turning tricks at sixteen. Forget about high school. Life was happening out there—on the street. My two kids are with my old lady. I lost 'em when I went into treatment. Treatment, yeah that's a laugh! As if I didn't feel badly enough about myself. The male staff and the residents made me feel like a two-bit whore. Maybe that's what I was, but they rubbed my face in it. I split and got high the second week I was there. I tried talking to a female staff member but she was meaner than the guys. Treatment—what a joke. Two staff members were trying to get into my pants! It would have served 'em right if I did ball them—I have syphilis and gonorrhea. Listen, I know I'm a dope fiend and a lousy mother. So why should I stop shooting drugs? Just give me my drugs and leave me alone. Who cares—do you?"

Joanie died of an overdose at age twenty-three. Her children were placed with her mother, who died two years later. The two children were then placed in foster care, in separate homes. Could a more sensitive, caring, and well-trained treatment staff have made a difference? It is hard to say for sure. Joanie had been through so much. But her sad story certainly makes the point that treating drug abuse has to do with a lot more than just drugs. Joanie and her children did not receive the help they needed.

What Is Known about Children of Substance Abusers?

Dr. Deren's review of the literature on the children of drug abusers dates primarily from the mid-1970s and points to the fact that most such work has concentrated on examining the effects of maternal heroin or methadone use on the neonate. Only in the last few years before the end of the review period in 1985 did Deren discover explorations of the consequences of maternal drug addiction on the older child—but these studies are still few in number. She also points out the major methodological weaknesses in the COSA literature. These weaknesses point to future directions for our research.

Weaknesses in the COSA Literature*

- □ Inadequate comparison groups
- □ Lack of differentiation of the mother's pattern of substance abuse (polydrug, single drug, various drug combinations)
- □ Lack of studies of COSAs whose mothers are not in treatment
- □ Lack of knowledge about families in which the father or both parents are drug abusers
- □ Small sample sizes that do not allow for within-group comparisons of generalization (high drop-out rates are also common)
- □ Lack of studies that control for characteristics of the mother other than drug use (maternal health, personality, parenting skills, and environmental factors)

*From Deren 1986, p. 90.

Deren further points out that, despite the review of a relatively large number of studies and papers, "little of a cumulative nature has been learned," and attributes this failure to "the lack of theoretical underpinnings and to the methodological problems which are to be found in the literature on COSAs." We must note that the apparent unanimity of the literature concerned with children of alcoholics stems from the fact that the field tends to be dominated by a single point of view—the disease concept of alcoholism—while the drug-abuse treatment field is characterized by far less agreement concerning the basic nature of addictive behaviors (chemotherapy model versus personality disorder model versus disease model). The children-of-alcoholics movement tends to be dominated by a nonscientific spiritual posture that is long on rhetoric and short on empirical data. It also suffers from the same methodological criticisms leveled by Dr. Deren against the COSA literature Woititz, 1983; Peele, 1989). The literature drawn from this era sheds the first light on the travails of the children of heroin.

The Effects of Opiate Addiction on the Pregnant Addict and the Fetus

"Yes, hope for a miracle, but as a Jewish sage suggested, don't depend on one."

Kaestner and her colleagues were among the first to document the rising number of women in the drug scene (Kaestner et al., 1986) and with them the rising number of children of drug abusers. Many of the addicted women we have known managed to escape detection and identification as addicted mothers by the medical and other authorities who track such things. Meyer and Black (1977) pointed out that addict women give birth more often than the general population. However, births to addicts go unreported as births by addicts due to physician reluctance to report addicted newborns, lying by mothers and fathers about their addictive behavior, births that occur outside hospitals, and the fact that an unknown number of pregnant addicts stop using drugs prior to or during pregnancy. We would add that drug screens (toxicologies) of the urine of newborns is a recent phenomenon. Cuskey and Wathey (1982) estimated that in the mid-1970s more than 234,000 children in the United States had mothers who were addicted to heroin. Carr (1975) estimated that in New York City, as of 1975, 93,000 children had mothers who were addicted to illegal opiates and 22,000 children had mothers undergoing methadone-maintenance treatment.

Dr. Deren in her review of the literature points out that we lack estimates for the number of children whose drug-abusing mothers abused multiple substances or for those children who come from households where the father or both parents are drug abusers. This is a serious gap in our knowledge base because other research has pointed to the fact that medical and psychological problems mount as the numbers of sustances abused sequentially or simultaneously rises (Barr & Cohen, 1979). Addicted fathers such as Slim and Icepick seem only to speak to us in whispers. Estimates of the number of children of drug addicts have increased with the advent of freebase cocaine and crack.

The proceedings of a symposium on comprehensive health care for addicted families and their children, published by NIDA in the mid-1970s (Beschner & Brotman, 1976), was among the first documents to pay serious attention to the needs of the children of drug addicts. George Beschner commented in the introduction, "Despite the overall reduction in the birth rate in the United States, many hospitals have reported sharp increases in one such group: drug-addicted mothers. The adverse effects of narcotic drugs on these women and their newborn has been well documented. . . . Children born to addicted mothers experience more physiological problems and have higher mortality rates than children born to nonaddicted women from the same socioeconomic class."

Concern for the children of drug addicts has never coalesced into a movement on behalf of these children; moreover, the literature on this subject remains in its infancy. In fact, prior to the advent of the crack epidemic of the 1980s, Beschner's hope for more scientific research on the children of heroin addicts was barely realized. They remained the forgotten victims of the drug-abuse problem in America.

The *Final Report of the White House Conference for a Drug Free America* was published with great hoopla and fanfare in June 1988. It contains literally hundreds of recommendations. Yet the education section contains no recognition of the problem or strategies for helping the children of drug addicts in school settings. The prevention section makes no mention of the children of drug addicts at all. The criminal justice system section makes no mention of addicts as parents or the fate of their children. The treatment section makes no mention of female addicts or of their children or of male addicts as fathers. These are the fruits of a negligent and barren national drug policy during the 1980s in America. Fortunately for the children, a few clinicians and researchers were studying and attempting to help children of drug-addicted parents.

Dr. Miryam Davis reported (in the 1976 symposium proceedings mentioned above) the results of urine surveillance randomly obtained once to thrice weekly, without prior notice, to pregnant patients enrolled in a Washington, D.C., methadone-maintenance treatment program; the samples were analyzed by gas-liquid chromatography for the presence of drug metabolites. Table 1-1 shows the patterns of prenatal drug intake for thirty-six women enrolled in two "low-dose" methadone-maintenance clinics (doses ranged from 5mg./day to 35 mg./day, with a mean dose level of 18 mg./day). Dosage was kept low to minimize risks to both mother and fetus. These women were volunteers in a NIDA-funded study on the long-term development of methadone-exposed offspring. They received

TABLE 1-1.

Incidence of Illegal Drug Abuse in Pregnancy
(Expressed in percentage)

	Clinic A Group (N = 21)	Clinic B Group (N = 15)
Polydrug abuse only, frequent	38.1	13.3
Polydrug abuse only, infrequent	9.5	0.0
Heroin abuse in early pregnancy only (up to 28 wks.), frequent	9.5	0.0
Heroin abuse in early pregnancy only (up to 28 wks.), infrequent	0.0	6.7
Heroin abuse in late pregnancy only (after 28 wks.), frequent	4.8	20.0
Heroin abuse throughout pregnancy, frequent	28.6	60.0
Heroin abuse throughout pregnancy, infrequent	4.8	0.0
No polydrug or heroin abuse	4.8	0.0

"personalized, high quality of obstretrical care" (Davis, 1976). Furthermore, all mothers were evaluated prenatally and the researchers followed the infants through serial neurological examinations from birth onward. Comprehensive pediatric care was also provided throughout the project. The table categorizes prenatal drug intake; the results speak for themselves. What is particularly notable is that 60 percent of the women in clinic B and 28.6 percent of the women in clinic A regularly and frequently supplemented their methadone dosage with heroin throughout pregnancy. Another 20 percent of clinic B women began frequent heroin use during the later stages of pregnancy.

It is important to understand that a totally drug-free environment would be the ideal state during pregnancy and just before delivery. However, few drug-free programs accept pregnant addicts, fewer provide for the needs of their newborns, and, as indicated earlier, these old-line heroin treatment programs are not well disposed toward recognizing and meeting the needs of women in general. Finnegan and Wapner (1987) inform us regarding abstinence during pregnancy:

> Unfortunately, the course of abstinence in heroin addicts during pregnancy is not smooth. Pregnant women recently detoxified from narcotics have the same high rate of recidivism as non-pregnant addicts and thus become resubjected to all of the attendant complications of illicit heroin use. The return to illicit heroin injection exposes the fetus to the risk of varying narcotic levels, which may well result in transient periods of fetal depression alternating with abstinence. Uterine contractions during maternal withdrawal cause an intermittent obstruction to placental perfusion resulting in intermitten fetal hypoxia [deprivation of oxygen]. (210)

Foremost among those studying and caring for the children of heroin-abusing and methadone-maintained mothers is Loretta P. Finnegan, M.D., founder and director of the Jefferson Hospital Family Center in Philadelphia, an outpatient facility offering comprehensive treatment for future, expectant, recent mothers and other women who abuse a variety of substances. Dr. Finnegan has authored a number of studies documenting the impact of opiate dependency on the fetus and neonate (Finnegan, Connaughton, Kron, & Emich, 1975; Finnegan, 1976; Connaughton, Reeser, & Finnegan,

1977; Finnegan, 1979; Finnegan & Fehr, 1980; Finnegan 1982; Finnegan, 1983; and Finnegan & Wapner, 1987).

The medical complications encountered in pregnant addicts have been well documented over several decades by Dr. Finnegan and her associates. She found medical complications in 40–50 percent of pregnant addicts. A list of the main complications appears below.

Medical Complications Encountered in Pregnant Addicts*

Anemia
Bacteremia
Cardiac disease, especially endocarditis
Cellulitis
Poor dental hygiene
Edema
Hepatitis, acute and chronic
Phlebitis
Pneumonia
Septicemia
Tetanus
Tuberculosis
Urinary tract infection:
    Cystitis
    Urethritis
    Pyelonephritis
Venereal disease:
    Condyloma acuminatum
    Gonorrhea
    Herpes
    Syphilis

Dr. Finnegan and her colleagues also documented the obstetrical complications associated with heroin addiction. They are summarized in the list below.

Obstetrical Complications Associated with Heroin Addiction†

Abortion	Intrauterine death
Abruptio placenta	Intrauterine growth retardation

*From Finnegan & Wapner, 1987, p. 207
†From Finnegan, 1982, p. 58

Amnionitis	Placental insufficiency
Breech presentation	Postpartum hemorrhage
Previous ceasarian section	Preeclampsia
Chorloamnionitis	Premature labor
Eclampsia	Premature rupture of membrane
Gestational diabetes	Septic thrombophlebitis

Addicted mothers often fail to realize that they are pregnant. The three classic medical indicators of pregnancy are a history of amenorrhea, a positive pregnancy test, and palpation of the gravid uterus. In the pregnant addict none of these indicators are reliable. Dr. Finnegan points out that some of the early signs of pregnancy experienced by the patient, such as fatigue, nausea and vomiting, headaches, hot sweats, and pelvic cramps, are often interpreted by pregnant addicts (and their physicians) as withdrawal signs rather than as indications of possible pregnancy. Unaware of their pregnant state, these women have continued to shoot dope! Continued drug use increases the amount of drugs delivered to the fetus as well as the dangers of secondary infections caused by drug impurities and unsterilized "works" (paraphenalia such as dirty cotton, bottle caps, hypodermic needles, etc.)—infections including hepatitis B, venous thrombosis, abcess, and AIDS.

Bi-annual pelvic examinations to palpate the uterus are difficult with addicted women. Generally, these women have poor relationships with doctors and do not react well to pelvic examinations. Pelvic infections, including pelvic inflamatory disease (PID), may lead to patient discomfort or distorting masses. Fecal impaction (constipation) from opiates can also lead to an inaccurate pelvic examination.

Dr. Finnegan and others emphasize that not knowing one is pregnant until one is "showing" at approximately five to seven months means not receiving prenatal care up until that point and almost always means continuous use of opiates. Rosenbaum (1979) studied one hundred women addicts and found that many often reported that they had assumed dysmenorrhea was due to being addicted and only became aware of their pregnancies when they began showing. All the studies we read and all the doctors we spoke to agree on one central theme: *The medical and obstretrical complications of pregnancy can be reduced with proper prenatal care.*

Several studies (Dickey & Hall, 1978; Suffet & Brotman, 1984) have shown that women heroin addicts in methadone-maintenance programs have a greater chance of having their pregnancies detected earlier. These studies also indicated that adequate prenatal care for methadone—maintained pregnant women led to a significant reduction in obstretrical complications. We could not find any reports on pregnant women participating in drug-free treatment programs. We certainly need to know the course of pregnancies in "clean" addicts, as contrasted with methadone-maintained women and of both groups in contrast to untreated women. Conspicious by its total absence from all of the literature we reviewed is what happens to those addicts Dr. Howard Shaffer of the Harvard Center for Addiction Studies calls "self-quitters" (Schaffer & Jones, 1989). That is, what happens to addicted women who successfully quit using opiates on their own? How eventful, by contrast with these other addicted women, is the course of their pregnancies? Clearly, the earlier women enter treatment and the earlier they receive prenatal care, the less likely the chance of their developing pregnancy complications.

Before moving on to consider the specific effects of heroin addiction on the newborn it is essential that we comment on an aspect of the problem only alluded to in the literature on the children of heroin addicts. The overall life-style of most addicts is detrimental to both the fetus and the children of heroin addicts. For example, fetal health is further compromised by the ravages of an *impoverished life-style* (Sowder & Burt, 1980). When a mother does not eat properly neither does her fetus. When a mother smokes cigarettes she harms her own health and that of her fetus. When a mother suffers from venereal disease so does her fetus. When a pregnant addict is battered by her husband or paramour (her "old man") or her trick (if she is a prostitute) the fetus is battered, too. When a mother lives in a filthy, vermin-infested apartment with no heat or hot water, and feels helpless and hopeless, her fetus suffers along with her. And, as Deren (1986) has so cogently pointed out, until studies compare addicted pregnant women with unaddicted pregnant women from the same community, we cannot determine what are the effects of addiction on the fetus (and neonate). A life spent in poverty in and of itself has adverse effects on mothers and their children. We cannot hope to tease apart that which is unique to additive behavior and that which is unique to other problems experienced in poverty (poor nutrition, venereal disease, smoking, poor health of the mother, etc.) without such well-controlled comparison studies. This was a serious problem encountered by Sowder and Burt (1980) when they attempted to study the children of heroin. They had a very difficult time finding adequate control parents and children to compare to the addicts and children of addicts in their study. We have every reason to believe that the independent variables of addiction and poverty interact to powerfully influence the dependent measures of fetal and neonatal health. But without adequate comparison groups the variables remain confounded.

Our point is that addiction is not simply about drugs: It is also about poverty and desperation. It is also about sexism, racism, and classism. It is also about continuing threats to our children and the perpetuation of cycles of poverty and despair. As we will point out in chapter 2, this type of impoverished life-style provided a perfect breeding ground for the explosion of cocaine HCL (powdered cocaine) and crack use, with its accompanying resurgence of heroin abuse, in the 1980s. The sociocultural, political, and economic roots of addiction in the slums of America threaten to perpetuate the problem forever. The weapons of neurobiological approaches will never prevail against the dismal reality of poverty and the culture of terror in America (Bourgois, 1990).

The lists of complications above give ample warning about the problems found in utero. Pregnant heroin addicts in great numbers are committing fetal abuse and little is being done to deal with this serious health problem. It must be kept in mind that the majority of women addicts are *not* in treatment and that the vast majority of pregnant addicts (some 97 percent) are *not* in treatment.

This fetal abuse is compounded by another drug often used in association with heroin. Dr. Jerome Carroll and his colleagues reviewed the literature regarding alcohol abuse by drug addicts (Carroll et al., 1977). They estimated that 80 percent, of all heroin addicts *had problems associated with alcohol before they ever used heroin.* Another 35 percent were using alcohol to "boost, balance, counteract or sustain the effects of other drugs including heroin." This type of abusive and destructive drinking does harm to the pregnant addict and to her fetus. It is estimated that in the United States in 1985 50,000 babies were born with permanent injury and disability from fetal alcohol syndrome (FAS).

Fetal Alcohol Syndrome (FAS)

Fetal Alcohol Syndrome is a cluster of severe physical and mental defects caused by alcohol damage to the developing fetus. While defects vary from child to child, the most commonly occurring major abnormalities include:

- Growth retardation before and after birth, with no catching up later even if the baby is well nourished. FAS children are typically small and thin.
- Facial malformations, including small, widely spaced eyes; short, upturned nose with a wide, flat bridge; flat cheeks; narrow upper lip that lacks a vertical groove; and a blunt, small chin that may appear large and pointed as the child gets older.
- Brain damage, including an abnormally small head and brain; mild-to-moderate mental retardation (I.Q. is usually 60 to 75); hyperactivity; poor coordination, and learning disabilities.
- Abnormal development of various body organs, including heart defects; underdeveloped genitals in girls; urinary tract and kidney defects, among others.

One study at Emory University showed behavioral problems in babies born to women who drank as few as two drinks a week throughout their pregnancy. Other studies have shown as little as two drinks a week leading to more miscarriages and stillbirths. Certainly, addicted women who drink are probably drinking at a higher volume than two drinks a week. More will be said regarding the cocaine/alcohol connection in chapter 2. FAS defects combined with the ravages of opiate ingestion during pregnancy can only compound and complicate all the negative effects. However, it is not known if the effects are additive or cumulative. Another important fact to note is that even if a woman drank during a previous pregnancy with no apparent ill effect on her child, subsequent children can be harmed by this practice. This is another good reason for insisting that women give up *all drug taking* (with the exception of legitimately prescribed medications) as part of their recovery and rehabilitation. Shockingly, not until 1990 did physicians decide to advise against any and all alcohol ingestion during pregnancy. Prior to that time some physicians were actually advising pregnant women, in all income categories, to take an occasional drink.

The leading cause of death among patients on methadone maintenance is AIDS. The second leading cause of serious medical complications in methadone-maintenance patients during methadone treatment, and during and following detoxification from methadone, is alcohol abuse (Kreek, 1978). Dr. Levy directed the Alcoholism Treatment Program at Beth Israel Medical Center in New York City from 1977 to 1982. During that time he trained many of the staff of the Medical Center's twenty methadone-maintenance clinics in issues concerning alcohol abuse and interviewed staff members of many of New York City's best-known drug-free heroin treatment programs. In 1982 he summarized his findings in an article entitled "Multiple Substance Abuse—Implications for Treatment" (Levy, 1982). He found that heavy drinking, alcohol abuse, and alcohol dependence was occuring among many staff members as well as clients in the majority of drug-abuse treatment agencies. The problem continues unabated. However, the children of heroin addicts are not the children of alcoholics in disguise. Although they share some issues and problems in common, they represent a separate, distinct, and multivariate population. The impact of multiple substance abuse and "dual addiction" to heroin and alcohol on the fetus and the children of heroin remains unstudied to date. Wilson and his colleagues (1981) found that at least 59 percent of a heroin-dependent group of pregnant addicts and 92 percent of a methadone-maintained group of pregnant women used other psychoactive substances, both prescribed and illicit, during pregnancy.

A major human rights issue is being defined by the phenomena of the pregnant addict. The rights of the mother are on a collision course with the rights of the fetus. The heroin "epidemic" of the 1970s and the growing intensity of the national abortion rights debate has set the stage for emerging court battles. Unfortunately, for unknown numbers of children born to these opiate-addicted women, the resolution of this complicated legal battle will come too late. We will comment further on this debate when considering legal rights issues in chapter 3.

The 1980s has witnessed a resurgence of heroin use stimulated by the marketing of smokable heroin combined with smokable (freebase) cocaine. The smokable heroin lengthens the crack high and reduces the intensity of the depression that follows it. Smoking opium, an ancient form of drug ingestion, is known as "chasing the dragon." Smokable heroin is new on the American drug scene. We can only wonder at the combined pharmacobehavioral effects this heroin/cocaine combination will have on the fetus and on children. We can only speculate on the new forms of fetal abuse that accompany each new development in the illicit drug scene.

The Effects of Opiate Addiction on the Neonate

"No wall can stop the coming of love, no clock can bring it back . . ."
—Rod McKuen

Most of the research done to date on the children of heroin deals with the newborn child. Neonatal outcomes for the children of heroin are fraught with complications, some of them quite serious (Deren, 1986; Finnegan & Wapner, 1987). The sidebar below shows the most significant of these complications.

Neonatal Outcomes for the Children of Heroin

- Infant withdrawal (estimates range from 70–90 percent)
- Low birth weight (50 percent are small for gestational age)
- Increased mortality rate (3X the general population in New York City from 1979–81)
- Longer postpartum hospital stays
- Increased fetal distress
- Increased incidence of sudden infant death syndrome (SIDS)—25 percent in children of heroin compared to 10 percent of the general population in New York City, 1979–81 (for children who died in the first year)
- Increased perinatal (at-birth) complications
- Increased neonatal complications
- Increased incidence of premature birth

No one who has actually witnessed the withdrawal of a newborn infant from opiates or methadone can fail to be profoundly moved. Dr. Levy first witnessed such births in Martland Hospital in Newark, New Jersey, in 1974. He describes the first such baby he ever saw:

> I was called to the patient's [an addict mother] room by her doctor because she was giving the nursing staff a real hard time—demanding drugs and being verbally abusive. This was 27 hours after delivery. After reducing the patient-staff friction I asked the head nurse if there were any problems with the baby. She said there were two problems—the baby was in active withdrawal from heroin and the mother was rejecting the baby. She then led me into the nursery. Nothing I had encountered in hospitals—personal experiences with medicine and surgery, work with adult addicts, firsthand observations of trauma in emergency rooms—none of this prepared me for the emotional reaction I was about to have. Nothing prepared me for the upset I was about to experience in viewing the newborn child of a heroin addict.
>
> The baby was quite small and was tremulous. She sucked frantically on a pacifier. When the nursery R.N. picked her up, she began to howl and cry. I have heard many babies cry but never like this. I can only describe it as an infantile howl that cut through me like a knife. When she finally stopped screaming she shook all over as the tremors and the frantic sucking resumed.
>
> I was overcome with sadness, followed by the rapid onset of feelings of intense anger toward a so-called mother who could subject her child to this outrage. I was overwhelmed by a sense of helplessness—should I take the baby home to nurture it myself? Should I place the mother in treatment immediately? Should I call the child-abuse authorities? All I could do initially was sit down in a chair and weep for this helpless child of heroin.

Dr. Finnegan has pointed out that an addicted woman may confuse the early signs of labor with signs of withdrawal and therefore present in labor a high level of narcotic drugs in her system. Awareness of the mother's drug addiction at the time of admission to the hospital will aid the obstetrician in managing the patient, and will later aid the pediatrician who will treat the neonatal withdrawal experience. Knowing a mother-to-be is maintained on methadone will alert the doctor to administer this drug to her to prevent her from going into withdrawal and will simultaneously alert the obstetrician to the impending withdrawal of the neonate. Narcotic antagonists should never be administered to mother or child because they will provoke withdrawal.

Listed below are the features of the abstinence syndrome in the newborn, compiled from a variety of studies (Chasnoff, Hatcher, & Burns, 1982; Stimmel, Goldberg, Reisman, Murphy, & Teets, 1982–83), described in detail by Green (1976), and reviewed by Deren (1986).

Green and Suffer (1981) developed a Neonatal Narcotic Withdrawal Index (NNWI). With its use they report that for infants exposed to methadone in utero the course of the subsequent withdrawal was less severe and the length of treatment shortened significantly.

Studies comparing heroin-using pregnant women, methadone-

Abstinence Syndrome in the Neonate

Withdrawal begins within 24–72 hours. Symptoms may persist up to several months and include:

Hyperirritability
Tremors
Hyperactivity
High-pitched crying
Frantic uncoordinated sucking and swallowing reflexes
Sleep problems
Feeding problems
Vomiting
Loose stools
Increased rooting reflex
Increased deep tendon reflexes
Exaggerated Moro response
Increased muscle tone
Changes in axillary temperature
Yawning
Sneezing
Mottling
Tachypnea (rapid breathing)

maintained unsupervised methadone-using pregnant women, and controls led Dr. Finnegan (1976) to state "that uncontrolled methadone use in pregnant women may be more harmful than illicit heroin." The highest rates of death for all infants and for low-birth-weight babies was for methadone-maintained women with little prenatal care. Finnegan (1976) found neonatal mortality to be higher for drug-dependent mothers, ranging from 66 percent for methadone-maintained mothers with comprehensive prenatal care to 81 percent for methadone maintained mothers with little prenatal care. The mortality rate for heroin-dependent mothers was 75 percent. A comparison of narcotic-addicted mothers to that of mothers in the general population in New York City in 1973 revealed a mortality rate *three times higher* for the children of heroin! Death is often brought about by such factors as hepatitis, syphillis, drug overdose, and AIDS.

In fairness to methadone-maintainance programs, it must be stated that for the pregnant addict who is likely to continue heroin use, methadone maintenance with accompanying prenatal care leads to the best outcomes for the babies—despite the incidence of the fetal abstinence syndrome. Finnegan and Fehr (1980) showed that infants born to methadone-maintained mothers had birth weights higher than those born to heroin-addicted mothers.

At the time the Finnegan and Fahr study was published little was known about the effects of other psychoactive drugs such as cocaine, marijuana, and hallucinogens on the newborn. This knowledge would not come until the advent of the cocaine babies described in the next chapter. We will have more to say about this topic in chapter 2, in which we describe what is being done for the children of cocaine.

A "cycle of despair" is generated by the abstinence syndrome in the newborn of addicts. Almost all the clinicians and researchers who work with addicted women and their children have commented upon the difficulties presented by babies in withdrawal and the negative effect withdrawal behavior has on bonding between the mother and child (Kaltenbach & Finnegan, 1988). Using the Brazelton Neonatal Behavioral Assessment Scale, the authors contrasted thirty-three methadone-exposed infants to ten drug-free infants (matched for socioeconomic, racial, and medical backgrounds). The results clearly showed that infants born to women maintained on methadone were deficient in their capacity for attention and social responsiveness and that "these deficiencies are present regardless of whether or not neonatal abstinence syndrome is severe enough to require treatment" (p. 227). Kaltenbach and Finnegan further point out that the infants' behavior remains effected until withdrawal is completed. They examined another group of infants born to addicted women who did not take methadone while pregnant, and found that these babies were more like the drug-free controls. This finding led the authors to state that given the fact that so many women are maintained on methadone in the United States the matter of which drugs are taken during pregnancy merits closer study. Further study indeed: the finding seems to point clearly toward the goal of drug-free pregnancies!

An already damaged self-concept is further assaulted by apparent "rejection" by one's own newborn child. These women often need to be taught that the behavior is driven by the withdrawal syndrome. The guilt attendant to this realization must also be carefully managed. The most wonderful mothers (those who had good parental models themselves and who have high self-esteem) would be put to the test by these withdrawing newborns. Having a child is a way for a woman to assume her place among other woman and for addicted women to approach "normalcy." The tremors and shrill cries that so powerfully affected Dr. Levy are far more devastating to the baby's own mothers (Escamilla-Mondanaro, 1977; Cuskey, 1982). The danger of a rapid return to active heroin use can be precipitated by such events. It is instructive to return to the mother of the withdrawing infant mentioned above.

> Because the infant in withdrawal could not respond normally to the mother's attempts to hold and nurture her, the nursery staff were complaining that the mother was trying to leave the hospital and did not want to take the baby with her. The staff suspected her sole motive was to get high [on heroin]. I walked into her room and closed the door behind me. "Talk to me," I said. She gave me a hostile glance and said "Why should I?" "Because they will take your baby and place it in foster care and you might change your mind!" Her look was hard and belied by the tears that gently rolled down her cheeks as she told a story I was growing too used to hearing. No husband, unsure of who the father is, strung out on heroin, poor, her mother refusing to raise the baby—she felt trapped and desparate. "How can

I take care of the baby when I can't even take care of me? That baby don't want me—she knows I made her sick and she don't want anything to do with me!"

Changing her mind took a lot of supportive counseling. I brought the maternal grandmother into the picture immediately. She learned that the baby's withdrawal would pass and that she needed "extra" loving. Mom agreed to take care of the child while her daughter went through detoxification and follow-up treatment. And then Mom said to her addicted daughter "You haven't named your child yet—the nurses are calling her baby Doe. Child's got to have a name." She named the baby "Faith" because she said that was all she had left!

The last topic to be covered in this section is in several ways the saddest and most disturbing of all the phenomenon associated with addictive behaviors. This is the topic of AIDS, in particular pediatric AIDS. Let us begin with some grim statistics.

The Evolution of Pediatric AIDS

1979: First cases of pediatric AIDS encountered at the Albert Einstein College of Medicine, Bronx, New York (Septimus, 1989).

1982: The Center for Disease Control (CDC) officially recognized acquired Immunodifficiency syndrome (AIDS).

1985: 217 cases of pediatric AIDS reported to the CDC. 48 percent of these cases are attributed to intravenous drug–using mothers. Seven percent of adult AIDS cases are women. Nearly 53 percent of them are IV drug users (Rutherford et al., 1987).

1988: 25 percent of AIDS cases in America and 20 percent of cases in Europe have IV drug use as a risk factor. In New York City over 80 percent of the perinatal AIDS cases involve IV drug use by the mother or a sexual partner of the mother (DesJarlais & Friedman, 1988).

1989: 1600 cases of pediatric AIDS have been reported to the CDC. Authorities project that as many as 10,000 to 20,000 children with AIDS will be detected during the next several years. Presently, approximately 78 percent of HIV-infected children have acquired their infection perinatally (Pizzo, 1989). At Harlem Hospital, in the heart of the ghetto, of 120 HIV-positive women who delivered, less than a fourth had been identified prenatally (Mitchell et al., 1989).

1990: By the end of the 1980s, 115,786 adults or adolescents in the United States had been diagnosed with AIDS, of whom 21 percent had the sole risk factor of injection drug use and another 9 percent had both injection drug use and another risk factor. Another 1,995 children under the age of thirteen had been diagnosed with AIDS, 826 of whom were born to female injection drug users according to the CDC. The majority of pediatric AIDS cases—58 percent—are associated with injection drug use (Sorensen, 1990).

The CDC estimates that nearly 6,000 HIV-positive women gave birth last year. A third of the babies will become infected. In some areas of New York City as many of 2 percent of all infants were born of infected mothers between November 1987 and September 1990.

Of 10,000 AIDS cases reported in New Jersey—most in Newark, Jersey City, and Paterson—53 percent have occurred among drug users. In Newark alone the figure is 69 percent.

The womb was not intended to be a breeding ground for acquired immunodifficiency syndrome and other immune systems disorders. The incubation period for pediatric AIDS is seven to nine months for perinatally acquired disease. Mortality rates range from 45–68 percent depending on which study one reads (Krasinski et al., 1989). The current number of older children with latent or asymptomatic infections is not known and neither is the incubation periods for children who are HIV positive. Dr. Keith Krasinski warns that because of the problem of viral latency, children who lose HIV-specific antibody and remain well cannot be regarded as HIV–infection free. Listed below are the diagnostic criteria for pediatric AIDS adopted by the CDC.

Diagnostic Criteria for AIDS in Children*

1. Disease indicative of defective cell-mediated immunity:
   a. Opportunistic infection
   b. Kaposi's sarcoma
   c. Primary malignant lymphoma of the brain
2. Absence of any cause of immunodeficiency other than HIV infection

*Adapted from Joshi, 1989.

3. Pulmonary lymphoid hyperplasia/lymphoid interstitial pneumonitis (PLH/LIP) complex with positive HIV serology in older children or demonstration of HIV positive in blood or tissues in infants up to fifteen months of age
4. Immunologic abnormalities outlined above
   HIV infection in children includes the following categories:
   a. Indeterminate infection (perinatally exposed infants and children up to fifteen months of age who have HIV antibody but who cannot be classified as definitely infected)
   b. Asymptomatic infection
   c. Symptomatic infection

Dr. Ben Katz (1989) has suggested guidelines for evaluating the children of HIV-infected mothers that we feel are important to share with you. AIDS is the *number one cause of death among children one to four years old.* When a mother is evaluated as HIV infected, her children must be evaluated.

Boland and Czarniecki (1991) warn that antibody tests for pediatric HIV should be interpreted with care. After an infected mother gives birth, the doctor should schedule the child for testing for the anti-HIV antibodies every three months. Within the first year, they warn, positive ELISA or Western Blot results do not necessarily mean a child has contracted the virus, "because even uninfected infants inherit maternal anti-HIV IgG antibodies. Nor do negative results prove the child is infection-free, since an infected child's immune system may take up to 15 months to manufacture antibodies against the virus." The only conclusive result obtained prior to the age of fifteen months is a negative test followed by a positive test (showing maternal antibodies have been used up and new infant anitbodies have been formed).

Boland and Czarniecki also point out that approximately half of the pregnancies of HIV-infected women do *not* result in HIV-infected infants. This prompts some HIV-infected women to conceive yet another child. Powerful motives that lead to the possible birth of yet another HIV-positive child include the desire to replace a lost baby, to create a healthy uninfected baby (to restore sense of competence as procreators), to satisfy a new partner, and to leave behind a living "legacy" after the mother's death.

Dr. Lori Karen (1989) reviewed the most salient issues of AIDS

Guidelines for Evaluating the Child
of an HIV-Infected Mother*

First Visit	Subsequent Visits	
	Thriving Child	Ill Child
Medical history—growth & development, intercurrent illnesses	Interval history	
Epidemiologic history		
Physical exam: height, weight, general appearance, neurologic & developmental evaluation, presence of parotitis, thrush, lymphoadenopathy, hepatosplenomaly	Physical examination	
HIV antibody determination (Western Blot) on index patient and all other household members-at-risk	Serial HIV antibody determinations (Western Blot)	
	Bordetella pertussis antibody titer	
	Pneumococcal and Hemophilus Influenzae (PRP); antibody titers (15–21 mo)	
	HIV antigen determination(s)	
	Quantiative immunoglobulins	Serial quantitative immunoglobulins
	B and T cell numbers and function	Serial B & T cell numbers & function
		Chest radiograph and/or pulmonary function tests
		Viral serology (e.g., EBV, VZV, etc.)

*Adapted from Katz 1989, 28.

prevention and chemical dependencey treatment needs of women and their children. Among the issues she highlighted:

- Female partners of male drug users may not recognize that they are endangered by sexual transmission of HIV.
- Males are unlikely to tell their female partners if they are drug users and/or HIV positive.
- Rates of AIDS are 11–13 times higher among black and Hispanic women—when adjusted for population size—than among white women.
- Women may risk a 30–50 percent chance of having a child with HIV infection and not opt for abortion due to their desire to have a child, religious beliefs, and/or family pressure.
- Drug-abuse treatment programs do not have specialized services for women and their children.
- Women with AIDS have compound difficulties including:
  - Grief reaction due to loss of their own health, positive body image, sexuality, and childbearing potential
  - Isolation from family and friends
  - Stigma for "immorally" infecting their child
  - Inability or unwillingness to parent their child
  - Little or no help from their child's father
  - Increased financial burden (on usually poor people)
- Pregnancy may mask nonspecific symptoms of infection and delay diagnosis of HIV illness.

Clinical staff working with adult drug addicts seem to practice a form of denial about the children of their clients. They do not want to hear about the horrors of pediatric AIDS. They can somehow handle the adults, but they shy away from their children. In 1989 Dr. Chavkin documented that of New York City's seventy-eight drug treatment centers:

- 54 percent refused treatment to pregnant addicts.
- 67 percent denied treatment to pregnant addicts on Medicaid.
- 87 percent denied service to pregnant women on Medicaid addicted to crack.

Susan Diesenhouse reported in the *New York Times* (7 January 1990) that "of about 7 thousand treatment programs nationwide only about 50 provide female patients with child and obstetric care and meet other special needs like counseling for sexual abuse."

"Mother" Clara Hale and her daughter Dr. Lorraine Hale provide us with a powerful example:

"Children become what they experience," she said. "My eight living children are all drug addicts. Six are HIV positive. Four of my grandchildren are HIV positive. . . . I've had 13 live births. Five babies died. Countless miscarriages, but no abortions. I was 13 when I began shooting drugs and prostituting. I don't know the father of any of my children; they look similar, like first cousins, not brothers or sisters." She continued: "My mother was an alcoholic. I was reared by, with, and around people who stayed drunk. Every disappointment was mourned by getting drunk; every success was celebrated by getting drunk. There were no in-between times. I don't think there was anything wrong in getting high. I was smoking herbs when I was 10 or 11 and went on to shoot up at 13."

"They finally took the kids away from me; that is, the Department of Welfare Social Services. I had been locked up for prostituting. I guess they had been gone for five days when I was released from jail. When I got home and they were gone, I almost went crazy. I called the police, told them someone had kidnapped my eight children. I soon discovered they had been placed in foster homes, separated from each other. It was inconvenient to get high during this period, so I remained sober through the ordeal. I wanted my children. I thought I was a good mother."

She paused for a moment, then said: "That can't be true. I can't imagine what motivated me to want to get the kids back. But I carried on. I had to go to court. There the children were taken from me until the next court date."*

According to Desjarlais et al. (1989), as of 14 September 1988, approximately one-third of all U.S. intravenous drug users with

*From *Mainliner Newsletter* (Hale House, October 1988).

AIDS lived in the New York metropolitan area. Killers like pediatric AIDS, child abuse, and substance abuse are replacing the traditional infectious diseases that kill poor children. In New York City alone there are about two million children, 60 percent of whom live in poor or near poor families, and 25 percent of whom do not have health insurance.

AIDS is also responsible for a growing generation of orphans. Dr. Pauline Thomas of the New York City Health Department estimates that by 1995 there will be 20,000 AIDS orphans who will need adoption or foster care placement. Says Chris Norwood, cochairwoman of the National Women's Health Network, "The family and social disintegration is almost unimaginable." Many of the parents developed AIDS after their children were born. Try to imagine all these children asking "When will my mother die? When will my father die?" Bernard's story, told below, is not unlike many we have heard.

Bernard (Age Sixteen)

"When I was a little kid me and my father were really tight. He played ball with me, told stories, and showed me off to his friends. He told everyone 'This is my son Bernard!' I lost my father twice. First, he became a junkie and I saw less and less of him. Then he got AIDS—he was real sick before he died. Like I said, I lost him twice."

At the end of her testimony before the Presidential Commission on the HIV Epidemic (Finnegan, 1987) Dr. Finnegan spoke for many of us who work with addicted families:

I want to underline for this Commission today the debilitating nature and long-range intergenerational effects of chronic drug addiction. It is even more devastating to drug-dependent women and mothers who so frequently do not have the resources for recovery available to them. Because of the lack of treatment services and research endeavors within the drug-addicted population for so many years, we are now plagued with rampant drug addiction in this country. We have fostered a spiraling legacy of addicts giving birth to addicts. This dark reality has now developed into the fact that soon we will have many thousands of babies at our doorstep who are dying of AIDS. If but only 10 percent of the resources for treatment and research provided for such conditions as cancer, heart disease and stroke had been applied to this population several decades ago, we would not have the overwhelming problem of rampant addiction, producing the concomitant tragedy of babies with AIDS. We are now confronted with the HIV epidemic, but we've had a drug abuse epidemic for a quarter of a century and we haven't done anything effective about it due to lack of funding. Will we permit the AIDS epidemic to reach uncontrollable heights? Must this generation and future generations suffer due to our willingness to act with urgency? We must make a sincere commitment that turns the course of this human tragedy. (5)

The First Year and Beyond

In reviewing the literature on the children of heroin, it struck us that little work had been done with children whose parent(s) had become or were at least struggling to become totally drug-free. Deren's comprehensive review of the studies done during the 1960s, 1970s, and 1980s demonstrates an interest in scholarship on the part of pediatricians and some methadone-maintenance programs. As we mentioned earlier, however, the drug-free programs are conspicious by their absence. One reason is so few actually seek to treat children. Even those that have produced some scholarship on topics such as family therapy with addicted families (Kaufman 1979, 1984) have done no empirical studies and share no data with us that sheds light on the children. Others, such as Odyssey House and Family House, although unique in the services they provide to women and children, have done no systematic studies such as those of Finnegan and her colleagues.

As you will see below, a mildly consistent pattern of deficits emerges during the first year of life for the children of heroin. However, little of a conclusive nature is known about these children beyond the first year. Data on the continuation of deficits is sketchy. One thing is clear: gross generalizations about the children of heroin are not possible. They do form a specific prototype. There is a great need for additional study with particular emphasis on research that compares these children to others matched for age, sex, education, socioeconomic level, and the like, whose parent(s) are not addicts.

The abstinence syndrome already discussed in relation to the newborn has been found by some authors to extend into the first two to four months. Householder (1982) reviewed the literature on infants born to narcotic-addicted mothers and described such withdrawal-related symptoms as sleep and feeding problems, hyperactivity, and colic. Householder also observed that as these effects wear off, the babies make rapid developmental gains between four and six months. However, the reviewers also found that developmental problems tend to reemerge at the end of the first year, and observed further that behavioral and psychological problems continue through early and middle childhood.

Dr. Sowder (Sowder & Burt, 1980), in reviewing the only six known follow-up studies of the newborns of opiate-addicted women, points out that the sample sizes are small and the measures of ability dissimilar, subjects are limited to preschool-aged children, and all but one study deals with children born to women maintained on methadone during pregnancy. The inconclusive results point toward some physical growth problems (impaired somatic growth and equivocal neurological signs) and contain indications of below-average motor development. Interestingly, all studies showed that the children scored average or above average on IQ tests.

A summary of eight follow-up studies of children born to methadone-maintained mothers was conducted by Dr. Deren. Bayley Scales of Mental and Motor Development indicate that:

- Opioid or methadone-exposed babies perform more poorly during the first year of life.
- Infants of opioid-using mothers are more likely to have poor motor coordination, high activity level, and poor attention.
- Problems that appear by the end of the first year involve attentional, visual, and fine motor coordination.

Once again, it is important to note that some results make these findings inconclusive. For example, Finnegan and her colleagues (Kaltenbach & Finnegan, 1974; Finnegan, 1983) reviewed many studies of methadone-exposed infants and found that they fall within the normal range of mental and motor development. When other factors such as parental poverty, parental I.Q., maternal psychopathology, parental marital status, and father in house are factored into the picture, a strong interactional effect becomes clear. Therefore, the evidence on the actual damage done by exposure to opiates in utero remains unclear.

In a strange way this makes sense. Using heroin leads one into a dangerous and unhealthy life-style. Few people actually die from the drug itself. One can die of an overdose (too much heroin heroin that is too pure, or heroin cut with toxic substances), of AIDS and other infectious diseases, of gunshots, and other dangers related to the heroin user's life-style. But there is no medical evidence that heroin itself causes any long-term damage to the human body. Contrast this reality with the effects of alcohol which can get into any organ system in the human body and reek havoc—in the short term, reversable, and in the long term, irreversible, damage. Dr. Mary Jean Kreek's many excellent studies of methadone have demonstrated the relative safety of that substance to the human organism. The life-style of the heroin addict is even more strongly implicated as the villain in the harmful sequellae to the children of heroin addicts than the pharmacology of the substance when considered alone. In any event, as Dr. Deren and others have properly cautioned us, many more studies are needed before we will know just how harmful these addictive substances are. It appears that the children are far more resilient than anyone would have thought given the "killer drug" used by their parents. Rescuing the children has less to do with drugs per se and a lot to do with the humanness of the children and their social, emotional, and cognitive needs.

An examination of the effects of heroin exposure on the older child does little to shed any light on the question as to the long-term consequences or the inconclusive findings reported earlier. Once again the number of studies is small, as is the size of the sample, and the study groups may not be comparable. Although inconclusive, studies show that children of addicts reveal:

- Deficits in somatic development (i.e., shorter stature and low birth weight up through age six)
- Poorer performance on tasks that require focused attention and persistence (through age six)
- Hyperactivity and impaired attention span (between ages one and two)
- Behavior and school adjustment problems
- Poorer performances on IQ tests and perceptual motor performance tests (for three-to-seven-year-olds)
- Increased anxiety, insecurity and shorter attention span; a

higher incidence of neurological deficits, mental retardation, and severe emotional problems (for three-to-seven-year-olds)
- More problems in school (for eight-to-seventeen-year-olds)
- A higher incidence of delinquent acts, and a greater likelihood to commit and these acts were more likely serious delinquent acts. Also these children were more likely to be using drugs and in drug abuse treatment.

This is where the formal empirical data on the children of heroin ends. However, our conversations with clinicians from many parts of the country over the past twenty years and our own work with addicts and their families reveal other equally disturbing findings. It is important to preface the account of these findings as being based on clinical observation rather than systematic studies. We believe that these impressions, anecdotes, and self-reports can form the basis for better controlled studies in the future.

Additional Clinical Impressions of Children of Drug Abusers

Many children of heroin come from dysfunctional families. Prominent in the array of dysfunction is parental drug use and abuse. Intergenerational drug use appears to be the product of social learning and is learned at a young age as a coping strategy for both relief and celebration of life. In the book *Life with Heroin: Voices from the Inner City,* Hanson and his colleagues (1975) point out that the life-style of the mole heroin addict, despite public stereotypes, is not completely dysfunctional, and that addicts are people who often romanticize their life-style and pass their ethos on to their children. So it is not suprising to find intergenerational addictive behavior, given the powerful early life–learning influences. The Odyssey House Parent's Program reported that 70 percent of their women had had disturbed maternal relationships in their own childhood (Carr, 1975). In contrast to the romantic fiction *is* the portrait of the addicted woman as a battered individual. Typically, the female addict grew up as the victim of strict sex-role socialization, suffered emotional neglect as an infant, and was criticized and punished for failing to live up to her parents' premature demands (Escamilla-Mondanaro, 1976).

Several studies have pointed to heroin addicts as mothers who are likely to exclude outside influences in their mothering role, and who try to totally control their children and their development. They tend to use a more threatening and authoritarian disciplinary approach that reinforces a disruptive method of attention seeking in the children. Our own clinical work has shown this to be true in a great many cases.

Addicted parents tend to feel inadequate as parents and therefore shy away from critical feedback and practical help. Methadone clinics that have tried to establish parenting programs have met with a lack of volunteers in their clinic caseloads. Therapeutic community programs have heard tearful confessions of inadequate parenting on the part of both men and women. Not surprisingly, these addicts also "confessed," quite often, to being poorly cared for themselves as children. Four-week "chemical dependency" rehabilitation programs that have "family week" or other types of family gatherings and confrontations are characterized by similar reports. The "rehabs" (as they are called within the field) have also reported great difficulty in getting family members to attend for reasons of exposure of these family "secrets" and the embarrassment and shame that accompany them.

Many addict families are single-parent families, in which the mothers often have little contact with their child's father. These women have few female friends and are often socially isolated. As a consequence, their children have few playmates. These women often turn to their own mothers to care for the grandchildren.

Many of the children are raised without fathers. If the mother is emotionally immature herself, the child may find himself/herself with a parent who cannot meet his/her needs psychologically. Indeed, some of these mothers act as if their child is supposed to "take care" of them, providing them with the emotional satisfaction and reinforcement so often absent in other areas of their lives. Very often these mothers are teenagers themselves. Thus, we have the phenomena of "children having children." When the children, acting in age-appropriate ways, fail to meet these needs, the mothers are driven deeper into feelings of despair and deprivation.

Marie Broudy (Levy & Broudy, 1975) has described what she has labeled the "pink fluffy" syndrome. Addicted women, shunning other women (regarding them with suspicion and jealousy) seek instead the attentions of male addicts, who tend to use, degrade, and ultimately reject them. Despite this harsh treatment, these women speak about boyfriends, fiancés, husbands, and babies as if they were participants in some crude television soap opera. Unfortunately, these are only fantasies. The real relationships are quite painful.

Hospital and childcare workers who encounter the children of heroin have reported many instances of abuse and neglect. The literature, while strongly suggestive of addiction as a major risk factor in child abuse and neglect cases, has yet to tease addiction out as a specific variable. As Dr. Deren reminds us, addiction does not exist as an independent factor. In addition to addiction the kinds of things that lead us to label a parent as "high risk" for abusive and neglectful behavior also includes poverty, multigenerational abuse and neglect, alcohol abuse, psychological problems, and family chaos. Another problem is that all parents responsible for such behaviors, not just addicts, *underreport it.*

In the absence of adequate data, we can only despair at the reported increase of such incidents among the children of heroin. Abuse starts with drug use in utero and can extend to lethal beatings of very young children. Neglect ranges from unpredictable meals to children left alone for days on end. Dr. Vincent Fontana (1983) of the New York Foundling Hospital found that during a six-month study period 25 percent of cases in which a child died from abuse or neglect the mother had been a drug addict. Dr. Judianne Densen-Gerber and Dr. Charles Rohrs (1973) consider children to be "at high risk" for abuse and neglect if a parent is an addict and even go so far as to suggest that "addiction must be designated as a prima facie criterion of unfitness as a parent." The addict life-style and responsible parenting are viewed by them as mutually exclusive.

The children of heroin are likely to have parents who shun routine medical care. Many of the women go without prenatal care. Infants are not exposed to well-baby clinics. Regular pediatric care is often absent up through adolescence. Emergency rooms take the place of family doctors for most poor people, including addicts and their families. Funds for medical care are either nonexistent or are used for drugs.

The criminal life-style attendant to heroin addiction often leads to incarceration. These and related events have caused many children of heroin addicts to be placed in foster care. Even among women on methadone maintenance, 40 percent had at least one child in some type of foster placement or living with relatives (Regan et al., 1987). Many children are placed in what are called "kinship" foster care, that is, they are placed with blood relatives. The most common placement is with the maternal grandmother. Sowder et al. (1981) found that children placed in such homes are at high risk for abuse and neglect (both children of heroin addicts and comparisons). We have already mentioned that addicts often come from families that are dysfunctional, families that are marked by poverty, alcohol abuse, physical abuse and neglect, and the like. Foster care placement of the children of addicts with their own grandparent(s) often exposes them to the same risks their parent suffered. Moreover, a grandparents resentment at having to care for a child's child often places the grandchild at extra risk. In the case of alcohol- and drug-dependent grandparent(s), the effects can be devastating. Since children are not necessarily placed with siblings, already fragmented families suffer further injury. Parents often seek to regain custody, without the benefit of appropriate treatment for their addiction. When custody is awarded, the spiral of heroin use, crime, and incarceration can lead to repeated placements in foster care. In some families, this means a pitiful parade from home to home, without the continuity and supports of normal family routines. These children are stripped of their right to have their basic needs met.

Children of heroin addicts are at great risk for sexual abuse, particularly incest. Few systematic studies exist, but clinicians in all modalities have encountered sexual abuse in two ways. First, adult addicts in treatment give testimony to their own victimization as children. Regan et al. (1987) surveyed 178 pregnant women who were drug- and/or alcohol-dependent and seventy pregnant drug-free controls attending the same prenatal clinic in Philadelphia. Subjects were matched for age, race, socioeconomic status, and prenatal care. The findings are summarized below.

*Violence Questionnaire Responses**

	Family Center (N = 178)	Control (N = 70)
Severely beaten as a child	19%	16%
Severely beaten as an adult**	70%	17%

Raped as a child**	15%	0%
Raped as an adult**	21%	4%
Molested as a child**	28%	7%

*From Regan et al., 1987, p. 317.
  (**p = <.01)

The women were beaten by their own parents. At least 8 percent of the rapes were incestuous. Dr. Judianne Densen-Gerber reported in the early 1970s that some 40 percent of the women in treatment at the MABON (Mothers and Babies Off Narcotics) Facility of Odyssey House in New York City were victims of incest.

Often, only vague but powerful emotional memories are recounted. At other times, fully detailed accounts of sexual exploitation, including rape, sodomy, and incest are available. In the second instance, clients have admitted to committing sexual acts with their own children. Sometimes women admit that their male companions or relatives have sexually abused their children and sometimes they admit that they were perpetrators themselves. Women drug addicts force their own children into prostitution to raise money for drugs. Such victimized children often grow up only being able to confront sexual feelings with drugs in their system. Heroin, which provides the feeling of not feeling, is ideal for the purpose of psychic numbing. Drug abuse clinicians need to learn when and how to take complete sexual histories, conducted in a caring and supportive manner, so that we can learn more about the relationship between drug addiction and sexual abuse of children.

Many of the children of addicts are victims of both verbal and physical violence. Certainly, violence perpetrated primarily against women and children interacts strongly with addictive behavior. In a perverse sense, drug use in the face of this madness becomes understandable. Altering consciousness to blot out physical and psychic pain "works" for short periods, but then exacts its own terrible toll. The child and the adult have fallen victim to the dual ravages of violence and addiction. From our own work with children and adults we know that violence is as much a cause of drug taking as drug taking is a cause of violence. In fact, in working with heroin addicts, who prior to the 1980s were known for crimes against property (not persons), and their children we came to realize that the crimes against persons are often committed by parents against their own children and did not appear in the usual array of police narcotics-related crime reports.

So much is still illusive and unknown. As Dr. Finnegan remarked in her testimony on pediatric AIDS, the investment of the federal government in studying and treating addiction remains painfully small when compared to investment in other public health problems such as heart disease and cancer. The financial and moral investment in studying and helping the children of drug abusers is smaller still.

In June 1990 the Human Resources Division of the General Accounting Office presented a report to the chairman of the Committee on Finance of the United States Senate. It was entitled "Drug-Exposed Infants: A Generation at Risk." On the following pages are several bar graphs that compare drug-exposed infants with those not identified as drug-exposed. They are compared on (1) likelihood of prenatal care; (2) birthweight; (3) prematurity; (4) hospital charges; and (5) likelihood of foster care placement. These graphs show the "price tag" for failure to invest in the children of drug abusers (themselves, their parents, and the family as a unit) for the last several decades. They are graphic evidence of what happens when needs go unmet.

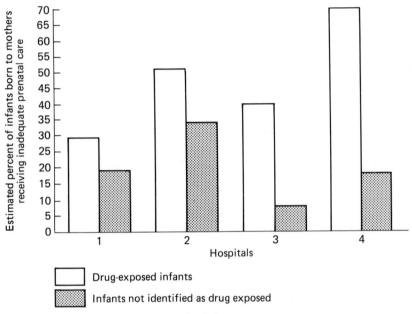

FIGURE 1-1.

Mothers of Drug-Exposed Infants Are More Likely to Obtain
Inadequate Prenatal Care (Comparison at 4 Hospitals).

Source: GAO, Drug-Exposed Infants, 1990.

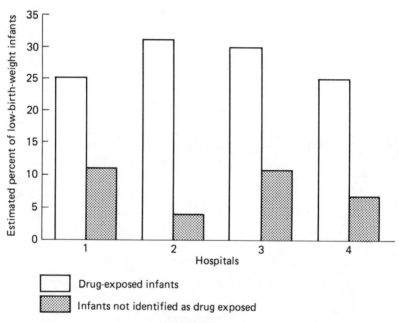

FIGURE 1-2.

Drug-Exposed Infants More Often Have a Low Birth Weight as
Compared With Nonexposed Infants (Comparison at 4 Hospitals).

Source: GAO, Drug-Exposed Infants, 1990.

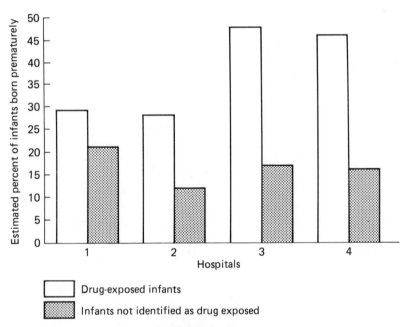

FIGURE 1-3.

Drug-Exposed Infants Are More Likely to Be Born Prematurely than Nonexposed Infants (Comparison at 4 Hospitals).

Source: GAO, Drug-Exposed Infants, 1990.

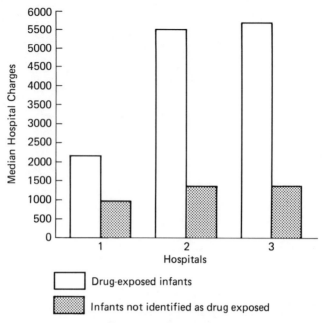

FIGURE 1-4.

Drug-Exposed Infants Incur Higher Hospital Charges than
Nonexposed Infants (Comparison at 3 Hospitals).

Over $14 million was spent on the care of drug-exposed infants at 3 hospitals where
we were able to obtain data. Hospital charges for drug-exposed infants at these
hospitals ranged from $455 to $65,325.

Because more than 50 percent of patients received public medical assistance in 7 of
the hospitals in our study, a large part of these costs was covered by federal assistance
programs.

TABLE 1-2.

*Estimated Hospital Charges for Drug-Exposed Infants at Three
Hospitals in 1989*

Hospital	Estimated no. of drug-exposed infants	Mean charge	Estimated total hospital charges
1	1,187	$6,914[a]	$8,206,918
2	400	8,939	3,575,600
3	440	6,520	2,868,800
Total	2,027		$14,651,318

[a]The charges at this hospital are based on a flat per diem rate and, therefore, may
be underestimated.

Source: GOA, Drug-Exposed Infants, 1990.

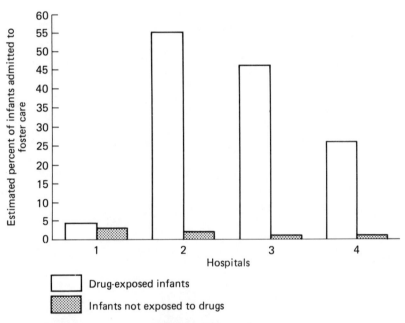

FIGURE 1-5.

Drug-Exposed Infants Are More Likely to Be Admitted to Foster
Care than Nonexposed Infants (Comparison at 4 Hospitals)

Source: GAO, Drug-Exposed Infants, 1990.

2

The Children of Cocaine

When Katherine looks into her infant daughter's large gray eyes, smiles and presents her with the new stuffed tiger a grandmother just left, the infant closes her eyes and turns her head to fall asleep. She's a healthy looking child, but will rarely, if ever, gaze back and gurgle like most babies. Usually, Katherine will keep coaxing the baby to smile, but then she howls. Fed up, Katherine put the infant in her crib and let her be. The baby quiets down and only when left alone gazes, seemingly happily, at the blank ceiling.
— "Cocaine Babies Face Behavior Deficits," *American Psychological Association Monitor,* July 1989

"Because they've got so much going on in their central nervous system, crack babies at one-month-old are equivalent to a two-day-old. . . . Children who are born addicted are slower reaching milestones. . . . We've had an opportunity to look at some kids for two years, and some of the delays are still apparent."
—Tresmaine Grimes, developmental psychologist, Hale House, New York City, September 1988

In a few months a new task force . . . is slated to tell President Bush what America should do about "crack babies"—the thousands born brain damaged, malformed or seizure-prone because their mothers smoked crack during pregnancy. The answers aren't obvious. Whatever the task force discovers, it is likely that the cost of helping crack babies will be high—but not as high as the cost of more children in foster homes, more babies tethered to tubes in intensive care units, more lifetime care for the irrevocably damaged. America pays a terrible price for cocaine addiction; children may pay the highest price of all.

—Editorial, *New York Times,* 7 August 1989

Maternal and perinatal addiction programs should be aimed at not only helping mothers to deal with their addiction but also teaching them the parenting skills necessary for proper infant stimulation and subsequent development. Future programs must develop methods to ensure adequate follow-up of all infants born to substance abusing mothers.

—Drs. Ira Chasnoff and Sidney Schnoll, "Consequences of Cocaine and Other Drug Use in Pregnancy," in *Cocaine: A Clinician's Handbook,* 1987

In Cities, Poor Families Are Dying of Crack. . . . Crack is rapidly accelerating the destruction of families in poor urban neighborhoods, where mothers are becoming increasing addicted and children are selling the drug in greater numbers than ever before.

—Front page of the *New York Times,* 11 August 1989

In the past, with heroin affecting primarily males, we saw the single-parent child. Now with cocaine affecting females as well as males, we see the *no-parent* child.

—George Will, syndicated columnist

Our Review of the literature on the children of heroin left us with a sense of despair because so little was and is being done: from birth to their majority, these children have few friends or advocates. And now our society is faced with cocaine hydrochloride and crack. Nasal cocaine (HCL) or "powdered" cocaine had already been gaining in popularity before the advent of crack and is not without recently discovered clear-cut dangers. In 1977 the director of research for the National Institute on Drug Abuse indicated that use of "two grams per week or less" of nasal coke was relatively safe. Little more than a decade later, we now know that the nasal ingestion of cocaine hydrochloride is a dangerous practice that can bring about serious health, behavioral, and life-style problems, particularly when cocaine use is combined with the use of other drugs such as alcohol. We have also learned that cocaine use carries devastating effects for the children of users.

Crack is the cocaine base separated (fractionated) from its accompanying hydrochloride salt. Originally, one required expensive, dangerous, hard-to-procure chemicals (like ether) to create "freebase cocaine." But then the drug dealers' chemists discovered how to achieve the same result with common baking soda (sodium bicarbonate) and tap water. To make crack, cocaine hydrochloride is mixed with water in a blender, baking soda is added, and the solution is heated. The hydrochloride salt and the contaminants settle to the bottom and the cocaine rises to the surface. The congeal is then skimmed off into a flat pan where it dries. When dry, it has a porcelain like texture and easily fragments into chunks and slivers. Dealers place the chunks, or "rocks," in vials of varying sizes with color-coded caps to indicate amount and the price of the vial. This process led to the creation of preprocessed, prepackaged cocaine in smokable form—the advent of crack!

The crack phenomenon is the "product of brilliant marketing." This mass-marketing scheme has stimulated the first true drug epidemic in American history. No one could have predicted the devastating effect of this new form of cocaine on crime, the criminal justice system, entire neighborhoods, our drug-abuse treatment system, hospitals, and the family—particularly poor families. While some may object to the use of the term "epidemic," we feel it is appropriate. We agree with the definition developed by Professors Craig Reinarman and Harry Levine (1989) in their searing critical analysis of politics and the media in the making of the crack cocaine scare:

> If "epidemic" is used to mean a disease (or even a disease-like condition) that is "widespread" or "prevalent," then one could say there never has been an epidemic of crack use or crack addiction among the broad middle-income majority of Americans. However, an epidemic of crack addiction and burnout could be an appropriate technical description for what has happened among a distinct minority of teenagers and young adult men and women from poverty families and neighborhoods. (551)

This is not to deny that crack has been tried by all classes—it has. Nor are we trying to suggest that white middle-class crack addicts escape suffering—they are just as much addicts as poor blacks and can suffer just as much. But their numbers are far fewer. And the resources available to middle-class addicts to help them to refashion a life ravaged by addiction far outstrip anything available to the poor. They have access, by means of health insurance benefits, to a system of private inpatient and outpatient care. A host of private "chemical dependency" rehabs and outpatient programs exist to tend to their needs. No such safety net exists for the poor.

Funding for publicly supported drug-abuse treatment programs has plummeted since the early 1980s. The system has been left to deteriorate. This drop in funding support coincided with the explosion in the use of cocaine HCL and crack. In 1990 a report ordered by Congress and funded by the National Institute of Drug Abuse, was issued by the Institute of Medicine's Committee for the Substance Abuse Coverage Study. It calls for a tripling of federal drug-treatment funding to reach more of the nation's 5.5 million addicts. Dr. Robert Hubbard (1989) of the committee specifically mentioned that public treatment programs need to be rebuilt after a decade of decline when the federal government shifted the burden of treatment to the states. To restore adequate funding for drug treatment programs Hubbard proposed "a one-time infusion [of $1.1 billion] for capital investments and training staff and program directors" on top of a permanent $2.2 billion increase for treatment itself (Youngstrom, 1990).

Our poor, nonwhite ghetto communities, already suffering from both overt and benign neglect by the government, were natural breeding grounds for the cocaine epidemic. Inadequate housing, poor nutrition, run-down schools, overworked health care agencies, crime, teenage pregnancy, high school drop-out rates, a growing homicide rate—all these things and more are the natural cauldron in which epidemics are made. Poor people are not eligible for the private rehabs, and they are met with long waiting lists for the publicly funded programs. As many as 65,000 addicts are on waiting lists across the nation. Our nation as a whole, according to the most recent 1990 Household Survey on National Drug Use, conducted by the National Institute on Drug Abuse (NIDA), seems to be entering a new period of declining drug use. But drug use in our inner cities is actually increasing, not decreasing. Just as our poorer citizens are more vulnerable to the onset and sequellae of an epidemic, they are also much slower to recover from one.

According to the 1988 Household Survey, 862,000 people used cocaine once a week (compared with 647,000 in 1985). In 1988 NIDA's Drug Abuse Warning Network (DAWN) reported 46,000 emergency room visits due to cocaine (compared with 8,831 in 1984). The NIDA also reported a 28-fold increase in the number of emergency room visits by people who smoked freebase cocaine for the same period. The 1988 Household Survey was the first to report on crack. Nationally, 2.5 million people reported using crack at some time in their lives (crack first appeared in late 1984). One million people reported using crack in the year preceeding the survey. The majority of these past-year users were aged eighteen to twenty-five. Crack use is most prevalent in large cities. Roughly 188,000 adolescents aged twelve to seventeen have tried crack (NIDA *Notes,* 1989/1990).

In contrast, the 1988 Household Survey found that 1.9 million Americans age twelve and older who live in households have tried heroin at least once. NIDA states that "it is generally thought, however, that the majority of heroin addicts in the United States are not among the population measured in this survey. From other surveys we estimate that there are approximately 500,000 current heroin addicts nationwide, a number that has not significantly changed over the past 10 years" (NIDA *Notes,* 1989/1990, 12). Interestingly, in 1988 "more people still used heroin heavily or daily than used cocaine daily [at least 750,000 for heroin, as opposed to about 300,000 for cocaine]," according to Reinarman and Levine (1989). According to the 1988 NIDA Household Survey almost *one million women* had used cocaine in the previous month! The news just kept getting worse for the children of addicts.

Those of us working with addicted women and their children have suffered anguish for several decades as our pleas for programs tailored to their children's needs fell upon deaf ears. We now see that our nation's failure to address the problems of addicts and their spouses, partners, and children has come back to haunt us tenfold as more women enter our programs and others can not find treatment because the cocaine epidemic has exhausted current public resources. Let us consider further the impact that drug abuse has had upon women and children in one state, New York. Once again, we turn to the work of Dr. Sherry Deren and her colleagues, who published trends and estimates for children of substance abusers in New York State in April 1988 (Deren, Frank, & Schmeidler, 1988).

Estimates of the Number of Children of Substance Abusers in the State of New York

- There are an estimated 467,000 children of substance abusers, aged seventeen and under, approximatly 1 out of 10 children in the state.
- It is estimated that 59,000 children have one or more parents in substance-abuse treatment in the state.
- It is estimated that there are 205,000 children of narcotics abusers who are not in treatment in the state.
- It is estimated that there are more than 203,000 children living in households with nonnarcotic-drug abusers who are not in treatment in the state.
- The age breakdown of these children in the state is:
  - 42% (196,000) are under the age of six
  - 32% (148,000) are between the ages of six and eleven
  - 26% (122,000) are between the ages of twelve and seventeen
- It is estimated that there were 24,000 births to substance-abusing women in 1986. This represents approximately 1 out of 10 births in the state. In Florida, 1 of every 7 babies is exposed to drugs before birth.
- The Drug-of-abuse breakdown for these births in the state is:
  - 2,600 to narcotic-abusing women
  - 2,500 to women who were users of cocaine
  - 18,800 births to women who were users of nonnarcotic substances
- The vast majority of these births, 97%, were to women who were not in treatment
- There appears to be an increasing trend in births to substance-abusing women—In New York City there were 781 births to substance-abusing women in 1978; by 1987 the figure had grown to 2,586.

Dr. Deren concludes:

> A wide range of services are needed to assist these families and break the cycle. . . . The magnitude and urgency of the problem indicates that services must be developed now. In addition, resources devoted to research and evaluation efforts are also needed. Research is needed in many areas, including further assessment of the nature and extent of this problem, evaluating the effectiveness of existing programs, and developing novel approaches to reaching and serving these children and their parents.

Habel, Kay, and Lee (1990) examined New York City Department of Health linked birth/infant death files. They report the number of infants born to drug-abusing mothers increased from 6.7 per 1,000 live births in 1981 to 20.3 per 1,000 live births in 1987. A recent study in Boston reported that of 1,226 pregnant inner-city women, 20 percent had used cocaine (Zuckerman et al., 1989). Between 1986 and 1988, the number of newborns in New York City who tested positive for drugs—mostly cocaine—almost quadrupled, going from 1,325 to 5,088. As many as 375,000 babies may be born each year to women who use and abuse drugs during their pregnancies, according to a study done by the National Association for Perinatal Addiction Research and Education (Chasnoff et al., 1989). They found that the birth rate for drug-exposed babies was similar in rural and urban hospitals across the country. In this study of thirty-six hospitals, high drug-related birth rates were also found in low- and high-income patients. According to *Crack Babies,* a report from the Office of the Inspector General of the Department of Health and Human Services (HHS), "The nation is only seeing part of the problem brought on by the 100,000 cocaine exposed babies that are born each year. . . . For the 8,794 crack babies identified in eight cities, the cost of hospital delivery, perinatal care and foster care through age five could be as much as $500 million" (*Focus,* 1990).

Another study done by the Justice Department in late 1988 showed that women were as likely as men to abuse cocaine. This finding stands in stark contrast to past findings with heroin, where 80 percent of users were men.

The literature on cocaine abuse and addiction is in its infancy.

There is no cohesive body of knowledge. Moreover, almost nothing has been published about the impact of cocaine abuse on the family. However, clinicians are beginning to share reports. The media's attention to "cocaine babies" and "crack babies" far outstrips any attention ever paid to the children of heroin addicts. The HHS 1990 study reports that we are only seeing part of the problem: "Most cocaine-exposed babies are not identified at birth, and there appears to be no *typical* crack baby."

The Devastating Impact of Crack Cocaine on the Family

Crack has its most devastating effects in poor minority neighborhoods where the population is most vulnerable. While poor whites are also affected, black and Hispanic communities are overrepresented in this public health problem. For example, in 1988 Hispanics accounted for about 10 percent of all drug-related emergency room visits in twenty-one metropolitan areas; nearly 18 percent of Hispanics who had medical emergencies had used heroin, morphine, or a combination of the two (this percentage is higher than for any other ethnic group); nearly 13 percent of of the 1988 deaths due to drug use in twenty-seven cities occurred among Hispanics (DAWN, 1988). In 1988, blacks and Hispanics in the United States who injected drugs constituted 80 percent of all intravenous drug users infected with HIV, according to the Centers for Disease Control. One study found that nearly half of the black drug abusers and 37 percent of the Hispanics injected cocaine, compared with only 30 percent of the whites (Chaisson, Bacchetti, & Osmond, 1989). Ethnic demographics do vary depending on the region of the country examined, but there is no doubt that cocaine addiction has hit blacks and Hispanics the hardest in poor America. NIDA had already documented that by 1978 44 percent of all admissions to treatment centers were from minority groups; blacks and Hispanics accounted for nearly 64 percent of all heroin addicts in treatment by 1980. During 1989 Odyssey House, a major drug-free therapeutic community program in New York City, reported that 74 percent of their clients were black, 16 percent were Hispanic, and only 10 percent were white (Ramos & Stone, 1989). Professors Reinarman and Levine (1989) inform us that "Alone with most other drug researchers and epidemiologists, we conclude that crack use has never been anything but relatively rare among middle-class and middle-income Americans. However, among the urban poor, especially lower class Blacks, Hispanics and youth, crack use has been considerably higher" (551).

Children, including newborns and infants, are being abandoned by their parent(s). This is unprecedented in the substance-abuse field. Crack addiction has led to the creation of the "boarder baby," that is, babies boarded in maternity, pediatric, and other settings because they have been abandoned by or taken away from their parents. By 1987, the height of the crack epidemic in New York City, many hospital wards were warehousing thousands of these boarder babies because the child welfare system was unable to place them in foster care. As more addicts have more babies the number of children entering foster care climbed steeply. Both the boarder baby phenomena and the rise in foster care provide evidence of addict parents who fail to provide for their children. This has led to a major increase in what are referred to as "kinship" foster care placement where blood relatives (often the mothers of crack addicts) are licensed and paid to act as foster parents. In less than three years, reported Suzanne Daley in the *New York Times* (23, October 1989), the number of children placed in kinship homes has grown to 19,000. The number of children in the entire foster care system in New York City has risen from 23,700 in 1977 to 38,000 in 1989. And the children are coming into the system at younger ages—58 percent of the entering children are now under six (an increase of 11 percent in just three years).

Grandparents, especially grandmothers, often of advanced age, are being forced to care for their children's children. Urban child welfare workers who deal with kinship placements estimate that 70 percent of the children they see are raised by grandparents or other relatives, after parents abandon them for drugs.

Dr. Ja J. Yoon heads the forty-bed Neonatal Intensive Care Unit of Bronx-Lebanon Hospital. In her article entitled "Hearing the Cries of Crack" (*New York Times*, 7, October 1990) Anna Quindlen spoke of her seven-year friendship with Dr. Yoon: "Like school chums we reminisce about the good old days, when the smallest babies were two pounds, when fetal alcohol syndrome and infant heroin addiction seemed the worst cases. Two percent of the babies went from the hospital directly to a foster home. The figure is now 15 percent. The reason is crack."

The violence attributed to crack use is leading to an unprecedented increase in child abuse. In New York City between 1987 and 1989 reports of drug-related child abuse and neglect tripled. Complaints of child abuse and neglect rose to 60,000 in 1989 in New York City, up from 18,500 in 1979. Most social welfare officials attribute this increase to the upswing in crack addiction. A congressional study in 1989 found that child abuse, drug and alcohol abuse, and homelessness are the major factors in the increase of costly out-of-home placements for children. Detailed and well-controlled scientific studies of the relationship between cocaine and crack use and violence are lacking. The term "drug-related" child abuse is often inprecise and differs from report to report. For an overview of the literature on child abuse and neglect, we suggest reading Gelardo and Sanford (1987). A study of 245,000 prisoners in state penitentiaries reported in 1990 that in two of every three violent crimes either the perpetrator, the victim, or both were under the influence of alcohol or other drugs at the time of the crime. Yet a more recent study of cocaine and crack arrests showed only 4 percent of those arrested were charged with felony violence (Fagin & Chin, 1989). Child welfare workers agree that crack is the major contributing factor to the increase in both the frequency and severity of abuse and neglect with children.

Does substance abuse cause violence or is substance abuse a symptom of an underlying social decay whose worst manifestation is violence itself? Either way, children are caught in a terrible cross fire between two incredibly destructive social phenomena: drug abuse and violence. The correlation between the two variables is positive and strong but the causal links have yet to be detailed. The individual story of each abused and neglected child is powerful and frightening and hurts us as a society. We remember in the summer of 1989 watching a report on prime-time TV news about a crack-addicted father trying to sell his infant in the street.

We could cite many similar stories. In June 1990 the abandoned child of a crack addict was awaiting adoption. The child had spent four months of placement with a single thirty-nine-year-old woman who had been approved by child welfare authorities. Then tragedy struck. The baby, one day short of her first birthday, began to cry and would not stop. Then, according to police, the woman, who had been drinking, shook the child, struck her, and dropped her on the floor twice. Twelve hours later the baby died. What really led to this tragic death: alcohol abuse, mental illness, a woeful lack of training to deal with a young child, a failure to understand the unique needs of a "crack baby," or perhaps a woman who herself was brutalized as a child repeating a multigenerational cycle of violence? The placement agency thought it had found a good home for this baby; the mother seemed to care a great deal for the child. There seems to be no "safety net" for these children. For too many of them the system is simply not working.

Often crack-addicted parents spend money on crack that should be spent on food and shelter. Children go hungry and families are put on the street because mothers use all their money to support their addictions. This is increasing the homeless population. Family members grow disgusted at the outrageous behavior of their addicted relatives and throw them out. Housing authority police in New York now have the power to evict tenants who deal drugs.

Life in welfare hotels is not much better. Children in particular report the squalor and violence found in these dreary social "institutions." Reporting in the *New York Times* (30 September 1990) Donald G. McNeil, Jr., tells us of the return of the welfare hotel in New York City. In 1987, there were 3,600 families in sixty-two such hotels. Authorities tried to close these awful places, and almost succeeded, but the surge in the homeless population has recently caused the number of welfare hotel placements to swell from 147 families in August 1990 to 427 families one and a half months later. Below is a picture drawn by Antoine, aged twelve, that accompanied McNeil's report. We believe this picture is truly worth a thousand words.

A resurgence of syphilis is being experienced in America. Dr. Ward Cates who heads the Federal Centers for Disease Control (CDC) program to prevent sexually transmitted diseases stated in early 1990 that "We've made major inroads in controlling gonorrhea, but we've seen much less success in syphilis and other sexually transmitted infections." The number of cases of syphilis hit a forty-year high in 1988 with 16.2 cases per 100,000, or 39,000 cases. Congenital syphilis rose 17.7 per 100,000 in the same year. This

FIGURE 2-1.

A Child's Drawing of Life in a Welfare Hotel.

Source: New York *Times*, September 30, 1990. Reprinted by permission.

increase is attributed to the widespread use of crack in urban ghettos. Dr. Stephen Joseph, then commissioner of health in New York City, stated that "the logical chain goes crack, syphilis, HIV. . . . there are now some very strong indications that crack and other forms of cocaine are a driving issue in HIV transmission." Syphilis has increased by 150 percent among blacks, risen 73 percent among Hispanics, and has more than doubled among women. Dr. Cates agrees, stating "In the crack house a number of factors combined to create a powder keg for the spread of HIV." This is contributing to a rise in pediatric HIV and pediatric AIDS cases.

One study done by the CDC surveyed ninety syphilis patients at treatment centers for sexually transmitted diseases in the City of Philadelphia. The results showed that patients with syphilis were at least twice as likely as other patients to have used cocaine; to have had sex with a partner they had met the same day; to have exchanged sex for drugs; or to have visited a crack house. Half of the patients admitted that they had used cocaine in the preceeding three months. During marathon crack-house sex and drug binges addicts do not use condoms, have sex with total strangers, and exhibit greatly diminished inhibitions, leading them to engage in high-risk sexual acts.

To us, the greatest source of alarm is the increased incidence of congenital syphilis, that is, the passing of the disease to the fetus. The number of babies born with syphilis in New York City has skyrocketed from 33 cases, to 126 cases, to 356 cases, to 1,017 cases in the period 1986–90. Dr. Woodrow Myers, commissioner of health for New York City, estimates that 20–40 percent of infants born with syphilis to untreated women are stillborn or die soon after birth. Many others suffer birth defects. Newborns who survive must remain in the hospital for ten days of intravenous antibiotic therapy. In September 1990 Dr. Myers called for required syphilis testing for all pregnant women after their sixth month of pregnancy. Such testing is unlikely to become a reality, but Myers's call does communicate the urgency of the situation for the children of New York and other cities where parental behavior endangers their very lives. A mother with syphilis who is treated with antibiotics usually prevents damage to the fetus.

Dr. Lawrence K. Altman, reporting in the *New York Times* (11 November 1990), refers to syphilis as "an ailment that is often misdiagnosed" and indicates that it is at its highest level since 1949." He also observed that "Syphilis, which is known as the great imitator because it mimics so many other diseases, is making its strongest comeback in forty years in the United States. And it is fooling a generation of doctors who have rarely, if ever, seen a

---

Some Facts about Syphilis*

Syphilis is caused by *treponema pallidum,* a spiral-shaped bacterium known as a spirochete.

The microbe is most commonly spread by sexual contact.

The disease appears in three stages:

Stage 1: Characterized by a painless sore, a primary chancre, that usually appears twenty-one days after exposure. The edges of the sore are hard, like cartilage, and can appear anywhere there has been sexual contact, such as the penis, vagina, cervix, tongue, or anus.

Stage 2: Untreated syphilis sores disappear after two to six weeks. Six to eight weeks later, the spirochete spreads silently through the circulatory system to cause the second stage. It often appears as a rash that may be accompanied by swollen lymph nodes throughout the body, a sore throat, weight loss, malaise, headache, and loss of hair. This second stage can also damage the eye, liver, kidney, and other organs.

Stage 3: If untreated, the second stage heals after two to six weeks. Then years to decades later it can damage the heart, aorta, bones, and cause paralysis and dementia.

The symptoms from syphilis are not only transient but can vary greatly, imitating many other illnesses, leading to misdiagnoses.

*Adapted from Altman, 1990.

case." For example, "Pediatricians have mistaken the sniffles that can result at birth from syphilis for the flu." The spirochete that causes syphilis can be transfered from the mother to the fetus. Babies born with syphilis often have a runny nose and can have a rash and other symptoms that resemble the adult's secondary stage of the disease. The congenital form of the illness can cause deafness, anemia, and permanent damage to the bones, liver, and teeth. If the illness is identified at birth and properly treated, permanent damage can be prevented.

The 1990 White House Task Force on Infant Mortality estimated that one-fourth of the 40,000 infant deaths and a large percentage of the 100,000 handicapped newborns that occur in our nation each year are "easily preventable." On 9 August 1990 a *New York Times* editorial stated:

> They've [health care professionals] known for years that poverty and accompanying ignorance, combined with cuts in Federal programs, have slowed America's steady progress in lowering the infant mortality rate. Today, instead of going down, it is being pushed up by crack, venereal disease and AIDS. By this measure the United State ranked 20th among industrialized nations in preventing infant deaths. The Task Force [on Infant Mortality] estimates that the steps it recommends would cost $480 million a year. Compare that with the lifetime medical costs for low birthweight babies; each can run $400,000. Such costs for children now being born to crack-addicted mothers are beyond reckoning. America can't afford not to spend more on prenatal care, not on economic grounds and not on the grounds of humanity.

Estimates of intensive care unit costs for "crack baby" care have run as high as $2.5 billion nationally. In a letter to the *New York Times* (28 August 1990) Jennifer L. Howe, president of the March of Dimes Birth Defects Foundation, stated, "It doesn't require new ideas or even new programs. But it does require budget priorities that will adequately finance existing, effective programs more fully to meet the needs of mothers and babies."

We have heard from children and adults story after story of how cocaine and crack have driven one or both parents into desperate addictive behaviors, leading to the actual demise of their families. The number of cocaine-exposed babies removed by officials has been one contributing event. Child abandonment has been another. Incarceration of the parent(s), being thrown out by relatives, entrance into long-term treatment programs (many therapeutic community programs require stays of twelve to eighteen months) that make no provisions to keep parents and children together, failure of other types of modalities to provide child care—all these things have led to the destruction of families.

Child welfare workers and drug-abuse treatment workers very often find themselves at odds. Treatment programs provide few services that include children or that take their needs and rights into account. Drug treatment programs often refuse to share information about parents with child welfare workers, invoking federal statutes on client confidentiality to justify their lack of cooperation. Family courts find the task of making rational decisions about families increasingly complicated by agencies that fail to cooperate.

Younger and younger children are being pulled into the cocaine and general drug trade to serve as look-outs, dealers, mules, and layaways. This tends to permanently distort and corrupt their value systems. Younger children see drug dealer affluence and become "wannabes": they "want to be" as successful as their drug-dealing entreprenurial neighbors. Children discover that they can earn more from the drug trade than their own parents can hope to garner from public assistance or marginal employment. These children undergo an emotional and financial "role reversal" with their parents. Adults find it difficult to reject sorely needed money even when it comes from the illicit drug trade. These children are exposed to the violence that surrounds cocaine dealing. Many are arming themselves and committing murder and becoming the victims of homicide, now an epidemic in our country.

Back in the sixties, H. Rap Brown said that violence is "as American as cherry pie." It seems his words were both accurate and prophetic. Powerful handguns, not inaccurate "Saturday night specials," but .38s, .45s, .357 magnums, .380s, 9 mms, and worse are becoming commonplace in America's ghettos. Drug dealers now carry automatic weapons (assualt rifles, MAC 10 pistols, Uzi submachine guns). These weapons tear bodies apart; their use has turned some city hospital emergency rooms into "war zone trauma centers." Drug dealers are becoming younger and younger. Many ghetto youth now perceive guns as something necessary to their daily survival—not merely the tools of the drug trade.

As we mentioned earlier, violence is a generic problem in the ghetto. Bob Maynard, a Newspaper columnist, told one terrible tale on 30 July 1990 Oakland (CA) *Journal News*):

Children and Guns, an Explosive National Tale. . . .

It was not easy to listen to Monica Reed on television the other night. She was eyewitness to a terror in our times. Her brother, 13-year-old Kevin Reed, had been walking on a quiet East Oakland street with two of his friends. A car drove by and a young man inside opened fire on the three children.

"I laid him on may lap," said Monica. She reached Kevin's side within minutes of the shooting. "I tried CPR, but it wouldn't work, and then his hands and arms got real cold and his head got heavy, I think then I knew . . . he was going to die."

Fifteen-year-old Varsey McClinton was shot to death on 8 January 1990, on the streets of Brooklyn's Fort Greene section for refusing to give a "high-5" sign to another teenager. Sherif S. Byrd, aged ten, was killed when he was caught in a deadly cross fire of dueling drug dealers on the streets of the Bronx. The summer of 1990 saw the number of children, many of them innocent bystanders, murdered by random and drug-related violence reach an all-time high. Law enforcement officials pointed to the crack trade as the cause of this violence. The Crime Control Institute, a Washington-based research group, reports an upsurge in the murder rate and homicide arrest rate for youth under age nineteen. This is the highest rate in the thirty-year history of the arrest reporting system. Dr. Lawrence W. Sherman, a criminologist at the University of Maryland, conducted a study of bystander shootings, and found that such killings had more than tripled in New York, Los Angeles, Washington, and Boston from 1985 to 1989. "Its like terrorism. . . . it disrupts your expectancy of safety in ordinary places" (*New York Times,* 12 August 1990).

We have met children of cocaine addicts who have been direct witnesses to this mayhem. Some of them have lost siblings, some have lost parents. We also know of children who have been shot. This is the real drug war, and the children of addicts are its victims. Unaided, the victims, in time, may become the next perpetrators of this violence.

What Is Known about the Children of Cocaine?

Innocent Addicts: The Fetus

> *"Do you believe that birth is an enjoyable experience for the baby?"*
> —Frederick Leboyer

Fetal abuse is the term used to describe the harm done to the unborn by drug-using pregnant women. Crack smoking, nasal cocaine use, and intravenous use of cocaine during pregnancy is increasing to frightening proportions in the poorer neighborhoods of our society. These mothers-to-be risk damaging their children for life. Research, in just the past few years, has begun to document the horrendous effects cocaine is having on the human fetus and the young child. Some pregnant crack and cocaine users are ignorant of these damaging effects. Others know they risk harming their babies but report feeling powerless to stop using drugs. We have also encountered cases where even after observing harmful effects to one child, women once again become pregnant and continue to use cocaine. And finally, when women themselves seek to stop this form of fetal abuse by attempting to enroll in treatment programs, many are turned away for lack of room.

Dr. Wendy Chavkin is a physician and Rockefeller Foundation Fellow at the Columbia School of Public Health. In the summer of 1989 she surveyed seventy-eight drug treatment programs in New York City. Her findings are both shocking and sad:

> Women claiming to be pregnant and addicted were refused service by 54% of programs; 67% denied treatment to pregnant addicts on Medicaid; 87% denied treatment to pregnant women on Medicaid addicted specifically to crack. Less than half of those programs that did accept pregnant women made arrangements for prenatal and only two provided child care, despite research by the National Institute on Drug Abuse demonstrating that lack of child care effectively precludes the participation of women in drug treatment.

Thus, pregnant women can not get help during the crucial nine months of their pregnancies, and those with children must be separated from them. This further contributes to a breakup of the remaining family unit. In New York State, where one child in ten is born to an addicted woman, we are speaking of some 25,000 new births per year! And only 3 percent of these women were in treatment!

Researchers tell us that crack and cocaine use cuts across all socioeconomic barriers, but the poorest and most alienated women in our society suffer the most. Addicts with adequate incomes and proper insurance benefits can arrange for private care. They often fail to inform their doctors of their cocaine use and the fetus goes unmonitored. Of course, obstetricians who treat middle-class women do not routinely inquire about their patient's patterns of illegal drug use. A conspiracy of silence exists between doctor and patient. Physicians are only just beginning to caution women about drinking alcoholic beverages during pregnancy. They had better add cocaine to their cautionary list because alcohol is often used in conjunction with all forms of cocaine to "smooth" out the high and forestall some aspects of the postcocaine "crash." The combination of alcohol and cocaine plans the fetus at risk for fetal alcohol syndrome (FAS) and whatever other harm is brought about by cocaine. Zuckerman and his colleagues at the Boston University School of Medicine (1989) and others have attempted to study women who smoked marijuana and used cocaine during pregnancy. These studies reveal that much work remains to be done to determine exactly which effects are associated with which drugs and what amounts are harmful to the fetus. In addition, work has just begun to determine at which points in the pregnancy (trimesters, for example) drug use is most harmful. All women of childbearing age need to be educated about the dangers of cocaine ingestion during pregnancy.

Crack/cocaine users are giving birth to a growing number of drug-effected infants (also referred to as drug-exposed infants). Constitutional makeup determines which babies will suffer the most. The regular crack and cocaine user often experiences a decrease in appetite, which can have a damaging effect on the nutrition of the fetus. Maternal malnutrition in the early stages of fetal growth is a decisive factor in the production of many congenital malformations. Dr. Ira Chasnoff and his colleagues at Northwestern University and the National Association for Perinatal Addiction Research and Education (NAPARE) have conducted a series of studies on the effects of cocaine use in pregnancy (Chasnoff, Hatcher, & Burns, 1982; Chasnoff, Schnoll, Burns, & Burns, 1984; Chasnoff, Burns, Schnoll, & Burns, 1985; Chasnoff, Bussey, Savich, & Stack, 1986; Chasnoff

& Schnoll, 1987; Chasnoff, Griffith, McGregor, et al., 1989).
Listed below are some of the early findings regarding cocaine use
during the various trimesters of pregnancy.

Use of Cocaine in the First Trimester of Pregnancy

- Associated with a 9 percent rate of abruptio placentae (mis-carriage), similar to the abruption rate for women who used cocaine throughout pregnancy (15 percent)
- Genito-urinary tract abnormalities (three out of seventy-five)
- Significant impairment in areas of orientation, motor ability, and number of abnormal reflexes.
- Motor ability was significantly below users of cocaine throughout pregnancy.
- Seven of sixteen newborns in this group were unable to reach alert states at all and consequently were unable to engage in any orientation.
- Compared to drug-free infants, crack/cocaine exposure in first trimester does place the newborn at risk for neurobehavioral deficiencies.

Use of Cocaine in the First, Second, and Third Trimesters

- Rate of premature delivery increased
- Lower birth weight, shorter length
- Small for gestational age
- Smaller head circumference
- Six of seventy-five had seizures during the neonatal period
- Two of seventy-five had suffered perinatal cerebral infarctions
- Six of seventy-five has genito-urintary tract abnormalities
- Eight of thirty-six infants were unable to reach alert states at all and were unable to engage in any orientation.

Other findings:

It is now known that crack/cocaine readily passes through the
placental barrier. A large enough binge can reduce the blood supply
so dramatically that the placenta may tear away from the uterus,
causing still births. In one study 15 percent of mothers who used I.V.
cocaine experienced premature separation of the placenta (this per-

centage is twice the rate of women addicted to other drugs and four times the rate of drug-free women). Risk of premature separation is directly reduced by ceasing cocaine use early in pregnancy. Cocaine ingested by parents) has been found in the urine of newborns twelve to twenty-four hours after delivery; cocaine metabolites (benzoylecgonine) continue to be excreted by infants for up to five days after birth.

A small "hit" is enough to cause spasms in the fetus's blood vessels, depriving the baby of the oxygen and other vital nutrients it needs. It is even possible for a fetal stroke to occur.

A higher number of spontaneous abortions and premature labors have also been reported. Nearly a third of the babies were born between the 20th and 38th week of pregnancy compared to only 3 percent preterm deliveries in a group of forty nondrug-using comparison women in one study.

The emotional consequences of crack/cocaine addiction cause great harm in the normal prebirth bonding syndrome. Expectant parents go through various emotional "trimesters" as they prepare to love their child to come. Early on, in normal pregnancies, the mother-to-be experiences an enhanced sense of narcissism. The physical reality of the bond between mother and fetus is often experienced as a fusion. Various ego defenses "loosen up" and early life emotional conflicts for the expectant mother may often emerge. The expectant mother must make the psychological effort to prepare herself to undertake the role of "parent" in an adaptive way. The psychological work of pregnancy is to *attach* the parent-to-be with the fetus.

Drug-dependent, expectant parents are delayed at these psychological tasks. They emotionally *detach* themselves from their fetuses. These parents are not anywhere near fully engaged in the process of expecting. Too often the mothers-to-be report no pleasure from their pregnancy, indicate that they feel like the victims of "bad luck," and suffer increasing isolation, depression, and guilt. Becoming a parent is often an incentive for terminating destructive behaviors. Indeed, we have interviewed many female addicts whose pregnancies were sufficient cause for them to stop using drugs—at least for nine months. Clinical interventions at this junction of the life cycle do have a great potential—if there are openings in the proper types of programs.

Case Illustration 1: Joyce

Joyce, age thirty-two, has one son in foster care. The social service department charged her with neglect; the neighbors indicated crack/cocaine abuse. Joyce denies both charges. Neighbors report that she left four-year-old Jimmy alone on the street all day while she got high. Joyce is severely underweight and looks much older than her stated age. A sympathetic woman, she brought Jimmy his favorite goodies and toys on the one supervised visit she made to the foster care agency during her son's eight months of placement. The putative father was dead, a murder victim.

Joyce stated that she had been given up for adoption when she was two years old. Her mother was an alcoholic. She was adopted by a middle-class family in suburban New York. Joyce claims that she was a poor student and never felt right in school. Her adoptive parents expected more from her. She dropped out of school in the 11th grade. Joyce tells of having many unskilled jobs until she became pregnant. The father of the child beat Joyce frequently. He was a drug user and seller.

She turned to her adoptive family for help, but they completely severed relations with her. Joyce states that she loves Jimmy. Social work staff requested Jimmy's immunization record and were surprised that she had it intact. She related to her child warmly, but warmth turned to anger when he was not responsive enough for her liking. She told Jimmy she would be back in a week, but she did not contact him again.

Joyce told the social worker she was pregnant again. The social worker made a few home visits, but Joyce was unavailable.

The Newborn: Babies at Risk

"The earliest, deepest wish of every newborn is for a loving, satisfying connection with the nurturing parent."

—W. Ronald D. Fairbairn, M.D.

Crack/cocaine babies are indeed "at risk." The enormous dependency needs of a healthy full-term baby are substantially less that those of a baby born after prolonged exposure to cocaine. Chasnoff and Schnoll (1987) report conflicting findings of teratorgenicity (the development of abnormal structures in an embryo) in animal studies involving cocaine. They conclude that cocaine clearly exerts a negative influence on pregnancy outcome and that there is a possibility that cocaine-exposed infants are at high risk for perinatal mortality and morbidity (a state of being diseased). However, Chasnoff Schnoll did not find evidence for congenital abnormalities in the newborns. Madden et al. (1986) found no teratogenic effects or any abnormalities born to eight women who had abused cocaine.

Many cocaine babies are quite small. Chasnoff reported that 25 percent of the babies born to cocaine-using mothers had decrements in birth weights (compared to only 5 percent of the babies born to drug-free women). Zuckerman and his colleagues questioned 1,224 mothers during pregnancy and after delivery. They found that cocaine-exposed babies were 93 grams lighter and 0.7 centimeters shorter than nonexposed babies. By way of contrast, they report that mothers who smoked marijuana regularly gave birth to children who were 70 grams lighter and 0.5 centimeters shorter than babies of drug-free women (NIDA *Notes,* 1989/1990).

About 15 percent of cocaine-exposed infants in the Chasnoff study died of sudden infant death syndrome (SIDS). The national average incidence is 0.5−1.0 percent.

Many cocaine babies are born HIV positive. In cocaine-exposed babies the number is about 60%. IV drug-related transmission of AIDS is especially significant for women. Of women who have AIDS, 51% are IV drug users, while approximately 20% are the sexual partners of IV drug users. Researchers believe that HIV-infected mothers will infect their infants prior to or at birth about 50 percent of the time (NIDA Capsules, 1990). Also indicated earlier, women with syphilis are more vulnerable to HIV transmission and AIDS.

The neurological system of a cocaine baby is hyperexcitable and can not process normal stimulation. Like other babies, cocaine babies tend to sleep when overstimulated. Cocaine-effected babies may be in a deep sleep up to 90 percent of the time, or they may act excitable and jittery. Some exhibit a combination of both types of behavior (Adler, 1990). Dr. Barry Lester, a psychologist at Brown University, and the staff of E.P. Bradley Hospital have found that excitable behavior, such as crying behavior, results from direct exposure of the fetus to cocaine. Lethargic or depressed behavior, such as excessive sleeping, results from indirect effects and is related to low birth weight (Adler, 1990). Cocaine babies advert their gaze. They have poor motor control that prevents them from exploring their own bodies and objects around them, thereby contributing to developmental delays. Data on thirty full-term cocaine-exposed infants and fifty full-term non-drug-exposed infants indicate a significant difference in mean total risk: 72 percent of the control group infants were assigned to the "no risk" category, while 43 percent of the cocaine-exposed infants were designated "high risk" for motor development dysfunction (NIDA Capsules, 1989).

Nesrin et al. (1987) studied birth defects among pregnant women in two large inner-city hospitals in East Harlem and the South Bronx. They examined fifty cocaine-only using women, 110 who were polydrug abusers, and 340 drug-free women (matched for ethnicity, SES, and smoking histories). They found that cocaine abuse significantly reduced birth weight, increased the number of stillbirths due to abruptio placentae, and was associated with a higher congenital malformation rate.

Habel, Kay, and Lee (1990) examined the records of the New York City Department of Health which maintains a linked birth/infant death file. This file combines the birth data and the death data of any infant who dies. They found the following:

- Reports of infants born to drug-abusing mothers increased from 6.7 per 1000 live births in 1981 to 20.3 per 1000 live births in 1987, with abuse of cocaine accounting for most of the rise.
- When standardized for race and ethnicity, the mortality rate for drug-exposed infants born from 1978 through 1986 was 35.9, or 2.4 times that for infants in New York City in general.
- Drug-exposed infants were three times are likely as infants in the general population to be of low birthweight.
- The association of both opiates and cocaine with increased mortality and low birthweight were similar.

- Death rates from SIDS and AIDS were especially high for drug-exposed infants, and were similar for opiate- and cocaine-exposed infants.

Dr. Daniel Griffith, a psychologist at Northwestern University Medical School, issued an important caveat concerning generalizations about cocaine-exposed babies: "Any attempt to describe categories is going to be too simplistic. One of the most important things to realize is there is no stereotypical cocaine-exposed baby."

Rosecan, Spitz, and Gross (1987), of the Columbia-Presbyterian Medical Center, New York City, rightfully caution us that there are difficulties in interpreting the available data on "the effect of cocaine on the fetus for the following reasons: small sample size, polydrug abuse and lack of long term data. Polydrug abuse makes it difficult to separate the teratogenic effects of cocaine from those substances like alcohol and cigarettes." The National Association for Perinatal Research and Education (NAPARE) has received a number of NIDA-sponsored grants which hopefully will address these concerns. NAPARE is entering its fifth year of a longitudinal study of infants exposed to cocaine and other drugs during pregnancy. They are also conducting a four-year study of drug use by women during pregnancy in twenty hospitals; a study comparing the impact of residential versus outpatient treatment for pregnant women and their families; and a one-year study of the prevalence of drug use by pregnant women in private and public hospitals in Illinois (UPDATE, 1990). Chasnoff and Schnoll conclude "only through further studies can the full impact of cocaine on pregnancy and the developing fetus be appreciated."

Chasnoff et al. (1990) report highly significant racial discrepancies in mandatory reporting of women who used alcohol or illicit drugs during pregnancy. According to objective urine testing conducted on a sample of 715 women, there was little differences between women tested in clinic settings (16.3 percent positive tox) and private offices (13.1 percent positive tox), and the frequency of a positive result was also similar among white women (15.4 percent) and black women (14.1 percent). During the six-month period during which these specimens were collected, 133 women in Pinellas County, Florida, were reported to health authorities after delivery for substance abuse during pregnancy. Black women were reported at ten times the rate for white women, and poor black women were more likely than other women to be reported!

Below are two case histories taken from our own work which will give the reader a feel for the human beings that are often lost in the statistical reporting of scientific studies.

Case Illustration 2: Jason

Jason, now age two and a one half, was born addicted to cocaine. Labor was difficult and premature, after a gestation period of thirty weeks. He weighed 1 lb. 15. oz. at birth. His APGAR score was 3-7. He was born with anemia, HIV(−), oral thrush, a head circumference of 23.5 cm (tangerine size) and soon required an inguinal hernia repair. The tubes in his ears were not fully developed. He was hospitalized from birth to six months of age. He mother left the maternity ward and never came back. Child welfare workers later found out that his mother died of AIDS.

Jason's development has been quite slow. At six months, he went to a caring foster home. Jason seemed to be continually sick, suffering from bronchitis, clinical pneumonia, and recurrent ear infections. He responded to the warmth of his foster family; after two months with them he weighed 14 pounds. Jason did respond with alertness but all his developmental milestones were delayed. He smiled easily, made good eye contact, and liked to play. He is active and it is still hard for him to gain weight; at two and a half he weighs 22 lbs. and appears much younger and smaller than his age. Jason has a moderate hearing impairment and has attended speech and language therapy. The foster parents are optimistic about his development and are considering adoption.

Case Illustration 3: Christopher Anthony

Christopher Anthony was born at thirty-five weeks gestation with a positive toxicology for cocaine. He weighed 5.7 lbs; head circumference was 35.5 cm. His biological mother disappeared. Christopher Anthony was discharged to a foster home where he slept all day and was up all night. He became rigid when the foster parents picked him up or touched him. He cried constantly. The foster parents used massage techniques to relax his rigid body. He had one brief period of playfulness each day; his foster parents would use this opportunity to talk to him. He ran a low-grade fever fairly regularly, but despite this continued to gain weight. There was speculation of neurological damage. Due to the adoption laws he had to be moved from a foster home into a preadoptive home. At the age of nine months, the preadoptive parents reneged due the child's difficulties. He was placed in yet another home. He has been freed for adoption and awaits a family.

These symptoms can persist up to four months and caretakers often have a difficult time with these babies. Attachment and bonding are frequently hampered. These babies are often unresponsive even when cared for by the most loving adults!

Both the biological mothers and their cocaine-exposed infants enter the mother/child relationship impaired. Addicted mothers quickly become frustrated by the task of caring for their infants. Like so many substance abusers, who themselves received so little love as children, they have little to give to these needy babies and easily become distraught and frustrated. The infants add to their mothers' problems by being so much more difficult to care for than infants born to non-substance-abusing parents. Crack/cocaine moth-

---

Observable Signs of Stimulus Overload

Hiccups
Change in color
Yawning
Sneezing
Trouble responding to voice and touch
Closed eyes
Uncontrollable crying

FIGURE 2-2.

A Cycle of Despair.

ers have low self-esteem to start with. When their babies turn away from them, they feel rejection. Their babies' actions are read as further evidence of their own worthlessness.

In most states, newborns testing positive for cocaine are referred to child protective services. Mothers who keep their babies—approximately 35 percent do—suffer increased loss of self-esteem and guilt, along with normal postpartum depression. Their babies are at continued risk for abuse and neglect.

Child welfare agencies are monitoring these families. These parents require massive amounts of support in order to be able to provide for their babies. With the aid of parent support/education groups, many parents begin to feel more competent about raising their children. When the parent experiences success and support, they gain self-esteem and are better able to master the tasks of parenting. The babies derive immeasurable benefits from parental pride.

However, some parents can not attach themselves to the constantly crying, often rigid, and ever-demanding newborn. The drug-dependent parent may try to escape deeper into their drugs to escape from this apparently unrewarding task, one that they are so ill prepared to handle. In the absence of social service supports, these children are often neglected. Rejection and frustration also provoke hostility and rage, making the children at risk for physical abuse.

Developmental pediatricians and other infant specialists have developed techniques for calming these babies down. Many of the techniques listed below are adopted from the work of Dr. Dan Griffith, a developmental psychologist (Update, 1989).

Techniques for Calming and Comforting the Cocaine Baby

- Don't allow the baby to reach a frantic cry state. Watch for distress cues.
- To help the baby master motor control you may use swaddling and offer a pacifier.
- Hold the baby closely and rock it in a vertical position. When the baby is agitated you can face it away from the parent (hard for them to orient when agitated).
- Orient the baby to face or voice contact when awake and calm. Use one stimulation at a time and watch for distress signs.
- You may need to stop what you are doing and allow the baby to recover.
- Gradually increase the amount of interactive visual, auditory, or tactile play. But play only when and as long as the baby is ready to accept it.
- Unwrap the baby when he/she is calm and allow to become accustomed to controlling body movements. When the baby signals loss of control, reswaddle and let the baby rest.
- Remove all stimuli if baby is displaying distress.
- If the baby is engaging in frantic sucking of fists use infant shirt (baby t-shirt) with sewn-in sleeves for mitts to prevent damage to the skin. If the skin is damaged, keep infected area clean with a mild soap and water.
- If the baby is sneezing, has nasal stuffiness, and trouble breathing: clean nose frequently. Be careful not to restrict chest movement with tightly wrapped blankets if the baby is having trouble breathing.

Mothers who follow these parenting tips should find them effective. These mothers will experience their overall parenting role as more positive and rewarding. Cocaine exposed babies do have responsive periods, although brief, each day. Parenting support groups that begin immediately after birth can offer emotional support and practical remediation. These groups can serve as a kind of extended family, often missing from the lives of the participants. The mothers share a sense of common purpose and mutuality. The common bonds of combatting drug dependency while mothering are shared. Increasing parental competence helps satisfy the wish of every baby to be nurtured and loved by an emotionally available parent.

Warning

Medical examiners in Philadelphia are investigating ten infant deaths from 1986 to 1989. All had chemical evidence of cocaine in their blood and died within several hours after cocaine exposure. Doctors theorize that passive crack smoke was the cause of death because the mothers were not breast feeding. The recent evidence surrounding passive cigarette smoke and its proven dangers raises the possibility of an even more lethal problem involving crack smoke. In an ongoing study, nearly six of every one hundred youngsters (aged one month to five years of age) treated in the emergency room of Children's Hospital of Michigan had cocaine in their systems from breathing the "second-hand" smoke of adult crack users. All the children who tested positive for cocaine (drug toxicology tests are done routinely upon admission to the ER) would have been exposed in the previous three days because cocaine passes through the body in seventy-two hours.

Preschoolers: Old Problems Persist and New Ones Arise

"The child indulges in fantasies of being a giant and a tiger, but in his dreams he runs in terror for dear life."

—Erik H. Erikson

Dr. Judith Howard and her colleagues at the University of California at Los Angeles (Howard et al., 1989) have found that toddlers who had been exposed to cocaine (or other drugs) in the womb are emotionally and socially underdeveloped and have difficulty learning. They compared eighteen prenatally drug-exposed eighteen-month-old toddlers with toddlers who had been born prematurely. The two groups came from poor, single-parent households. Their mothers were undereducated. All the babies had received little pre-natal care, although after birth, both groups of children received excellent health care and were not abused or neglected.

The drug-exposed children did not show strong feelings of plea-sure, anger, or distress. When playing alone, these toddlers were less creative and purposeful. They scattered or batted toys and dolls, picked them up, and soon laid them back down again. In compari-son, the non-drug-exposed children would sit a doll at a table, stir a pot, or make motorlike sounds with a truck. Another striking obser-vation was that most of the children subjected to drugs prenatally seemed unattached to their caregivers. They exhibited no emotion when their caregivers left or returned, an unusual reaction for eighteen-month-olds, who normally are upset when their mothers leave.

The two groups of children were given standardized developmen-tal assessment tests in which an examiner guided activity with the child. Although the drug-exposed children scored significantly lower on the developmental scale, their results were still within the "low average" range. Dr. Howard notes that "The children appeared to be more competent then we clinically judged them to be." We can only wonder what "experimenter bias" may have crept into this type of study, for many of the measured differences were quite subtle. Dr. Coryl Jones of NIDA's Prevention Research branch has stated that "Researchers and clinicians often observe difference between drug-exposed and non-drug exposed infants but have trouble describing these differences. Tools need to be developed to standardize how clinicians and investigators record neurobehavioral effects. When assessment instruments are inadequate, results indicate few or no long-term effects."

In an unpublished study comparing normal children with two- and three-year-old cocaine-exposed children, Drs. Chasnoff and Griffith found no difference between the two groups as a whole on the Bayley Scales of Infant Development. They did find, however, that about one-third of the cocaine-exposed two-year-olds had real difficulties on the items that measure beginning language development and the ability to sustain an activity in the face of distractions. Similar results were also reported for the three-year-olds. Cocaine-exposed children responded well to the same sort of help that other children would receive for similar developmental problems reports Dr. Griffith. He stated "It's not a new breed of child." Dr. Griffith was quick to note that the findings must be qualified by the fact that the mothers of the cocaine-exposed children had volunteered for treatment and the infants received good pre- and post-natal care and nutrition.

NIDA program staff point out that "despite the recent flurry of research findings, there are still gaps in knowledge that must be filled". Specifically, we need empirically derived, longitudinal studies, employing matched controls to determine:

1. What is the effect of dose and duration of drug exposure on newborns?
2. What, if any, are the delayed effects due to prenatal drug exposure? And are these effects reversible?
3. How does drug exposure in the womb affect a child's behavior or performance at home and school?
4. How does maternal drug use affect child rearing?

In the absence of these types of large sample studies, actual case histories are instructive.

Case Illustration 4: Jonathan

Jonathan F., age four and a half, was born with a positive toxicology for cocaine. His sixteen-year-old mother smoked crack throughout the pregnancy. His father, age forty-six, and the mother were looking forward to the birth and participated in prenatal classes. The father also smoked crack several times a week and maintained a job as superintendent of a large apartment building.

Jonathan seemed to escape any affects of the drugs until he was sixteen-months-old, when he began having seizures. His mother left and married a man who would not accept Jonathan. The biological father, still smoking crack, attained custody. Mr. F. attended a Veteran's Administration drug rehab program three times. During these absences Jonathan was left in the care of a babysitter.

Unsuccessful at rehabilitation, Mr. F. continued to smoke

crack. He stated that Jonathan's only toys were a radio and VCR. Jonathan often observed his father engaging in various sexual acts with a variety of partners. Jonathan's seizures increased and his father did seek neurological help. Because of his continuing drug use, he could not follow the doctor's orders and administer his son's medication on a regularly scheduled basis.

Mr. F. finally requested foster care for Jonathan. He now visits him on a weekly basis. During these supervised visits, a male case worker played with Jonathan and provided modeling and parent education to his father. Mr. F. confided that he still smokes crack "a few times a week."

Jonathan's adjustment to his foster home was difficult. Immediate neurological workups were needed because the boy was measured as having 150 petit and grand mal seizures a day! Medication regimes to stabilize the seizures are still being evaluated nine months later. Socially, Jonathan was quiet and fairly obedient to his foster parents. He would act out sexual behaviors on his foster siblings. The parents worked hard to deal with their own strong feelings about this precocious and provocative behavior. They set limits in a compassionate manner. The agency staff were sensitive to the needs of his other caretakers (especially the nursery school) and gave frequent consultations until Jonathan's sexual acting out subsided.

Developmentally, Jonathan was environmentally delayed in the areas of eating skills, exhibited deficits in fantasy and play, had delayed fine motor skills, undersocialized, and experienced lags in speech and language. Frequent aggressive behavior was also documented. Emotionally, Jonathan was highly guarded and slow to trust people. Separation anxiety from the end of supervised visits with his father did not occur until four months into placement. He is very quiet and still does not feel comfortable sharing his feelings and a sadness exists in his emotional posture. In his special education, prekindergarten class, he is liked by his teachers and peers.

He receives physical therapy, occupational therapy, prescribed special education, and play therapy.

Mr. F. appreciates all the help his son is getting. He is trying to get into drug rehabilitation treatment again. He states that he longs to be reunited with his son.

Mr. F.'s addictive life-style became unmanageable. His extended family lives in other states and he was unable to create informal supports systems. His case is unusual, as the more common profile of a crack-addicted parent appears below.

Profile of the Average Crack-Addicted Parent

- Female
- Age twenty-five
- On crack for one to five years
- 11th grade education
- 44 percent on public assistance
- Tenuous self-esteem; if child is placed in foster care, self esteem is even more difficult to retrieve
- Involvement with public agencies infantilizes parents by assuming too many of their adult responsibilities
- Mothers have usually suffered from sexual abuse, incest, substance abuse, domestic violence, emotional neglect, poverty, and racism

All of this adds up to parents whose egos have disintegrated. It seems fruitless to expect these parents—without the benefit of drug-abuse treatment that also addresses parenting skills—to be able to provide the nurturance and support their children are entitled to.

Latency: Families Lost, Often Forever

> "Love is more than simply being open to experiencing the anguish of another person's suffering. It is the willingness to live with the helpless knowing that we can do nothing to save the other from his pain."
>
> —*Sheldon B. Koop*

Crack/cocaine addicts have not been present long enough to have historical examples of latency age children being born with positive cocaine toxicology. Today, in New York State alone, there are an 148,000 children between the ages of six and eleven who live with substance-abusing parents.

Many of these children live with grandmothers or other relatives. Thirty percent live with their biological mothers. The rest of these children flood the foster care system. Since babies and younger children have priority for foster homes placement, latency age children live in foster boarding home settings, called group homes.

Unlike other dysfunctional family behaviors, these children do not deny their parents' drug problem. They have witnessed their mothers and fathers smoking crack. Many of these children talk about cooking crack: "Take a big pot, put in the powder (cocaine), heat it up with water and baking soda and wait 'til it pops!" They have seen their parents high, depressed, paranoid, and violent. These children live with an unusual amount of violence in their lives. Their parents will often resort to burglary, prostitution, and mugging in pursuit of money to buy drugs. It is painful for these children to talk about their mother's prostitution. Children used as pawns in prostitution rings, to help the family "drug economy," have great difficulty describing their life circumstances.

Case Illustration 5: Charlie

Charlie, age eight, came into the group home reluctantly. He had been truant from school for several months. Child welfare officials placed him in care due to parental neglect. His mother had begun using crack two years prior to his group home placement. Her relatives had pitched in to help care for her children, but eventually gave up.

The group home staff was worried because Charlie regurgitated everything he ate. He had a dietary need to be on soft food unknown to the group home staff. The child admitted that for the past few months he ate what he found in garbage cans. Charlie also had head lice, was quite thin, and very dirty. An eye examination revealed that he was in need of glasses.

Charlie responded quickly to the structure and guidance of the group home. He was academically delayed and required remedial help. Having the friendship of the other boys, in care for the same reasons, lessened his shame.

Charlie's most painful times were weekends and holidays when he remained at the group home while others visited parents. His mother became homeless and could not be located. Charlie would confide in a trusted staff member that he thought about his mother constantly. Little wonder his teachers reported that Charlie seemed distracted in class.

Charlie, in a desperate effort to find his mother, brought staff members to his former neighborhood. Gunshots were heard in the background, as Charlie and staff members threaded their way up dark apartment house stairways littered with crack vials and other drug paraphernalia, carefully avoiding couples engaged in sexual activity on the stairwells. These impediments did not stop Charlie's search, but he failed to find his mother. Upon returning to the group home, the child welfare workers offered Charlie a hug which he eagerly received. He was promised a visit with his only known relative, his younger brother Allen.

Allen, a developmentally disabled five-year-old-child (born with a positive cocaine toxicology) was initially placed in care along with Charlie. Allen's low level of functioning precluded his remaining in community-based care. Allen was placed in an institution for developmentally disabled youngsters. After sibling visits, Charlie verbalized feelings of loneliness. He spent a great deal of his eight years taking care of Allen. His longing for a real family is pervasive.

A great aunt came fourth ten months after Charlie was placed in care. This elderly woman and her husband wanted to become his foster parents. After the casework interviews, visitations began. Charlie's mood lifted. He looked forward to being discharged. The elderly couple were, sadly, rejected as foster parents. Unfortunately, the blood relationship between Charlie and his aunt was too far removed and, as a result, her home standards would have to meet numerous fire, safety, and space standards.

Faced with meeting such standards the aunt withdrew her application. Charlie was heartbroken. His hopes for finding family were dashed once again.

The next step for a chilld like Charlie would be to free him for adoption. He would be photolisted and attend "adoption parties" where adoptable children are placed on view for perspective adoptive parents. Very few children of Charlie's age are actually adopted. Moreover, adoption often does not work out for those who are adopted. When an adoption fails children are returned to a foster or group home. Competition for group home beds is so intense that places for children cannot be reserved, so the children of failed adoptions often end up worse off, for they lose the friends they made in their original group home.

Twenty-five percent of latency-age children of substance abusers will have similar histories. They are tormented by abandonment, repeated loss, rage, and indifference. Sadly, increased intellectual understanding usually brings with it increased emotional trauma. They are children in search of parents, feeling rejected and unwanted.

Developmental lags in expressive and receptive language make it hard for the "Charlies" to make sense of their world. Relationships with love objects continue to be shallow.

Thirty-five percent of latency-age children living with drug-addicted parents were abused. Drug use thrives on isolation. The more isolated the parents, the more severe the abuse. Take for example a reclusive family with nine children living in the Bronx. The children lived in squalor and were abused and neglected. Neighbors rarely saw the children and a few reports to the authorities went unheeded. Parents addicted to cocaine demonstrate higher levels of violence than those addicted to other drugs. Children develop survival skills to cope with such violent, neglectful homes—survival skills ill-suited for success outside the home.

Latency is usually a time of action. Running, jumping, ball playing are all part of latency. Children become part of a peer group. In order to be successful in such peer group activities, a child must develop social skills and group morality. Proficiency in language helps in mastery of socialization and group morality. Other major tasks of latency include learning to read, developing scientific approaches to problem solving, distinguishing between right and wrong, learning to tell the truth, and forming close, same-sex friendships.

Children of substance abusers do not experience latency as a highly productive period of childhood. Their addicted parents often failed to master these same latency tasks and therefore are not a resource for them.

At best, these vulnerable children get inconsistent nurturance and praise. Isolation becomes soothing as the child avoids painful contacts with other people. These children growup to expect less. Their fragile egos implode, making aloneness and isolation seem more attractive. Such children are "bad seeds" for drug addiction and gang activity, both of which thrive on suspiciousness and lack of trust.

Adolescents: A Tormented Leap into Adulthood

> "*Adults rarely see the young clearly. We fantasize about them, we project onto them our own dreams and phobias and needs; we tell ourselves stories about them and devise programs to solve what we call 'their problems.'*"
>
> —Peter Marin and Allan Y. Cohen

Adolescence is a time of resolving identity issues, of separating from one's parents. In completing a successful adolescence the child must integrate his/her past with the coming future. Children who in their earlier years have failed to acquire the problem-solving, intellectual skills of latency struggle mightily with adolescence. Negative identities are formed when growth possibilities are restricted by environmental, intellectual, and psychological limitations.

Children of substance abusers are often confronted with all of these limitations. The myriad of choices in adolescence can be very confusing even to children from high-functioning homes and close to impossible for the limited children of the drug addicted.

Educational and occupational success, clear gender identity, positive self-esteem, and a positive body image form the basis of adult personality. Parental influence is especially important during this tumultuous time as adolescents seek validation and celebration of their emerging personalities. Good-enough parents facilitate development throughout this period, but drug-addicted parents exacerbate difficulties by being unavailable or abusive.

Case Illustration 6: Jamal

Jamal, age fourteen, claims that his mother was a nice normal mom until she started using crack. She held a job as a bank teller until cocaine addiction overpowered her. When she smoked crack Jamal would flee the apartment, because his mother transformed from the stable bank employee—"Mrs. Jekyll"—into the verbally and physically abusive addict—"Mrs. Hyde."

Neighbors reported Jamal's situation to the authorities and he was placed in a group home. His mother promised to enter a drug treatment program. She was quite upset that her child had been removed from her home. Jamal longed to be reunited with his mother and verbalized to the staff that he would only be in a group home "for a short time."

A year passed. Jamal remained preoccupied with thoughts of his mother. In the group home he acted out his frustration and loneliness. His sweet innocence and dreams had been replaced by bitterness and confusion.

Case Illustration 7: Desiree

Desiree, also age fourteen, had a mother addicted to crack. Desiree was overweight and grew heavier each day. Her grandmother sent her to live in the South with her aunt. Desiree got along with everyone there, but was obsessed with checking on her mother. Her remarried father shunned her as well as her three younger siblings.

Desiree's aunt took her back North to visit her mother who was still actively using drugs. Desiree was offered the choice of returning to her aunt's custody or placement in a group home. She choose the group home to remain geographically close to her mother, indulging her dream of a reunited family. The group home staff made it clear to Desiree's mother that she could only visit when not using drugs. Drug testing was part of the agreement. The child agreed to the plan because she feared her mother when she was high.

Many months passed before the first visit, but Desiree

finally began to enjoy visits from her mother. At this point, the mother began to displace a lot of anger on the group home staff. Desiree aligned herself with her mother against the staff and planned to return to her mother's home. Her disappointment was immense when her mother relapsed into active addiction.

Desiree identified strongly with her mother. She assumed the role of the responsible oldest child and visited her younger siblings at their foster homes. At holiday time she went so far as to reach out to the father who had rejected all of them.

She excelled in school and was admitted to a special high school for the gifted. She was not comfortable attending school with other gifted youth and began to feel uncomfortable with her own success. Who had ever been so successful in her immediate family? Desiree was guarded. Accustomed to relying only on herself, she trusted no one. She had uncomfortable feelings about herself and her new classmates. She retreated into obesity, chronic headaches, and backaches.

Christmas time revealed Desiree's extreme need when the tough teenager asked Mrs. Rutter for a box of crayons and a coloring book for her present.

It is important to reflect further upon Desiree. A main task of adolescence is formulating an independent identity through accomplishment and psychological separation from the parent(s). Desiree's inability to embrace her positive accomplishments, coupled with her inability to separate from her drug-addicted mother, made the formulation of an independent identity very difficult. Her continued pursuit of a relationship with her addicted mother did little to relieve Desiree's deeply embedded sense of shame.

She sought to combat painful affects through overeating and prematurely adopting a parenting role with her younger siblings. However, these strategies did little to help her establish positive ties with her peers. Lacking the skills derived from successful completion of adolescence, a child like Desiree will go on to be haunted by loneliness and unmet dependency needs for the rest of her life. This is nothing short of a tragedy: her family's inability to love her leave Desiree without the resources needed to connect to other people. This is the profound price that children such as Desiree pay for their parent's addiction. Their ability to form close relationships is severely undermined regardless of their intelligence or abilities.

Accomplishing such developmental tasks of adolescence as peer group identification and bonding is made more difficult by the suspicion and fear that drug-addicted parents engender in their children. The child must mistrust the addicted parent in order to survive and can not easily give up a basic mistrust with either their peer group or adult authority figures.

Case Illustration 8: Emanuel

Emanuel, age seventeen, lived with his mother and her family of origin in a wealthy New York suburb. Emanuel was referred to counseling by his high school teachers. He is a street-smart teenager. He did well in school on the few days a week that he attended. He never came to school before 10:00 A.M. He knew how to get by in school without getting himself thrown out.

Emanuel's mother was involved in a dual addiction to heroin and cocaine. He was her only child. She often robbed her son of his cash to support her habit. Emanuel has been self-supporting for four years, working first as a dishwasher and later as a delivery boy. To protect himself from his mother's robbery attempts he invested in locks for his bedroom door and a safe. His grandparents, who shared the apartment with Emanuel and his mother, were not strong enough to protect him from his mother's invasive behavior. Occasionally the grandparents gave Emanuel money.

Emanuel was depressed and angry. He alienated several counselors before reaching the beginning phase of psychotherapy. He would show up for only one out of every four scheduled sessions and be late for that one. His case was transferred to a social work intern who had far fewer cases than the other counselors, and perhaps more desire to help. Through her empathic persistence,

Emanuel got past the "testing" phase and tentatively began to form a trusting relationship.

One of his greatest fears was contracting AIDS because of his mother's irrational behavior and intravenous drug use. He believed he was at "high risk" when he engaged in sexual intercourse. He wore three condoms simultaneously. He never brought friends to his home, and never gave anyone his phone number. His dream was to rent a room in the community, get his high school diploma, and join the armed forces.

His therapist encouraged him to pursue those dreams. It was touch and go for a while as truancy, delinquency, oppositional behavior, anxiety, and rage often interfered with Emanuel's progress. Emanuel did graduate from high school. The only person present was his therapist. She gave him a set of flatware for his furnished room. Emanuel was appreciative but still refused to give his therapist his new address.

Children like Jamal, Desiree, and Emanuel are at risk for serious occupational, emotional, and social problems. Their inability to satisfactorily master the developmental tasks of adolescence leaves them highly vulnerable despite their considerable abilities and survival skills.

The children of cocaine addicts need more than spot psychotherapy to survive. They need ongoing support to help them negotiate life's passages. The stark reality is that these children have no real families and no real parents. Will Desiree ever complete her education? Who will be waiting for Emanuel when he returns from military service? The same family that did not show up for a major life milestone, his high school graduation?

Affluent, middle-class children often have great difficulty coping in our high-tech, high-skills, competitive, and often uncaring society. Middle-class parents worry about how their children will deal with drugs, AIDS, school, and getting a good job.

What chance do the children of poor, drug-addicted, minority parents have in such a world as we have built for them? As Philadelphia school principal Madeline Cartwright stated in the *New York Times Magazine* (25 November 1990):

The preachers and doctors and all the rest of the black middle class that once set examples for children, those people are all gone. I don't have enough working families to use as role models. So my role models are my welfare families who take care of their children, who keep a clean house, who keep the children dressed up, who send the kids to school. Now I'm seeing these role models go right down the crack drain.

These children need life support systems to take the place of the parents and families they do not have. We all need to have someone at our graduations and other milestones—loving us, validating our efforts, and cheering us on to greater heights! These children cannot "Just Say No!" This nation needs effective leadership to provide the funds and other resources to help these young people cope with the economic and emotional poverty of their lives. Families of origin can not be replaced. We must find the courage and the funds to help these children become normal functioning adults in our society or risk losing them permanently to the impoverished lives led by their own lost parents. Failing schools, overcrowded jails and prisons, an overwhelmed criminal justice system, rocketing drug abuse—all are signs of societal failure. We ignore the children of substance abuse at our own peril.

Caring and effective intervention and support are vital for these children. We have to rethink current clinical intervention programs that treat adult addicts as patients, without also thinking of them as parents of dependent children. Maria Vandor is director of Women and Children's Services for the New York State Division of Substance Abuse Services. A knowledgeable professional, she had this to say during our interview in 1990:

These kids are survivors. They are far tougher and more resilient than the media gives them credit for. They have been labeled and stigmatized. And gross overgeneralizations are being made. Even some of the early researchers like Dr. Chasnoff are now reporting that what originally looked like horrific problems are appearing milder—with good assessment and intervention most of the children turn out better than originally anticipated. I get calls from school officials who, frightened by media reports of permanently damaged children, want to know what to do about the "crack kids" now that some of them are old enough to enter the school system. They are expecting an onslaught of a new wave of difficult children. It's just not the case. I tell them to assess and provide services where needed as they would with any other child experiencing developmental delays or behavioral problems. I am more concerned about the "lost children," aged birth to five years of age, who are not picked up by any system unless the family is grossly dysfunctional.

In the following chapters we consider the system(s) in detail and then discuss both traditional and innovative approaches to helping and healing the children. Our review of the literature on the children of heroin and cocaine has revealed that a great deal remains unknown. All that is known is not doom and gloom. Very often, in our work the children themselves have provided us with examples of both courage and optimism. The population of children of drug abusers is diverse, multivariate, and hard to stereotype. This is perhaps their greatest strength and hope for their own futures. Professionals in the fields of substance-abuse treatment, child welfare, child mental health, and family practice must stay tuned into these individual differences.

We must protect them from those who would see them as stereotypically coming from a single "cookie cutter," permanently damaged, "diseased," and hopeless. This is not what the literature to date tells us. We must have the courage and the wisdom to avoid the pitfalls and gross generalizations so often imposed on the children of alcoholics, who are so often asked to formulate their entire self-concept around the one historical fact of their parent's destructive drinking behavior.

3

The Current State of Affairs

Flaws in the System

Here the world is divided in two: the children of the light and the children of the darkness, the sheep and the goats, the elect and the damned.

—*Martin Buber*

This chapter is devoted to exposing the serious flaws in the substance-abuse treatment, child welfare, and family and criminal justice systems. Today all these systems find themselves overwhelmed and wholly unprepared to address the needs of the children of addicts. In the next chapter we will propose solutions in the form of a new child advocacy system that can work. In the final chapter we will cite examples of some treatment programs that are keeping parents and children together and working to strengthen families. It is important to note now that within the existing substance-abuse treatment system in America, programs and agencies that direct their energies toward addicted families as a unit or children in particular number fewer than 1 percent of all modalities.

How Drug-Abuse Programs Fail the Children of Drug Abusers

A bias in the field of drug-abuse treatment further aggravates a bad situation. Until the drug abuser is successfully treated for his/her addictive behavior, all other matters are considered secondary. If an addict focuses attention on anyone but himself or herself, he or she is being distracted from the main business at hand: treatment (recovery, sobriety, etc.). In twelve-step circles it is often said that "Recovery is a selfish program." Because addicts are viewed as selfish and self-centered to begin with, a treatment that emphasizes the individual's needs seem to make sense to most treatment personnel. Traditional drug-abuse agencies stress the idea that clients have to be "ready" before they can assume other responsibilities such as parenting and employment. This view is often shared by case workers in the child welfare system. In a paper on permanency planning for children from chemically dependent families, Brian Kugel (1989) wrote:

> An important distinction, which is not often made in child custody decisions is the distinction between chemical sobriety (characterized by abstinence from alcohol and other drugs) and recovery; chemical sobriety is a sine qua non for recovery. Recovery describes the process of emotional healing and restoration of emotional growth and learning from the point of arrest. Parents who may have been abstinent for a period of time must not be presumed to have regained (or developed) the emotional ability to parent.

Kugel makes an important point. But we think it only brings the need for *family-centered treatment* to center stage. Addicts do not need additional reasons for delaying active and responsible parenting. Again and again we must make the same point: children need clean and sober parents but cannot be asked to sit on the sidelines while mom and dad "get well." At some point parents must be compelled to make a responsible choice for themselves and their children.

Conjoint treatment of parent(s) and child has never taken root in the male-conceived, male-dominated treatment system designed for heroin addicts in the 1960s. Findings of several national surveys conducted by NIDA indicate that drug treatment program staff are often hostile to women and do not address their special educational, gynecologic, or parenting needs, and that many of the drug treatment programs specifically geared to women do not provide contraceptive or gynecologic care (New York Academy of Medicine, 1989). When such programs began, the male to female ratio was 4:1 and 5:1. By 1981 the modalities studied by Hubbard et al. (1989) in their national study of treatment effectiveness, showed that for a study population of over 10,000 clients, women represented 31.6 percent of methadone clients, 22.3 percent of therapeutic community clients, and 33 percent of outpatient drug-free program clients. Unfortunately, Hubbard et al. reports no data or findings on addicts' parental status or roles. Phoenix House, the largest therapeutic community program in America, reported that the number of women seeking treatment tripled between 1972 and 1987. But despite increased numbers of women in drug treatment programs, the National Association of State Alcohol and Drug Abuse Directors (NASAD) in a 1990 survey estimated that 280,000 pregnant women nationwide were in need of drug treatment. The survey estimated that only 11 percent of this number were actually receiving care. It was not reported how many of these women had sought care and had been turned away for lack of openings.

The types of treatment programs offered to addicts in the United States reflect this bias. This spells bad news for addicts as parents and their children.

Primary Types of Drug-Abuse Treatment Modalities

RESIDENTIAL THERAPEUTIC COMMUNITY PROGRAMS (RTCPs). Usually twelve to eighteen months in length. Client lives in extended-family, "tribal" setting with a highly structured regime. There is an emphasis on work as therapy. RTCPs are renowned for a form of "attack" therapy known as the encounter group. Emphasis is placed on a personality disorder model of addictive behaviors. The immature, selfish, hedonistic addict strips away deviant street behavior and works toward achieving a middle-class work ethic and value system. The basic goal of RTCPs is for drug abusers to undergo a "complete change in lifestyle: abstinence from drugs, elimination of antisocial (criminal) behavior, development of employable skills, self-reliance and personal honesty" (DeLeon & Rosenthal, 1979). Residents live in the treatment community until close to the end of treatment, when they move into a "reentry" mode of living. Few RTCPs utilize family therapy and even fewer offer parenting or parent/child programming as part of their approach. In all of New York City there is only one such program, the Family Center at Odyssey House (founded in 1971).

METHADONE-MAINTENANCE TREATMENT PROGRAMS (MMTPs). This is an outpatient modality in which people with a history of opiate addiction are given a synthetic narcotic, methadone, which acts as a "narcotic blockade" if the client tries to use opiates (Dole & Nyswander, 1965; Lowinson & Millman, 1979). When taken in the proper therapeutic range, methadone creates a state of being far below the euphoria of a heroin high but far above the terrors associated with full heroin withdrawal. It is the treatment of choice for addicts themselves. For example, in the State of New York, some 35,000 people are maintained on methadone while only 10,000 people are in drug-free treatment. Nationwide, more than 100,000 people participate in methadone-maintenance treatment. Over the years, due mainly to cuts in funding and the AIDS crisis, "support" services for methadone-maintenance clients (counseling, vocational aid, educational assistance, child care, family services) have been severely reduced. MMTP clients have rarely shown interest in group counseling. Parenting and parent/child programs for MMTP clients are almost nonexistent; virtually no day care services for working MMTP clients are provided by their own agencies.

INPATIENT CHEMICAL DEPENDENCY PROGRAMS (ICDPs). The inpatient chemical dependency program model was developed in the Midwest and rests solidly upon a biologically oriented disease model. Originally designed for the treatment of alcoholics, it borrows the "folk wisdom" of alcoholics anonymous (Alibrandi, 1985). Most ICDPs are expensive and are therefore only available to those with the proper insurance coverage or adequate income. Some of these programs include a family day or family week as part of their therapeutic offerings. However, this modality is too brief for in-depth family restoration. Moreover, many clients relapse. No follow-up studies have been published, but it is hard to imagine a direct positive impact on the lives of an addict's children. ICDPs are notorious for making unsubstantiated positive claims for their treatment outcomes. However, they do not figure conspicuously in the largest comprehensive study devoted to treatment outcomes, the Treatment Outcome Perspective Study (TOPS) conducted by the Research Triangle Institute under contract to NIDA (Hubbard et al., 1989). Few ICDPs emphasize parenting skills and very few offer a residential setting for parents and children to live together. Here the bias mentioned above is very strong in terms of focusing on the addict/ alcoholic to the exclusion of all else. The notion is that anything that upsets a person threatens his or her sobriety; the client is to avoid that which is experienced as "uncomfortable." ICDPs, due to their short duration, typically four to six week stays, rarely participate in arranging child care for parents. ICDPs will refer clients to Adult Children of Alcoholics (ACOA) groups but rarely provide any direct help to clients as parents. They have been known to refer children of alcoholics and addicts to Alanon and Alateen. We could not find references for any work with children of addicts done by this type of modality.

OUTPATIENT TREATMENT PROGRAMS (OTPs). These vary greatly in the types of services offered. Most, with the notable exception of methadone maintenance, heavily emphasize a drug-free approach to treatment. Some OTPs employ a day hospital or evening hospital regime, while others offer intensive outpatient rehabilitation programs. Most OTPs offer some combination of individual and group counseling, but the group component is emphasized. Our review of the literature and discussions with informants indicate that few OTPs do much in the way of family programming; a women's group or family therapy is sometimes offered. The vast majority do not provide formal parent educational programs or parent/child interactive programs. Where such programs do exist, they are usually available only to adolescent clients and their families. Younger children are rarely included. Very few OTPs provide child care services such as baby sitters or access to day care. It is only now, at the beginning of the 1990s, that such help is becoming available.

Why Women Do Not Enter or Fail to Remain in Treatment

Studies of women who use heroin, cocaine, and other drugs have shown that many stay away from treatment and others leave prematurely because they feel torn between their desire to join a program and their desire to be with their own children. Our own clinical work with heroin and cocaine–abusing women resulted in the same clinical observation. Some women report that their primary motive for stopping drug use, entering treatment, or "cutting down" on drug use is concern for their children. Though drug addicts, these women are also parents and they do not part company easily with their children. The crack epidemic has generated a myth that drug-addicted women do not care for their children and will not be motivated to bond or properly parent until they are have "completed" treatment. No matter how many women (and men) fail to act as responsible parents while actively addicted, it is wrong to assume that their parenting instinct is dead and never to be retrieved. Remember the rampart sexism and double standards common to of drug treatment programs. Women do not feel safe, understood, and supported in most drug treatment programs. Therapeutic communities are famous for their assaults on the damaged egos of these women. Lesbians—and gay men—are particularly discriminated against in these agencies. This discrimination is important to note because an unknown number of addicted lesbians are raising children in single-parent and partner-relationship families. In a word, many women are being told to *ignore* their children while in treatment. Women are being told "Get your act together and then become a parent." These are not mutually exclusive endeavors. Fierce attachment to their children combines with many practical problems to keep women away from treatment.

Reasons Why Women Do Not Enter or Remain in Treatment

- Children's fathers not available for sharing of child-care responsibilities.
- No responsible relatives, friends, etc., to care for their chilren if they enter residential treatment.
- No responsible relatives, friends, etc., to care for their children if they enter four- or five-day-a-week day or evening hospital model programs.
- No responsible relatives, friends, etc., to care for their children or money to pay for babysitters so they can attend evening outpatient programs.
- No car, rides, or reliable public transportation to get to treatment sessions on a regular basis (programs usually have rigid rules for attendance).
- Many programs forbid bringing children, especially those that are highly active or otherwise require continuous supervision, to individual or group counseling sessions.

- Husbands, boyfriends, or paramours refuse to allow "their woman" to enter a program, especially if there are male counselors.
- Many women fear that "exposure" to the authorities, including treatment personnel, will result in having their children taken from them. They fear urine analyses that might reveal continuing drug use.
- Some women avoid programs with female counselors or women's groups because they would rather deal with males, whom they perceive as easier to manipulate and "get over on." They know that women are less likely to be sympathetic to such attempts to manipulate and can see through their defenses and excuses.
- Other women avoid programs with male counselors because they have been brutalized by men in the past. Women who have been beaten, raped, molested, subjected to incest, and otherwise abused and neglected have reasons to be particularly leery of male "ex-addict" or "recovering" counselors.
- Many women avoid treatment because confronting the consequences of indiscriminate sexuality can induce powerful feelings of shame and guilt. Many female addicts suffer from STDs, AIDS, pelvic inflammatory disease, etc., but this is only part of the problem. Objectifying one's body into a vehicle for sex for drugs (cocaine whoring) or money for drugs (more common to heroin addiction) leads these women into feelings of a "depraved humanity" caused by participation in sexual "freak shows" (put on for men for money or drugs) that can only be dealt with by skilled and sensitive counselors (sorely lacking in most drug abuse treatment programs).
- Many women shun treatment for fear of having their poor parenting revealed. Because their children exhibit more problems than those of nonaddicts, they are fearful of being judged and tend to keep to themselves. When their children's problems go untreated or get worse, addict mothers sink deeper into depression and drug abuse.
- Some mothers fear detection of child abuse and neglect. They are afraid of being reported to government authorities. They know that if such action is taken and they drop out of treatment, their children can be placed in foster care.

In the field of alcoholism treatment, primary efforts to treat the alcoholic have led to significant "spinoffs" that have directly benefited large numbers of family members. Most notable among these spinoffs are Alanon and the children-of-alcoholics movements. Clinical programs for children of alcoholics such as Project Rainbow in Rockland County in New York State have been replicated in other parts of the country (Oliver-Diaz & Slotwinski, 1984). Alanon and Alateen organizations are active in all fifty states (O'Gorman, 1984). National and state associations exist to promote help for both young and adult children of alcoholics (Cermak, 1985). While there have been significant drug-abuse prevention projects, operating primarily through school settings, there are few clinical programs for young children of drug addicts, and no national or state associations designed to help children of substance abusers. Groups such as Narcotics Anonymous and Cocaine Anonymous have yet to emulate the success of Alanon in drawing significant numbers of active, steady participants. We hope that the recent media focus on the plight of cocaine-exposed babies will signal the beginning of services for children. Time will tell us whether this is just more media hype or a turning point in serving the previously invisible children of drug abusers.

Two Women's Stories

Joann violated her probation by using cocaine once too often. Random urine testing revealed her cocaine use. The judge ordered her to enter a long-term, residential, substance-abuse treatment program. When she protested that there was no one to care for her two young children, they were placed in foster care by the family court. Although everyone in her drug treatment program told Joann that if she succeeded, she could be reunited with her kids in a year, she split after three weeks. She abducted her two kids from their foster home. They willingly joined her because they missed her greatly. The three are now living in a shelter for homeless families under an assumed identity. Joann was reported to be trying hard to stay clean.

Bonita had been on the streets for years. When she finally entered treatment she was emotionally and physically exhaused and sick. Her three kids had been taken away from her years earlier and she has not seen them since. The program psychologist felt that she was at risk for suicide. A Hispanic, hooker, junkie, she told the staff she had nothing left to live for. Bonita died of a heart attack on her third night in treatment. She was a mother dead before her time. Her three children were cast into the foster care system, permanently cut off from their family of origin.

How Child-Welfare Agencies Fail the Children of Drug Abusers

Child welfare agency workers are encountering mounting difficulties in contending with addicted parents. Heroin-addicted parents are often hard to locate, may fail to show for scheduled child visitations, and can be very immature and defensive in their behavior during their visits. The crack-addicted parent exhibits these behaviors, but also presents more serious problems. They are even harder to locate, sometimes leading child workers to search for them in dangerous neighborhoods. They are more likely to show up while under the influence of intoxicating drugs—exhibiting agitated, paranoid, and belligerent behavior. They sometimes directly menace their own children and the workers. All too often their children are in great emotional turmoil before and during an actual visit: they desparately crave their parent's attention and yet they may fear the parent in the very same instant.

Searching for Mom

A brave child welfare worker was looking for the mother of one of his charges. The child, age two, had been removed on a neglect petition and placed in a group home. The worker was required to make a "vigorous effort" to locate the mother (the father was unknown) so that "failure to plan" could be established. Once this was done, the child could be free for adoption. The worker climbed four stories into a ghetto tenement in an almost all-black neighborhood. He asked several people in the building if they could direct him to Ms. X, explaining why he was there. They stared at him in amazement and said "Are you crazy? You better get out of here!" He was then told that the seminaked women reeling at the top of the stairs, blitzed on crack cocaine, was the mother he was seeking. "Her boyfriend is on the way up here, you better leave now." As the worker headed down the stairs he was met by a large man over six feet tall and weighing about 250 pounds heading up the stairs. "What the hell do you want here?," he demanded. The worker was barely able to pass this massive form on the staircase and was glad to have escaped unharmed.

A powerful and moving letter to the editor appeared in the *New York Times* on 22, December 1990. It was written by "Jane Doe" who requested anonymity for fear of reprisals for her efforts to adopt a "boarder baby." The *Times* editors pointed out that "Crack has changed the old rules." Jane Doe's tale offers another story about a search for a family that is nowhere to be found.

Why Should I Give My Baby Back?
by Jane Doe

As work on a corporate project wound down, I made the call. I was ready to take home a "boarder baby."

Boarder babies are primarily victims of the crack epidemic, born in New York City hospitals of mothers who test positive for cocaine and cannot take care of them. They are taken by private agencies operating under the supervision of the city's Department of Social Services and given to foster parents temporarily, until they can be placed with relatives. Unless people open their homes to them, the babies languish in institutions, unloved, untouched, apathetic, cast off.

I had requested a boy. Having raised daughters of my own, I wanted the experience of a son. Next to "race" on my application I wrote "no preference," which meant he would most likely be black. My only other request was that he be healthy, as crack babies go. I didn't have the courage my first time out to deal with the effects of extreme damage.

"Who do we have today?" the cheerful voice on the telephone cried out to someone in the office. "Any newborn boys?" Moments later he was back on the line with news of an available four-week-old boy with a "positive tox" from crack cocaine weighing considerably more than his birth weight of six and a half pounds and ready to leave the hospital.

Two days later, he was delivered to my apartment by a young man who had been commandeered as a messenger for the trip from Brooklyn to Manhattan by an overworked social worker friend. He put the infant in my arms and laid his worldly possessions down next to us: two small bottles of formula, one gray cotton sweater, one nightgown, three Pampers and the bright and pretty comforter he was wrapped in, made lovingly by a volunteer from some charity group.

In addition, there was a paper with his name, his mother's name, the hospital he was born in, date of birth and the information that he was on a three-hour feeding schedule. Then the messenger left. I don't remember if I signed a receipt. I think I did.

There we sat, this little being and I. How did I, after years of husband, children, and they very mixed blessing of domesticity, end up with another baby in my arms? If I had called yesterday or tomorrow, who would have been my baby then? What was I doing with a newborn infant that I had never seen before?

Despite the oft-voiced concerns of my loved ones and friends, I felt perfectly capable of giving him up when the time came, knowing that I had saved him from living death. I'm a big girl, I said, I can handle it. Not without some pain and loss, of course, but I can always take another child and do it again. I'm not about to bring up a child to maturity. Not at my age. I've done that already. Besides, deep down I believed some loving grandmother would come looking for him, eager to return him to the welcoming arms of his family.

Well, my son has celebrated his first birthday. He's a real hunk with "thunder thighs" and a smile and a squeal that sets my heart afire. His early, uncontrollable muscular tremors are gone, and he is filled with the boundless excitement of discovery that all children feel when they are loved. I have gone back to the gym to be able to keep up with him.

No grandma has come to fetch him. No aunts, no uncles, no cousins. No mother. No one has even come to see him. Teams of social workers do tireless outreach work, and every few months I am told that they have found someone who "wants him." Translation: They have contacted some overburdened relative who is tempted by the monthly payments to take yet another unwanted child. But these families never request a visit, and each is ultimately rejected as unsuitable.

In my boy's case they seem to have run out of relatives, and the focus now is on his mother. No one is supposed to tell me much. Strict confidentiality and all that. But I was recently warned that she had entered drug rehab and wanted her baby back. I was told to bring him to the agency for a visit with her, and to be prepared for her taking him on weekends until she was well enough to keep him for good.

"Keep him up all night, make him crabby so she won't see that irresistible smile." "Dont' feed him too much." "Dress him in throw-up clothes and pray that he cries for the entire visit." Such was the friendly advice from family and friends—people he had regularly reduced to blithering, ga-ga blobs of ecstacy.

But we showed up for the visit with him sweet-smelling, smiling and full of trust, and me a teary, anxious mess. She never showed up. Neither did her social worker. We made another appointment for two weeks later. Again, she didn't show. Neither did her social worker.

The pain of these episodes is indescribable. To be a mother, to have that ferocious instinct of protectiveness and to be rendered impotent is truly hell. Rather than surrender to my helplessness, I spent days on the telephone seeking the best advice I could find on my rights. Here is what I learned: I was as helpless as I felt.

The sanctity of the family rules supreme. Before the agency can go to court to have the mother's right terminated, they first have to exhaust every effort the law requires. Until he was with me for a year, I had no rights whatsoever. I was a paid baby sitter for New York City, bonding or no bonding.

I understand that these laws were created for another time, another world, when mothers with emotional or financial problems deserved every opportunity to get their beloved children back, when grandmothers did come to fetch their precious babies if the mothers couldn't get it together. But that was another time, before crack. The grandmothers are getting used up, and statistics on getting clean and staying that way are hardly encouraging.

My heart goes out to this community of devastation and despair, one that we must look at long and hard and not turn away from. However, the beautiful child who so magically entered my life is my first priority.

Now that he has been with me a year, I have engaged a lawyer and am seeking to terminate the mother's rights. I will do anything I can within my power and possibly beyond to insure him a life where he will be valued and appreciated for the pure love and joy that he is.

Rigorous compliance regulations, created before the current cocaine epidemic, stipulate that children in care visit their parents once a month, creating a serious dilemma for child welfare staff. There are no stipulations in the current law that require addicted parents to undergo urine surveillance or other measures to ascertain their drug-taking status. As the system is presently constituted, such surveillance would require agencies to refer prospective visiting parents to hospitals or drug clinics for such testing. The logistics and turnaround time for knowing the results would make the system unworkable. However, when parents are known to have recent, active, drug-taking histories some mechanism for mandating relative sobriety and monitoring compliance must be established for the sake of the children and the case workers. It seems to us that such a system, with realistic logistics worked out, should be mandatory before the child visits the parent in the drug treatment community, or before the parent(s) comes to visit the child in a group home or similar setting. This approach may appear radical to some, but keep in mind that the rights and safety of children are at least as important as the rights of the biological parent(s).

Things were even worse before 1990. According to a report from the New York Academy of Medicine, despite the fact that the New York State Child Welfare Reform Act of 1979 mandates that preventive services be provided to families at risk of having children placed in foster care, drug treatment was *not* specified to be such a preventive service until the very end of the 1980s!

If a parent or relative can not be found as the result of a "diligent search," children under the age of fourteen can be placed for adoption. In New York State a diligent search consists of phone calls, letters, home visits, contacting relatives, and leaving messages in places like neighborhood markets. The search includes attempts to locate the "putative" father as well as the mother. Brave agency workers go into drug and crime–infested communities to conduct their search. They have little training, if any, in dealing with addicted parents and often perform their work at great risk. Due to episodes like the one reported above, workers are now advised to travel in coed teams because such teams are deemed safer. After a diligent search, the courts may proceed to terminate the rights of the biological parents.

Parents also have the option of making a "voluntary surrender" of their child or children to the courts. Even in circumstances where parental rights have been surrendered, however, parents are expected to participate in life planning for their child every three to six months. When they can not be found, their "failure to plan" may serve as grounds for a permanent loss of rights.

Other parents plan haphazardly, and allow their children to be slotted for "independent living." This means that at age fourteen, the child will have to begin to prepare for a totally independent life which begins at age twenty-one. Assignment to independent living precludes the possibility of adoption. Upon discharge these "independent" children surrender all rights to emotional and financial support from child welfare agency staff and the system.

The laws that we refer to above are unique to New York but other states have similar laws. These laws were enacted to prevent the "warehousing" of children in institutions. Efforts at the federal level have also been made. Federal guidelines in the form of Public Law 96-272 were promulgated in June 1980. The intent of PL 96-272 is that each child is entitled to a plan that creates permanency in his/her life. The hope is that with permanency a strong bond is formed with a parent or parent substitute. Reunification with biological family is given the highest priority and "warehousing" of children is to be avoided at all costs.

We agree that "warehousing" is objectionable. By the summer of 1986, when the so-called crack epidemic had reached a "fevered pitch" (both in reality and media hype), dozens of group nurseries were established in the New York area to deal with the "boarder baby crisis" of the children of cocaine. The child welfare system prefers that children live in foster care. The state generally prohibits group care for children under five, but at that time there were not enough foster homes in which to place the children of cocaine. Barbara Sabol, the commissioner of New York City's Human Resources Administration, the agency responsible for these children, was quoted in the *New York Times* (23 September, 1990) as stating that "Even a bad foster home is preferable to good group-home care. Even if the congregate care is good, it is not the best place to rear young children."

We note with alarm that the number of people—whether relatives or strangers—willing to provide foster care fluctuates unpredictably. The spread of pediatric AIDS has frightened away many potential foster care providers. The quality and the relative permanence of foster care placements also varies greatly. However, we are compelled to agree with Barbara Sabol that a family placement, with a relative or even with a stranger, is preferable to institutional care even when these institutions have a caring staff and are not simply warehousing children. No agency staff can substitute for a mother or father or the continuous presence of parental surrogate(s).

The Council of Family and Child Caring Agencies (COFCCA) located in New York City and Albany, conducted a review of the city's preventive services initiative, designed to provide preventive services for boarder babies discharged to their biological families, after its first year of operation. They published their report in June 1989 (COFCCA, 1989). Below is a summary of their findings, "which validate the notion that there are families dependent on drugs who are amenable to participating in services with a community-based preventive provider and who in fact benefit from the services provided." They point out further that there are often multiple and extreme service needs of families who are drug dependent and that interagency and intersystem response are needed to maximize chances for intervening with this "most at-risk" population.

Summary of Preventive Services Findings

1. A relatively high percentage of families referred to service agreed to participate in preventive services, often after extensive outreach by preventive services staff.
2. A high percentage of families who in participating in preventive services accomplished one or more of the agreed-upon treatment goals.
3. A significant number of vulnerable children benefited from the timely professional assessments conducted by preventive case workers which resulted in workers immediately advocating for their placement into foster care where indicated.

4. A high percentage of families with children were able to remain safely within their home environment during the course of the family's involvement with the preventive services program.

Judges, in conjunction with social workers, legal guardians, and families of origin often order parents to attend such therapeutic activities as psychotherapy, family counseling, and A.A. meetings. They are also ordered to participate in treatment planning for the child at child welfare agencies, and to attend a parenting skills class. The judge usually hears and reviews the progress of the case after six to eight months. Judges will refer a parent to a program for incest, sexual abuse, child abuse, or other mental health programs, if necessary. Upward of 70 percent of child sexual abuse and incest is directly related to families with drug addiction. The exact relationship between substance and sexual abuse is not yet precisely understood. But as Dr. Edward Schor of Stanford University notes, "During the past several decades the reasons for children to enter foster care have changed. Absence of the parents, impoverishment, or physical or mental instability to care for children was previously the most common reason for placement. Increasingly, children enter dependent care for reasons of neglect or physical or sexual abuse."

The recent introduction of crack has wrought further havoc on the children. The Council on Family and Child Caring Agencies pointed out that with crack addiction the earliest possible interventions are needed to help save the children. Judges often fail to recognize parental drug addiction and make recommendations without taking this important fact into account, thereby missing a golden opportunity to make strong addiction treatment recommendations. The obvious problems of fragmentation and destruction of family life brought before the court often obscures the underlying addiction. Is a system designed in response to the "client's rights deinstitutionalization movement" of the 1960s appropriate for dealing with the children ravaged by the crack epidemic of the 1980s? We think not. Some of these children will require continued therapeutic and educational services into early adulthood. What will become of these parentless children, who lack skills, resources, and support? What kind of future do we hold out to them? No other agencies are sanctioned to assume responsibility for these children when child welfare agencies discharge them. As Maria Vandor, director of Women and Children Services for the New York State Division of Substance Abuse Services, told us, children through age five are "lost children" because they rarely receive needed assessment and intervention unless their families are totally dysfunctional. If family court judges are not made aware of parental addiction so that they can make vigorous efforts to impose treatment participation, more families will be destroyed. In practice, decisions for permanency often defy social and legal resolutions. The additional burdens of object losses, loyalty conflicts, shifts between biological home, foster home, preadoptive home, and group home dynamics are likely to create a physical and psychological pathogenic separation experience for an already vulnerable child. Despite laws such as PL 96-272, the foster care dependency system has not worked. It is a system overwhelmed by unmanageable caseloads and increasingly difficult cases. Since passage of this law, child welfare agencies have been successfully sued in federal court for failing to meet their responsibilities under this statute.

By December 1990 18,000 children (42 percent) out of a total foster care population of 45,500 in New York City lived in kinship homes. A *New York Times* editorial (16 December 1990) expressed concern that while a New York State Task Force concluded that kinship placements offered real advantages—it is easier to keep siblings together; relatives tend to be stable and hard-working, though poor—the task force also found problems with the system:

> But the task force wasn't satisfied. For one thing, the program's rapid growth has outrun the Child Welfare Administration's capacity to police it. Costs have soared. In some cases, relatives are not properly monitored. Drug-abused infants are not getting the special services they need. And because relatives seem to offer stability, caseworkers may be less aggressive in seeking to reunite children with their parents or give children a permanent home with adoptive parents. . . . The task force urged more supervision of kinship homes and more planning for a child's future. . . . Ideally all foster children, whether living with relatives or strangers, would eventually be reunited with their rehabilitated parents. If that's not possible, every child deserves to be placed permanently in a stable home.

This New York State Task Force on Permanency Planning took an intensive look at one hundred cases, of which forty-two involved drug-exposed infants and another twenty-three involved abandoned children. The tast force found almost no evidence that these infants were receiving special help or that any "concerted efforts" were being made to link parents to rehabilitative services. Here are some of the other findings of that task force:

- Although poor, the majority of the kinship caretakers were "stable and hard-working families who cared a lot for each other," and who provided a "decent" home away from home.
- There was "little evidence" that caseworkers complied with requirements for supervising kinship homes. If such supervision was provided, it was not properly documented in most instances.
- Because of "weak" case records, it was impossible to tell whether children in kinship homes were visited more frequently by their parents than those in conventional foster homes. "Little evidence" indicated that, where a court order barred unsupervised parental visits to kinship homes, arrangements had been made for monitored visits.
- The paucity of information in case records about fathers was "truly shocking." Many forms in the files did not even have a space for the name of the father.
- Ninety-five of the one hundred kinship caretakers were female, including fifty-three maternal grandmothers, and eighteen maternal aunts. Paternal relatives included fourteen grandmothers, one great-grandmother, and four aunts. Despite concern that kinship parents might be too old for the young children in their care, the mean age of the caretakers was only 45.9, and few were older than sixty.

The younger child who becomes "freed" is eligible for agency adoption efforts. These younger children have a slim chance of being adopted, especially if they present a less-than-perfect physical and mental health profile. Rejected by the family of origin, these children suffer another ego-bruising injury when they fail to present an "attractive" adoption package.

Case Illustration: Esther

Esther came into the foster boarding home system at the age of ten. Her addicted mother was a transient, who never made contact with her daughter following placement. Esther was lonely and depressed.

The agency offered Esther a volunteer who spent weekends and vacations with the child. But, quite naturally, Esther longed for a family of her own. Esther refused to sign papers for independent living status. She went through the necessary procedures for finding an adoptive family.

An adoption agency that deals with hard-to-place children collaborated on Esther's cases. But, photo listings, adoption parties, and multimeetings—all recognized adoption techniques—have failed to produce a recreated family for Esther. Supportive psychotherapy and a caring group home staff can not produce a drug-free mother for this needy child.

When asked how well the agency had done trying to help her, Esther replied that she felt the agency had done everything it could for her drug-addicted mother, but had failed painfully in its efforts to find her an adoptive home.

Earlier intervention, prior to Esther's entering placement, could have reunited Esther and her mother. At least Esther can visualize her mother. Many of the babies of crack-addicted mothers will never have even a memory of their mothers.

Agencies need to fundamentally rethink the role they play in the lives of the drug-addicted family population. Resources are needed to promote new ways of helping drug-addicted parents and their children.

Child welfare agency workers need to do more extensive outreach work to engage the addict-parent. But they must be aided by a move away from the philosophy of PL 96-272 and the creation of newer guidelines that jibe with the reality of crack, cocaine, and heroin in American society. A great many states are beginning to consider and/or to pass legislation that impact on the children of drug abusers. At least ten states now have laws that require health care practitioners to report drug-exposed neonates to the state health officials (there is great variability in reporting requirements from state to state). Public Law 99-457 (and 34 CFR Part 303) has prompted the states to develop standards for a "timely, comprehensive, multidisciplinary evaluation of the functioning of each infant and toddler with disabling conditions and the needs of the families to appropriately assist in the development of the infant or toddler." In New York State the Early Intervention Services Act of 1990 was passed to meet this mandate. But we can only wonder where the funds for its implementation will come from during a nationwide recession. At this writing, the only part of the act being carried out is the "cataloging" of needs.

Staff selection and training for both child welfare agencies and drug treatment agencies need to reflect a greater concern for assessment and treatment of the whole drug family of drug-dependent persons.

Again and again we have underscored in this book the desperate wish of children to be reunited, in almost any way possible, with their parents. Child welfare agencies can simply not replace the priceless gift of a natural parent. Thus, they must make a greater effort to keep these addicted families together; they must stop making an artificial distinction between drug treatment and childrearing. Assessment of individual needs of the child and a recovery process involving both parents and children must be developed.

A plan must be devised for an extensive revamping of the current system that focuses on the drug addiction of the parent and child welfare as totally separate entities. Intervention should be directed toward preventive services. Policies must be developed now because implementation may take as long as five years. Child welfare agencies and drug rehabilitation agencies must work together with a coordinated plan and a common goal: the uniting of a child with his or her own drug-free parent! Nothing else will adequately address the pain and hardships these children of sustance abusers are currently suffering.

The mission statements of child welfare agencies are beginning to change. To a vast extent these changes are motivated and prompted by the children of drug addiction.

Some Facts About the Child Welfare System*

- About four children enter care for every 1,000 children under the age of nineteen.
- There are between 250,000 and 300,000 children in care in the United States.
- Boys and girls are equally represented.
- Minority ethnic groups are overrepresented in foster care.
- Girls are more likely to be in care because of sexual abuse. Boys are more likely to be physically abused or to be physically, cognitively, or emotionally impaired.
- Adolescents make up more than 50 percent of children in foster care.
- Approximately 73 percent of foster children are placed by court order.
- When in independent care, 70–75 percent of children reside in foster family homes; the remainder live in group homes, emergency shelters, or residential treatment settings.
- 20–30 percent of children returned to their biological family eventually return to foster care. Inadequate help given to the family to improve their situation or poor evaluation of the family's resources and potential are the major causes of such negative outcomes.
- Annually, about half of the children placed in care return to their biologic families, most within thirty days of placement. The median duration of placement for children leaving care in 1985 was nine months.
- About 25 percent of children remain in care after two years; those who remain for two years are likely to remain for many years thereafter.
- Slightly more than half of children experience only one foster care placement setting while in care; more than one-fourth experience three or more placement settings.
- Approximately 20–25 percent of dependent children reside in group home settings.
- Children in foster care have significantly greater rates of chronic health problems than the general population of chil-

*Adapted from Schor, 1989.

dren, with 40–76 percent of these reportedly affected. Few children entering foster care will be entirely normal physically.

- The most frequently identified health problems of children in foster care are mental health disorders. Prevalence data for serious emotional problems among foster children range from 35–95 percent. A study done in 1989 at one foster care agency of 220 children revealed that all had DSM-IIIR axis I diagnoses and that 80 percent had significant chronic medical problems.

Dr. Schor goes on to point out that the greatest administrative crisis facing the foster care system is the identification and recruitment of suitable foster homes. The crack epidemic has led to the increasing placement of children in kinship foster care. This is deemed more desirable than placement with "strangers." But this presumption may be flawed: many kinship homes are not suitable for proper child care. If the kinship homes were subject to more careful scrutiny many children would be moved to "out-of-home" placements.

We note that many child welfare agencies are moving further away from custodial care and more into the realm of child mental health. This is a profound and necessary shift of emphasis. Clinical intervention and ongoing treatment are needed by most of these children. The system is also beginning to move from a child-based orientation to a family-based orientation. Preventive services must strive to keep families in the community and in outpatient treatment for substance abuse and related problems.

How the Court System Fails the Children of Drug Abuse

As background to the specific problems involving families and addiction, let us first consider some recent facts concerning the impact of addiction on the criminal justice system in general.

Some Sobering Facts about Drugs and Criminal Justice

Fact: Drug cases have overwhelmed the national justice system. In 1987 police made 352,612 drug arrests, an increase of 24 percent over the previous year.

Fact: As recently as June 1985, New York police had not made a single crack arrest. In the first ten months of 1988, they made 18,074. The number of people arrested in Washington, D.C., who were high on cocaine increased by 40 percent between 1984 and 1988.

Fact: Crack has forced the criminal justice system to spend furiously for police, prosecutors, courts, and judges, but the system has not been able to keep up with crime. California has built 21,000 new prison beds since 1983 and plans 16,000 more at a total cost of $3.2 billion. Since 1983 New York has spent $900 million to build 17,780 cells, but officials say 9,000 more are needed. It costs New York taxpayers $2 billion to run the prisons each year, and the state has borrowed $1 billion more to build them. Even if federal prison cells were increased by 24,000 cells (at a cost of $1 billion), federal penitentiaries would still be overcrowded by 25 percent.

Fact: World drug production, particularly for opium, coca leaf, and marijuana, is up sharply according to the State Department. There are 600 gangs in Los Angeles with some 70,000 members; it is estimated that they make $1 million per week selling drugs. These gangs are moving into smaller cities and towns. Crack is sold by young, wild, heavily armed, and murderous youth gangs.

Fact: Ther murder rate is rising due to drug abuse and drug trafficking. New York City, in 1988, broke the all-time murder rate that was set in 1981. In August 1988 alone, 201 people were slain (a 74.8 percent incease from the previous year). The increase in violent crime is directly attributed to the infusion of crack into the inner city.

Fact: It would cost some $15 million to provide 1,500 crack addicts with residential treatment, but these same 1,500 addicts will commit $45 million in crime if left untreated.

Fact: In 1989 59 percent of the males arrested in New York City tested positive for cocaine. In other areas of the country, 80 percent of the males arrested tested positive for cocaine. Almost half of all criminal trials in federal courts now involve narcotics prosecutions.

Fact: Treatment remains elusive and "treatment on demand" an illusion. Some 600 to 700 addicts were waiting to enroll in methadone-maintenance programs and some 2,500 were writing to enroll in residential drug-free programs in New York State alone during 1990.

Fact: In 1985 New York State prisons had 27,000 inmates. By 1990 the prison population had increased to 58,000. In New York City, in 1985, the number of prisoners awaiting trials in Rikers Island Jail was 10,000. By 1990 21,000 prisoners were being held for trial.

Fact: According to Sterling Johnson, special narcotics prosecutor in New York City, there were 2,000 narcotics felony indictments in 1985. Felony drug indictments reached 7,000 in 1990.

Fact: Drug courts are a treadmill, where the name of the game is plea bargaining. Most drug dealers plead guilty to lesser charges and return quickly to the street to resume business as usual. A review of court cases completed in Brooklyn, New York, in 1987 revealed that:

- 6,621 people were arrested on felony narcotics charges.
- 2,983 were actually prosecuted on misdemeanor charges.
- Nearly 50 percent of these mmisdemeanor cases were dismissed.
- Of those arrested on felony drug charges and later convicted of some offense, 1,302 were placed on probation, fined, ordered to perform community service, sentenced to time served, or had their cases dismissed. Another 1,772 received less than a year in jail.
- Of an additional 6,647 people arrested on misdemeanor narcotics charges, only 1,340 received jail time.

Fact: In places where special police units, such as New York City's much-heralded T.N.T. Squads (Tactical Narcotics Team) sweep an area clean of drug dealers, they return as soon as the police are gone.

Fact: As jails and prisons become more and more overcrowded, judges make rulings that populations must be reduced. To more room for new inmates, others must be released. Most return immediately to drug dealing and addiction. Overcrowding also influences the plea-bargaining process: the more crowding, the more likely criminals are to be offered the chance to plea to lesser offenses. The average probation officer in the City of New York carries a case load of 250 probationers. Most of the supervision is done by phone.

Fact: In New York City, there are only 150 spaces in public treatment programs for people under sixteen. The New York State Divisions of Substance Abuse Services estimates (conservatively) that there were 97,000 crack users under the age of sixteen in 1989. A study by the federal Justice Department found that many juvenile offenders had criminal histories just as extensive as those of adults in state prisons (about 39 percent had been incarcerated for violent crimes and nearly 43 percent had been arrested more than five times). Nearly half were under the influence of alcohol or other drugs when they committed their offenses. Studies repeatedly show that prisons are full of criminals "who started early and stayed late."

This sad and frightening litany of facts is the background against which the drama of the family court judge unfolds. Most family courts in America are understaffed and have overburdened calendars. Judges must adjudicate cases which, in rapidly advancing numbers, are the outgrowth of the drug epidemic in America. The judges themselves have received little or no training in drug abuse and must do the best they can without benefit of rational input. They are besieged by emotional appeals from addicted parents, biased attorneys, and harried social service agency workers. Even where legal guardians are appointed to represent the rights and needs of the children, there exists an abysmal ignorance regarding the impact of addiction on family life and sensible strategies for effective intervention. Yet these judges are expected, Solomon-like, to fashion fair responses to adults and children alike.

Family courts are the setting in which every conceivable type of strife and mayhem are given their day in court. The first way in which the system breaks down is the concept of "court-ordered" treatment. Judges often sentence people to enter drug-treatment programs without regard for the offender's motivation or interest in stopping drug use. Many weeks or months may pass before an addict, who has avoided actual treatment, is once again brought before the court. Addicts are particularly clever and manipulative. Listed below are some of the "scams" used to avoid treatment.

Ways to Avoid or Delay Involvement in Drug Treatment

• Addicts have their lawyers seek delays in making court appearances, often using excuses like feigned illness or the need to work.
• Addicts often simply do not show up for court dates.

• Addicts ordered to go for a "drug evaluation" simply stay clean until after the evaluation (usually involving urine screening).

• Addicts adulterate urine specimens or use another persons's clear urine for testing (especially if the giving of speciments is not observed).

• Addicts claim to be attending Alcoholics Anonymous or similar self-help meetings. Since these are anonymous meetings, anyone can sign the addict's "attendance sheet."

• Addicts often refuse to sign releases allowing drug-abuse treatment staff to give reports to the court. Addicts are notorious for playing agencies against one another.

• Addicts first delay entering a program. Next they minimally comply with program expectations. Finally, they may switch programs. All this time they continue using drugs.

• The "split" rate (leaving against staff advice) is very high for some drug programs (therapeutic communities often lose 50 percent of new members in the first month of residence). Alcoholics Anonymous acknowledges that 50 percent of newcomers are gone after four months. Only 34.1 percent of methadone clients and 6.6. percent of outpatient drug-free clients stayed in treatment at least one year (Hubbard et al., 1989).

• Addicts rely on naive judges and long waiting lists. They con judges into sending them to the least restrictive treatment agencies so that they may continue to have access to drugs and the people who sell them and use them.

• Addicts tell the court they are seeking a "geographical cure" and ask to be sent out of town (further abandoning their children).

• Addicts often join treatment programs to hide from the criminal consequences of their addiction. Federal laws governing the confidentiality of such clients prohibits any disclosure without written consent by the addict.

• Judges often fail to stipulate the signing of releases as an important part of the court-ordered treatment. The courts are lax in monitoring attendance or drug-taking status. This system has unleashed thousands of "pseudo clients" on already overburdened drug-treatment staffs whose burnout is only hastened by unmotivated and hostile clients (whose only motive is to fool the courts).

• Family courts often rely on probation officers to monitor treatment involvement. Few probation officers are trained to deal with drug abuse and many have case loads that do not allow the type of intense supervision that addicts require. Many officers are easily manipulated by clever addicts, especially women with children, who lie and scheme to maintain their addictive life-styles. Few probation departments rely on random, unannounced, and observed urine testing as an objective indicator of a person's drug-taking status. Too many probation officers hear only what they want to hear; as long as probationers do not hassle the officer, he or she is too ready to assume all is well. They also assume that because a person is "enrolled" in treatment they must be doing well. They do not realize that for most addicts, the most frequent outcome of treatment is relapse (it is the nature of addictive behaviors that repeated attempts are required to achieve a sober life-style).

• Addicts often find that family court judges will not take severe action against them, and therefore continue using drugs.

• Women addicts find that judges are reluctant to separate them from their children, so they use their children as pawns in a destructive game of "pseudoparenting" and active drug use. Because so few programs treat women and their children together, "childcare" becomes an excuse for no real treatment.

The whole system is being crushed under the weight of the inner-city crack epidemic. Crack has also exposed the weaknesses and lack of responsiveness of the child welfare system in terms of handling reported abuse and neglect. How many more children must be brutalized before we realize that we are losing an entire generation of children in this country? While politicans play a shell game with desperately needed funds for courts, treatment, protective services, and child welfare, the children are waiting and waiting for someone to help. No one seems to be a position to make change! William Bennett, President Bush's former drug czar, did not help the dialogue between the fields when in July 1990, in referring to the children of drug abusers as "orphans of the living," he indicated that the children of drug addicts should be taken away from their parents and placed in orphanages. He further proposed that this effort be paid for by depriving delinquent parents of welfare support. Needless to say, this pronouncement, made before the Urban League, a social service and advocacy group, received a cool reception. This type of flimsy social policy shows the real failure of government officials to understand the complex nature of the problem and a further failure to propose helpful action.

Rights of the Mother versus Rights of the Fetus

A new battlefront is heating up. The rights of a prospective mother are being pitted against the rights of the fetus. In July 1989 a Florida woman, Jennifer Johnson, was convicted of child abuse for using cocaine while pregnant. She was found guilty of delivering drugs to a minor via the umbilical cord in the moment after her child was born and before the cord was clamped. In Michigan, prosecutor Tony Tague charged Kimberly Ann Hardy with the same felony charge: "delivering drugs in the amount of less than 50 grams" to her son through her umbilical cord during birth but before the cord was cut. Since then similar cases have been brought in Massachusetts, Florida, South Carolina, and Virginia. In a case in North Carolina, a prosecutor charged an addicted mother with "assault with a deadly weapon" on her newborn. According to the newletter of the American Council on Obstetrics and Gynecology (May 1990) by February 1990, at least forty-four women had been prosecuted for "fetal abuse" from cocaine use during pregnancy. Professor Alan Dershowitz at Harvard Law School sees the issue as a surrogate of the national abortion debate: "Although pro-choicers are sympathetic to prenatal issues, they are terrified to give in at all on fetal rights for fear of providing grist to antiabortionists."

How far should the state go in protecting an unborn child from drugs? If a woman can be jailed for exposing her fetus to cocaine, why should it be legal for her to abort it? According to Janet Dinsmore, a spokeswoman for the American Prosecutors Research Institute, such questions have created "horrendous factions": "Suddenly people who were allied on feminist, health and child welfare issues are split down the middle between those who advocate for children and those who advocate for women."

Voices from Two Sides of a Difficult Issue

To legislate what a woman can or cannot do when she is pregnant would be a gross violation of her right to privacy. Criminalizing is a barbaric approach to deal with someone who is sick.—Eve Paul, Planned Parenthood Federation, New York

We thought we were getting tough when we tried voluntary contracts that required the parents to go into drug treatment, gave the state legal custody, or allowed it to monitor the child. But it doesn't work. In a few weeks, the family disappears from the system and the child protection agencies are too overwhelmed to follow through. In a year, the family shows up again with another drug-affected baby.—Dr. Jan Bays, director, Child Abuse Programs, Emanuel Hospital, Portland, Oregon.

This is a short-term, knee-jerk solution. The temperence movement is creating such a level of frustration that people are beginning to lash out at the group with the least defenses—women, especially the minority poor. If these were white middle-class women, wouldn't they be talking about Betty Ford treatment programs rather than jail?—Dr. Ira Chasnoff, president, National Association of Perinatal Addiction Research and Education, Chicago, Illinois.

I'd much rather see this problem dealt with by the more subtle systems of public health, social services, and education. But, damn it, we've had nothing but failures. This country has gone from 1 in 1,000 babies being born with controlled substances to 1 in 10. It's time to invoke the mechanism of last resort.—William O'Malley, prosecutor, Plymouth County, Massachusetts.

The Supreme Court in 1925 declared drug addiction to be a medical, not a criminal, matter. The court reiterated this decision in 1962, stating that "We forget the teachiungs of the Eight Amendment if we allow sickness to be made a crime and sick people to be punished for being sick." This age of enlightenment cannot tolerate such barbarous action.—Dr. Wendy Chavkin, Rockefeller Foundation Fellow at the Columbia School of Public Health, New York City.

These cases for the first time force a pregnant woman to act in the service of another, the fetus. If you see a child in a burning building, you are not required to risk your life to save the child. These cases ask a women to sacrific her right to privacy and open herself to policing during pregnancy. All of a sudden the behavior of pregnant women is open to state controls to which no one else is subject.—Kary Moss, A.C.L.U. Women's Rights Project, New York City.

Mother and child are really one unit and should be treated together. When you create an adversary relationship between women and their fetuses, neither one wins. We're all concerned about the increasing numbers of drug-addicted babies and there's nothing wrong with referring the mother for treatment when you find a baby who's has been exposed to drugs. But we shouldn't intervene in a punative way, especially when we have no services to offer, and we put babies in foster placements that pose a greater peril than staying with their mothers.—Judith Rosen, attorney, San Diego, California.

The issues are complicated and are most often without legal precedents. Prosecutors, judges, and child protection officials say they feel an obligation to protect fetuses and newborns from the ravages of drug abuse. But some critics point out that in their attempts to accomplish this worthwhile and important goal, rights are being created for fetuses that have no foundation in law. Public health officials and women's rights lawyers perceive many of the law enforcement efforts as unconstitutionally applying laws more harshly to pregnant women than to others.

In 1990 a thoughtful paper was presented before the American Society of Criminology in Baltimore (Mahan & Hawkins, 1990). The authors conclude:

> Despite the well-publicized outrage over "crack babies," there has been increasingly outspoken opposition of public health organizations to prosecutions of cocaine-addicted pregnant women. Whatever action criminal justice authorities may take will only be possible with the cooperation and support of health care providers. Rather than simple criminalization, a more comprehensive and complex policy is needed to address not just the social problems involved for cocaine-abusing pregnant women, but also the multiple health problems of all childbearing women.
>
> On the structural level, laws relating to family life are not important because of their direct effect in coercing compliance, but because

they set the outer limits of what the community regards as morally tolerable. Drastic action toward cocaine mothers, while alcoholic mothers and those exposed to toxic substances in the environment are seldom mentioned, illustrates the public outlook toward personal responsibility and general fear and loathing of crack cocaine abusing pregnant females. A broader perspective is in the greater interest of society. (17)

The criminal justice system is confused by a multifaceted modern dilemma. Uncertain whether addictive behavior represents a crime, and/or a life-style, and/or a disease, the system is trying to find ways to defend the rights of the children—whether fetus or born child. In the November 1989 issue of *Update,* the newsletter of the National Association for Perinatal Addiction Research and Education, Dr. Sandra Garcia reviewed several of the models involving pregnant women and their unborn or newborn children.

MEDICAL MODEL. Starts with the premise of addiction being a disease but there is no consensus that totally supports this notion. Model is saddled with an interesting paradox: if "loss of control" is the main symptom of the disease, the addict is told to maintain total abstinence for an indefinite period. As Marlatt and Gordon (1985) point out, "surely the intention or commitment to abstain is, itself, a form of control."

SOCIAL PATHOLOGY/SOCIAL DEVIANCE MODEL. Attributes the addict's antisocial behavior to environmental stresses and debilitating social forces—what one judge has called "rotten social background"—especially evident among minorities in the inner cities. This model recognizes the need for a far-ranging attack on the problem.

FREE WILL/PERSONAL CHOICE MODEL. Based on the American majority opinion that people are free to choose to do right or wrong and are responsible for what they choose to do. Mitigating circumstances can be physical compulsion, deficits of will or knowledge, and irresponsibility based on incapacity, such as insanity. Main reason for confusion is that recovery from addiction actually does involve choosing to be drug-free. At what point is the addict free to make this choice?

What is often missed when people take a rigid position is the simple truth that many of the women addicted to crack do not follow through on efforts to get them into treatment even when such treatment is available. What measures should then be taken to ensure the safety of fetuses, newborns, toddlers, young children, or older children? Is failure to comply with treatment sufficient grounds for placing the rights of the fetus before the rights of the addicted mother? During what trimester? After how many treatment "failures"? Answers to these questions remain elusive for the moment. Whatever the are, the criminal justice system's response to addiction among women must include the needs of the children. It must also recognize what Charlene Johnson pointed out in her testimony before the House Select Committee on Children, Youth and Families, "Real solutions must address the drug problem on all fronts at the same time. People need jobs, housing, education, counseling, coaching, child care, health care, skill training and food all at the same time" (Johnson, 1990).

On 11 August 1990 Dorothy Roberts, associate professor of criminal law and civil liberties at Rutgers School of Law summarized another aspect of the probem in a letter "The Bias in Drug Arrests of Pregnant Women," a letter published in the *New York Times:*

> The overwhelming majority of the defendants (about 70%) are poor and black. The wisdom of the prosecutors cannot be assessed honestly without first confronting their racial dimensions. . . . The reason African-American women are the primary targets of prosecutors is not because they are more guilty of fetal abuse. Rather, the discriminatory enforcement is a result of a combination of racism and the mothers' poverty. . . . Because poor women are in closer contact with governmental agencies, their drug use is more likely to be detected and reported. . . . Moreover, hospitals decide whom to screen for drug use by applying criteria, such as the mother's failure to obtain prenatal care, that are more likely to select poor women of color. According to the Children's Defense Fund in Washington, only half of black American women get adequate prenatal care. For whites the figure is 72.6 percent. . . . Private physicians who treat more affluent women tend to refrain from testing their patients for drug use because they have a financial stake in securing their patients' business and referrals. . . . Poor black mothers are thus made the scapegoats for the black com-

munity's ill health. Punishing them assuages the nation's guilt for an underclass of people whose babies die at rates higher than in some third world countries. Making black mothers criminals appears far easier than creating a health care system that ensures healthy babies for all of our citizens.

As the economic situation in our nation grows worse, the health of children deteriorates and the medical, psychological, educational, and social services for them, already woefully inadequate, suffer further budget cuts. But what the *New York Times* calls "Islands of Illness" are mainly inhabited by racial minorities, blacks and Hispanics. It is estimated that 50 percent of addicts are black and another 25 percent are Hispanic. These groups are always overrepresented statistically in the list of social welfare ills. Pressure to find real solutions is mounting daily as more and more drug-exposed babies are born.

An honest appraisal of our current social welfare policy leads one to understand that the truly disadvantaged in America are the residents of our inner cities, primarily black and Hispanic minorities. Since the mid-1960s, the social condition of poor urban blacks has continuously deteriorated. We quote from the overleaf to *The Truly Disadvantaged: The Inner City, the Underclass, and Public Policy* by William Julius Wilson(1987):

> Inner-city decay cannot be explained by racism alone, Wilson argues, but instead is related to a complex web of factors involved in the urban economy, the most important of which is the changing class structure of ghetto neighborhoods. The movement of middle-class black professionals from the inner city, followed by the exodus of increasing numbers of working-class blacks, has left behind a concentration of the most disadvantaged segments of the black urban population. At the same time, urban minorities have been particularly vulnerable to broader changes in the ecnomony that have produce extraordinary rates of joblessness, which in turn has exacerbated other social problems.

When the National Institute on Drug Abuse announced in December 1990 that there had been a major drop in casual cocaine use (72 percent over five years) according to the latest Household Survey on Drug Abuse, addiction workers in the inner city reacted in a predictable manner. They noted that the survey only covers households where there are telephones: many addicts do not have phones. If a social perception grows that the "war on drugs" has been won, less money will be allocated for treatment. This could occur at a times when the needs of addicts and their children are largely being unmet! All the problems thus far outlined in this book do not speak to a reduction in the problem for the children of drug abusers! We think the evidence is massive and overwhelming for major changes and additions to the treatment and child welfare systems to meet the needs of both the children and the adults. And the main need is for family-centered treatment.

4

Healing the Children
A Call for a New Advocacy System

Who will speak for the children of drug abusers? The hour grows late and the workers in the three fields of substance abuse, child welfare, and child mental health grow weary. If we are to gather strength and do what must be done for the children, the time to act is now! As Lisbeth Schorr exhorts us in the conclusion to her excellent book *Within Our Reach: Breaking the Cycle of Disadvantage:*

> Knowing now that effective social interventions can reduce the number of children hurt by cruel beginnings and simultaneously promote the national welfare, we must be certain that these newly available tools are put to work. We have the knowledge that we need. We know how to organize health programs, family supports, child care and early education to strengthen families and to prevent casualties in the transition from childhood to adulthood. We know how to intervene to reduce the rotten outcomes of adolescence and to help break the cycle that reaches into succeeding generations. Unshackled from the myth that nothing works, we can assure that children without hope today will have a real chance to become the contributing citizens of tomorrow.

On 9 September 1990 a frank but encouraging article "Why Is America Failing Its Children," written by the famed pediatrician Dr. T. Berry Brazelton of Harvard Medical School appeared in the *New York Times Magazine*. Brazelton states:

As a pediatrician with forty years' experience with 25,000 children, I have begun to regard the growing neglect and poverty of the young as the biggest threat to the nation's future. (One in five children in America live in a household below the poverty line.) I also see evidence that we could start preventing this terrible waste, with remedies available right now—but we seem to have lost the will even to think about it.

He concludes the article with the following remarks:

The challenge for the National Commission on Children is to come up with ways to strengthen families and to support them as they nurture their children's development. We can do it, but it will be expensive and difficult. American leaders seem able to focus only on danger from outside the country, not yet recogniziing in any committed way that the greatest threat is from within, in the breakdown of families and in the growing numbers of poor. The anger and addictions of the impoverished and the harm being done to their children are a national crisis. If we want poor children—and therefore all children—to have a future in this country, we have no choice but to make families our top priority.

In this chapter we call for a major rethinking of present systems that fail to serve the children of drug abusers. We issue a challenge to all three fields to venture beyond their conventional boundaries and fiefdoms and to emerge into a braver, albeit less comfortable, service arena where they join hands in the name of an improved child care system. Nothing less will work. Children can not vote, they do not have the funds to influence society, they are impotent with regard to the control of their own destiny. The societal problem of drug abuse must be managed in new ways to save the children, lest they become overwhelming burdens on society during their childhood and far into their adult years.

Personnel Needed for the Real War on Drugs

To move forward with a chance of real success, it is important to know to whom we must appeal for immediate involvement. Necessary participants in the combined war to end drug addiction and save the children of drug addicts include:

- Drug abuse treatment personnel
- Child abuse specialists
- Teachers and pupil personnel service workers
- Child and adult mental health workers
- Child welfare system workers
- Law guardians
- Criminal and family court judges
- Pediatricians and other child and family health care workers
- Clergy
- Commited legislators, lawmakers, and political leaders

Unfortunately, most of these people work only within their own separate and unique settings. In order to come together to tackle the multivariate needs of the children and adults we have mentioned in the last three chapters, they will have to begin making true interdisciplinary efforts. They will have to move beyond traditional agency boundaries and traditional job descriptions. They will have to confront powerfully entrenched attitudes and prejudices and learn to purposefully blur boundary distinctions. They will have to be willing to say what they know and what they do not know. The information we have already shared clearly indicates where knowledge gaps exist. They can be filled by the efforts of energetic open-minded professionals.

The Establishment of Residential Treatment Settings for Addicts and Their Children

There are very few residential programs for families. Programs for women and their children do exist, but they are pitifully few in number. Some examples are Odyssey House in New York City and Family House in Pennsylvania. There are lengthy waiting lists for the few beds available. In addition, most programs will not take women with older children. Programs should develop therapeutic nurseries where newborns and infants can be evaluated and treated. Both parents and children should be medically, psychologically, and developmentally evaluated. Individualized treatment plans that take the needs of parents and their children into consideration must be developed. Programs can be developed with educators on the premises who can work together with substance-abuse counselors and child care personnel. In other words, instead of separating out the adults and placing the children in foster care, the elements of joint care could be developed in a single setting. Such facilities would not be cheap. But it is foolish to conceive of "treatment on demand" when we insist that parents (mostly mothers) must automatically be separated from their children in order to receive treatment. Most federal and state agencies involved in the funding of drug-abuse treatment have historically been mandated to work with individual addicts, thereby deemphasizing family-oriented treatment approaches.

If we could assure women the kind of treatment options listed below, would they not come to treatment in greater numbers and be more likely to stay? What if we promised drug-addicted mothers that they could:

- Remain with their children
- Be assured of the physical, emotional, and spiritual health of their children as well as themselves
- Learn more effective parenting skills while simultaneously receiving treatment for their addiction
- Learn how to integrate a healthier family life with the prevention of relapse to drug use
- Be trained for today's job market

We must not allow the crack generation to become the "no-parent" family without making a mighty effort to attract and maintain women and men in treatment. This will not be easy: all addiction treatment modalities are faced with high attrition rates either prior to, during, or following the active treatment phase.

Half the clients in drug-free therapeutic communities leave within the first month; 50 percent of the newcomers to Alcoholics Anonymous drop out within the first three to four months; a review of 500 studies of alcoholism treatment outcomes studies concluded that over 74 percent of clients relapsed in the first year of treatment; the 1981 Califano Commission Report in New York State showed that only 10 percent of opiate addicts were clean one year beyond treatment; similar statistics are being revealed regarding attempts to treat cocaine addiction; 85 percent of the alcoholics in America are untreated. These statistics point to relapse as a natural phenomenon in addictive behavior and indicate the need for new treatment strategies to intervene more effectively. Despite these rather grim-sounding statistics, treatment does work for those clients who stay (Hubbard et al., 1989). In fact, the main variable that contributes to positive treatment outcomes is time in treatment—that is, the longer one stays in treatment, the more likely one will have a good outcome.

The authors believe that one of the greatest barriers to treatment for women is the requirement that they be separated from their children. Hence, our call for a meaningful increase in the number of residential programs for women and their children with age-appropriate programming for children of different ages. An unknown number of addicts, especially those who smoke cocaine, find their lives so debilitated that they can not hope to gain abstinence without some period of stabilization in a residential program. For impoverished minority women this problem becomes even more critical. How can they resist addiction in the emotional and physical climate of inner-city ghettos? How can they hope to properly nurture their children when so few of them have ever been properly nurtured? We must create settings where the parent and the child receive the nurturing, support, and basics for life they require. With a solid beginning—free of the pull of the street—and the mastery of basic coping skills we can not expect these people to adapt long-term, drug-free life-styles.

The media has portrayed crack addiction as a chronic, hopeless condition. A dark tunnel with no light at its end. An intractable condition without hope of recovery. It is useful to understand the power of metaphor in our society. In her book *Illness as Metaphor* Susan Sontag cautions us, "Any important disease whose causality is murky, and for which treatment is ineffectual, tends to be awash in significance. First the subjects of deepest dread (corruption, decay, pollution, anomie, weakness) are identified with the disease. The disease itself becomes a metaphor."

The public is bombarded with articles about addiction and disordered brain chemistry or disordered personality. But addiction in the Western world seems more and more to be a response to deteriorating social conditions. The babies in Hale House, the boarder babies in hospitals, the newborns struggling with cocaine withdrawal are as much the victims of society as they are the product of addictive behavior. Treating poor women and their children together will give us an opportunity to dispel the myth that these women do not care about their own children or that the children are better off raised by strangers outside their natural family. Despite the high relapse rates that accompany addiction it is a noble and necessary endeavor to unite families in treatment. Follow-up studies may indeed reveal that for addicted women with children, this is not only the treatment of choice, but the most successful as well!

Comprehensive Multiservice Centers for Women and Children

When addictive behavior becomes the driving force in a person's life it must be prioritized into the first target behavior to be addressed by any service agency. But it should not be the *only* need to be met. By breaking up service components into different bureaucratic strata we create too many false dichotomies for women and we create too many hurdles for them to climb over. While theorists and ideologues thrash out the "true nature" of addictive behavior (biological disease, personality pathology, sociocultural deprivation, etc.) a truly wholistic view needs to be taken of the women and the children to be served. Addiction itself is a metaphor for many things in our society at all socioeconomic levels. But nowhere is it as devastating as it to the women who are already facing a melange of social, medical, psychological, nutritional, domicile, educational, and vocational problems. While we must admit that some of these problems are the usual outcome of an addictive life-style, they can also serve as the causes for the addictive behavior.

Centers can be developed to focus on evaluation of a women's functioning in all these areas. Needs can then be prioritized and treated. This approach can cut through the wasteful squandering of valuable resources. For example, providing food, clothing, and temporary shelter to an active addict only prolongs his or her active drug use. Thus, we should make reception of other services contingent upon active participation in drug-abuse treatment. Such a system can work if it is set up so that the current interagency lack of communication is eradicated from the outset. If a women takes advantage of the multiple resources presented at the proposed multiservice center as an outpatient, then she may indeed be on the road to true independent living. If she can not, and continues to use drugs, then she can be referred for more intensive care, through a day treatment, evening treatment, or inpatient program). The staff of the center can help her and her children during the transition and make sure that treatment for mother and children happens as a joint experience, wherever that may be.

Furthermore, if there is a need to separate mother and children for a period, the mother's frequent visitation and awareness of adequate child care will help her to concentrate on addiction treatment. Too many women lose their ability to focus because they are worried about their children. The center will see to it that both parties' needs are being addressed. No longer will the children be lost in the shuffle of "adult only" concerns.

The multiservice center can be a "soup-to-nuts" delivery system. The idea of multiservices centers is not new to the addiction field. Such centers were proposed for youth as early as 1975 (Crupi, Schwartz, & Weiss, 1975). An excellent example of such programming is "The Door," a comprehensive multiservice center for youth developed in the 1970s and lauded by the National Institute on Drug Abuse as an innovative model for working with youth. The Door offered its youthful clients medical and dental care, psychological and addiction counseling, recreational activities, and related services. The Door was a hybrid model that borrowed from the free clinic model and the old settlement house approach to children. During the late 1980s and 1970s in New York City, The Door boasted of over 150 *unpaid* volunteer professionals. In this way otherwise highly expensive professional staffing costs were significantly reduced. Hundreds of clients received hassle-free treatment and developed the kind of trusting relationships that can lead to movement into more enduring and tradition treatment.

Considering the high degree of addiction among the homeless, many of whom are family groups consisting of mother and children, the multiservice center will need a residential component just to get folks off the street into a safe and drug-free environment. Mahatma Ghandi said "Where there is bread there is a country!" But bread alone is not the solution. The center must have strict rules forbidding drug use, and violence or the threat of violence, to ensure the safety of its residents. This component of care would be a cross between a shelter, a therapeutic community, and a halfway house.

We must begin to create hybrid programs, facilities that borrow from the best of several worlds. Even the lowest rungs of the social service ladder are marked by real-world distinctions: not every "shelter" receives equal funding or provides equivalent services. Those shelters for women and their children must be *safe:* safe from drugs, safe from violence, and safe from the men who so frequently victimize both women and children.

These comprehensive women's service centers could create a breakthrough on another important issue: the separation of women and their children. Women in the centers will not have to move from place to place for various kinds of treatment and help, and their children will not need to be placed in foster care throughout the treatment process. A model along these lines is emerging at the "Women in Need" program directed by Claire Reilly in New York City. Once female clients begin to avail themselves of the basic services Reilly's program provides, they are encouraged to accept preventive services. Women In Need seeks to bolster women's self-esteem by providing preventive services to avoid placement of their children. This is accomplished by providing housing and housing referrals, child care, referral to drug-abuse treatment programs, etc. The program offers relief from the pain of life on the street and the vicious cycle of addictive behavior. They hold "survivors groups" for women who survived drug abuse and homelessness. They provide child care while women are in group or out seeking permanent housing or visiting the welfare office or interviewing for jobs. They have client advisory and advocacy groups so that clients can learn to advocate for themselves. They have been able to prevent removal of children by child protective servives by simultaneously helping mothers to address their addictive behavior and the needs of their own children.

Making sure that women and their children will receive needed medical screening and care will be an essential goal of such centers. Crack cocaine and AIDS has changed the face of the drug scene and treatment programs. In the State of New York, where treatment programs in 1989 were at 107 percent of capacity, as many as 63 percent of clients have tested HIV positive. The number of pediatric AIDS cases as well as the number of children born with sexually transmitted diseases (STDs) is rising among the addict population in

America. Yet, as of this writing, few programs in the entire State of New York provide joint treatment for new mothers and their children. Even with plans for five new programs to open in 1990 the population of addict mothers and children will continue to be underserved. Thus, the need for comprehensive multiservice centers for women and their children is acute.

Another important goal of these proposed centers would be to help women and children socialize. Addicted women and their children do not lead normal social lives. Many of these women do not have even a single friend. Moreover, friends and acquaintances are usually also caught up in the world of drug use. Several years ago one of the authors had an opportunity to visit the PACE Program in the South Bronx. Directed by Dr. Carolyn Goodman, a clinical psychologist, PACE is a day hospital program with a genuine child care component that serves mentally ill women, many of whom are alcohol and drug abusers, and their children. Dr. Goodman pointed out the need to set up social networks between these women, many of whom lived isolated in their own aparments, cut off from family and friends. Simple home visits between these women, chats over a cup of coffee, shared-baby sitting, and other friendly exchanges—taken for granted by middle-class people—begin to form the fabric of a richer drug-free existence. The PACE program is an oasis in the middle of an urban desert.

In the fall of 1990 the State of New York, through its Division of Substance Abuse Services, acknowledged the importance of such centers with the issuance of a "Request for Applications" to receive funding support for establishment of *Family Support Communities*. With the issuance of this call the state legislature provided capital construction funds for the development of comprehensive multiservice centers for chemically dependent women and their children. Operational funds for these specialized Family Support Communities (FSCs) will be provided by the State Drug Agency (DSAS) with similar funding available from the New York State Division of Alcoholism and Alcohol Abuse. One FSC is to be located in New York City with four others located in other parts of the state. This is an exciting initative and one that we believe speaks to the true spirit of keeping families with addiction problems united and in the care systems that they need.

In-Home Interventions

Dr. Levy was the clinical director of an outpatient crack cocaine program in Rockland County, New York, from September 1986 through September 1989. During that time several of the counseling staff had the opportunity to visit with clients in their homes. These visits turned out to be revealing and helpful in formulating realistic treatment plans. As the reader knows, addicted clients can be quite manipulative, playing fast and loose with the truth in an attempt to disguise their true life-styles. Viewing a person's home and all his/her possessions (or lack thereof) provides a realistic portrait of his or her day-to-day reality.

Staff were able to note the relative state of the following by doing home visits:

• Cleanliness of dwelling
• Adequacy of furnishings
• Level of nutritional food supplies
• Privacy for adults and children
• Drug paraphernalia and presence of alcohol
• Adequacy of clothing for adults and children
• Presence of toys and games
• Physical safety of dwelling

After noting these things, counselors were able to raise some survival issues that were being ignored or hidden by their clients. Treatment plans often took on a new urgency and linkages to other social service agencies were quickly made. we soon stopped taking for granted assumptions about our clients concerning basic competence in cooking, cleaning, shopping, budgeting, and child care. The program philosophy evolved from an addict-centered approach into a family-centered approach. We were able to identify the covert antecedents—the otherwise hidden triggers—to relapse. Almost by accident, we had stumbled "back" onto an old tradition of the family doctor making a house call. Home visits also come from other traditions such as settlement house social work, real community mental health, and visiting nurse services. Too many drug-abuse treatment programs adopt a private practitioner mentality: "Come back next week at the usual appointment time." More program staff have to be willing to go where "the rubber meets the road."

Eileen Rutter's foster care staff at Saint Agatha's Home of the New York Foundling Hospital aggressively pursues parents in drug-infested communities to seek their involvement in planning for their children. The authors believe that a more aggressive drug scene requires a more aggressive approach by treatment and child welfare personnel.

Child protective services and preventive services for families in need are usually different branches of the social service system; drug abuse treatment programs are part of an entirely separate system. As more addicts have babies, the foster care burden mounts, the number of abused and neglected children continues to soar, and the age of children entering the foster care system continues to drop (58 percent of those entering the system in New York City are under age six). The *New York Times* (24 December 1989), in an editorial entitled "The No-Parent Child," pointed to this problem:

> As caseloads grow, so do horror stories from the City's Human Resources Administration. Children are removed from abusive parents and placed with poorly supervised foster families who often abuse them more, sometimes to death. . . . Children languish for years in foster homes when they could be adopted. . . . City Council President Andrew Stein cites heart-rending cases of children placed with foster parents prepared to adopt, only to be yanked away and returned to their severely troubled natural mothers.

Addicted parents count on a lack of communication between agencies to keep their behavior hidden from officials. They count on addiction-treatment workers not following procedures for reporting suspected or actual child abuse and neglect. When social service workers visit their homes, addict parents carefully orchestrate such visits to hide their addiction and any harm that may have befallen their children. The National Committee for Prevention of Child Abuse estimates that one out of every 13.3 children with a substance-abusing parent is seriously abused every year (NCPCA, 1989). In-home visits made by teams trained in assessment of both child abuse and drug abuse can cut through a lot of this deception. The team could consist of workers from the fields of child welfare, child mental health, preventive services, and family-centered addiction treatment.

The State of Hawaii has taken this idea one step further: Hawaii intends to screen all new parents for the danger signs of abuse. The program is called "Healthy Start" and has already screened about 60 percent of new parents in the state. The program works through a structured interview designed to reveal histories of abuse, trouble relating to children or adults, hostility or impatience with babies, or violence directed toward children in the past. Sometimes danger signs are gleaned from hospital charts, which may contain such evidence of life-style problems as no permanent address or lack of a telephone. Parents who are identified as being prone to commit abuse are offered the services of Healthy Start home visitors. The visitors follow the family with visits and phone calls during the years that children are at the highest risk of serious abuse: from birth to age five. About 20 percent of the parents screened have been offered services thus far. State officials state that only about 5 percent of parents approached had declined participation. About three-quarters of the parents served by this programs are mothers on welfare.

Reducing and preventing abuse and building families has been proven to work when intensive early intervention in the home is provided. There were 2.2 million reported cases of child abuse in 1987 alone (this is the most recent year for which figures are available, according to the American Association for Protecting Children, a division of the American Humane Society).

Mrs. Rutter met with Betsy Pratt, Program Development Specialist, of the Family Stress Center in Honolulu. This center conducted the three-year pilot program upon which Healthy Start is based. The biggest problem they have encountered thus far is "finding more severely high-risk families than we expected because of the spread of drug abuse." She agrees that interagency communication is essential to combat the growing problems of addiction and child abuse: no one agency can hope to do it alone!

Client Confidentiality

In order to maximize communication between agencies the very sensitive issue of confidentiality must be addressed. We need to make our position clear from the outset. While we have no desire to violate the rights of addicts, this present emphasis on addict rights must be changed. The rights of addict's children must also be met. Very often the rights of both parties clash head on and the burden of resolving the dilemma must fall squarely upon the shoulders of legislators and agency policymakers.

Currently, federal law protects clients in alcohol and other drug-abuse treatment programs from any disclosures without their written consent. Title 42, Code of Federal Regulations, Part 2, entitled "Confidentiality of Alcohol and Drug Abuse Patient Records" covers treatment agencies that (1) receive federal funds, (2) have a federal license or authorization, (3) or are considered tax-exempt by the Internal Revenue Service, or (4) allow income tax deductions for contributions. This law also covers what is known as redisclosure. Even if your agency does not fall into one of the just-mentioned categories, if you receive information from one that does, that information must be protected in accordance with federal regulations. State and local laws also apply. Under these regulations no staff member may even reveal if someone is enrolled in a treatment program—or any other information about that person—without the written consent of the client. Violation of this law makes the offender vulnerable to stiff fines and possible imprisonment. Drug-abuse clinicians and administrators have been known to staunchly defend this law and protect patient rights at almost all costs. This attitude has led to a serious problem regarding the protection of the rights of the children of drug abusers. When child welfare, child mental health, social service, family court, medical care, probation, or other workers representing the interest of the children seek information from a treatment agency, the client can simply refuse to grant permission and the staff are powerless to release any information about their client.

Even child abuse does not have to be reported under these regulations. We quote from *A Practitioner's Guide to Alcoholism and the Law* (Evans, 1983):

6. Do you have to report child abuse on the part of a patient?

No, you do not have to, even if there is a state law mandating reporting. If you want to report child abuse, you must first set up a written "qualified service organization" agreement between your agency and the child abuse and protection agency in your state that will allow you to report the abuse, but only if they agree to use the information for treatment and not prosecution. If they wish to prosecute, they will have to seek a court order under Subpart E. Some authorities, however, argue that child abuse can be reported anonymously as long as you don't reveal that your patient is in treatment. (24–25)

Maria Vandor, director of Women and Children's Services for the New York State Division of Substance Abuse Services, using a methadone program as an example, explained what life was like under these old regulations. A methadone program located in a hospital could only report as the hospital, not as the program; the report had to be made anonymously; or a complaint could be made by a "concerned citizen." Under newer federal regulations—PL 99-401—providers, including alcohol and drug-abuse treatment agencies, are mandated to make an "initial report" when child abuse or neglect is suspected. Failure to do so is punishable by six months of imprisonment and a fine of $2,000. Those agencies, mandated as reporting institutions under the law, must provide training for their employees. It is hard to know how many agencies will overrule client protests and report suspected abuse or neglect. Child abuse and neglect is another one of those thorny and complicated issues that pits parental "rights" against the need to protect children.

Laws on child abuse, mistreatment, and neglect differ from state to state. For purposes of exploring this important issue we believe it is instructive for the reader to see how the law actually reads in the State of New York (Social Services Law, Section 412)

Child Abuse, Maltreatment, and Neglect
Social Services Law—Section 412,
State of New York

Definitions of What to Report
A. Abuse
1. Pursuant to Social Services Law, Sec. 412, an abused child means a child under eighteen years of age who is defined as abused by the Family Court Act. Section 1012(e) of the Family Court Act further defines an abused child as a child less than eighteen years of age whose parent or other person legally reponsible for his/her care:
- Inflicts or allows to be inflicted upon such child physical injury by other than accidental means, or
- Creates or allows to be created a substantial risk of physical injury to such a child by other than accidental means

- Which would be likely to cause death or serious or pro-tracted disfigurement, or protracted impairment of physical or emotional health or protracted loss or impairment of the function of any bodily organ, or
- Commits, or allows to be committed, a sex offense against such child, as defined in the penal law, or
- Allows, permits or encourages such child to engage in any act described in sections 230.25, 230.30 and 230.32 of the penal law (i.e., prostitution), or
- Commits any of the acts described in section 255.25 of the penal law (i.e., incest), or
- Allows such child to engage in acts or conduct described in article 263 of the penal law (e.g., obscene sexual performance, sexual conduct).

2. In addition, pursuant to Section 412.8 of the Social Services Law, an abused child can include a child residing in a group residential care facility under the jurisdiction of the State Department of Social Services, Division for Youth, Office of Mental Health, Office of Mental Retardation and Developmental Disabilities, or State Education Department. The definition of an abused child in these settings is virtually identical to the above definition of abuse occuring in a familial setting (see Appendix D, Selected Sections of Laws).

3. Pursuant to Section 412.1(c) an abused child can include a handicapping condition, who is eighteen years of age or older, who is defined as an abused child in residential care, and who is in residential care provided in one of the following:

- The New York State School for the Blind (Batavia, NY) or the New York State School for the Deaf (Rome, NY);
- A private residential school which has been approved by the Commissioner of Education for special education services or programs;
- A special act school district; or
- State-supported institutions for the instruction of the deaf and blind which have a residential component

B. Maltreatment and Neglect

1. Social Services Law, Sec. 412, states that a maltreated child includes a child under eighteen years of age: (a) defined as a ne-glected child by the Family Court Act; or (b) who has had serious physical injury inflicted upon him/her by other than accidental

means. Section 1012(f) of the Family Court Act defines a neglected child as a child less than eighteen years of age:

* Whose physical, mental or emotional condition has been impaired or is in imminent danger of becoming impaired as a result of the failure of his/her parent or other person legally responsible for his/her care to exercise a minimum degree of care:

(a) in supplying the child with adequate food, clothing, shelter or education in accordance with provisions of part one of article sixty-fixe of the education law, or medical, dental, optometrical or surgical care, though financially able to do so or offered financial or other reasonable means to do so; or

(b) in providing the child with proper supervision or guardianship, by unreasonably inflicting or allowing to be inflicted harm, or a substantial risk thereof, including the infliction of excessive corporal punishment; or by misusing a drug or drugs; or by misusing alcoholic beverages to the extent that he or she loses self-control of his/her actions; or by any other acts of similarly serious nature requiring the aid of the court; or

* Who has been abandoned by his/her parents or other person legally responsible for the child's care.

2. The circumstances which constitute impairment of mental or emotional condition, more commonly referred to as emotional neglect, are also defined below as follows:

"Impairment of emotional health" and "impairment of mental or emotional condition" includes a state of substantially diminished psychological or intellectual functioning in relation to, but not limited to, such factors as failure to thrive, control or aggression or self-destructive impulses, ability to think and reason, or acting out and misbehavior, including incorrigibility, ungovernability or habitual truancy, provided, however, that such impairment must be clearly attributable to the unwillingness or inability of the respondent (i.e., parent or other person legally responsible for the child) to exercise a minimum degree of care toward the child (Family Court Act, Sec. 1012(h)).

3. Pursuant to Section 412.9 of the Social Services Law, there is a separate definition of a "neglected child in residential care." Such definition pertains to children residing in group residential facilities under the jurisdiction of the State Department of Social Services, Division for Youth, Office of Mental Health, Office of Mental Retar-

dation and Developmental Disabilities, or State Education Department. Section 412.6 defines a "custodian" as a director, operator, employee or volunteer of a residential care facility or program. A neglected child in residential care means a child whose custodian impairs, or places in imminent danger of becoming impaired, the child's physical, mental or emotional condition:

(a) by intentionally administering to the child any prescription drug other than in accordance with a physician's or physician's assistant's prescription;

(b) In accordance with the regulations of the state agency operating, certifying, or supervising such facility or program, which shall be consistent with the child's age, condition, service and treatment needs, by:

(i)   failing to adhere to standards for the provision of food, clothing, shelter, education, medical, dental optometrical or surgical care, or for the use of isolation or restraint; or

(ii) failing to adhere to standards for the supervision of children by inflicting or allowing to be inflicted physical harm or a substantial risk thereof; or

(iii) by failing to conform to applicable state regulations for appropriate custodial conduct.

4. Pursuant to 412.2(c) a maltreated child can include a child with a handicapping condition, who is eighteen years of age or older, who is defined as a neglected child in residential care, and who is in residential care provided in one of the following:

• The New York School for the Blind (Batavia, NY) or the New York State School for the Deaf (Rome, NY);

• A private residential school which has been approved by the Commissioner of Education for special education services or programs;

• A special school district; or

• State supported institutions for the instruction of the deaf and the blind which have a residential component.

5. It is important to emphasize that abuse or maltreatment can result from the acts of parents or person legally responsible for a child's care, and suspected incidents should be reported accordingly. In accordance with Sec. 1012(g) of the Family Court Act:

"Person legally responsible" includes the child's custodian, guardian, or any other person responsible for the child's care at the relevant time. Custodian may include any person continually or at regular intervals found in the same household as the child when the conduct of such persons causes or contributes to the abuse or neglect of the child.

It is clear that in New York State children are to be protected from such behaviors from all perpetrators including the state's own agencies. This law allows the state to intervene in a drug user's family life if it is able to demonstrate that the offending parent is an addict, or that the offending parent is a drug user and the child's condition is impaired (or in danger of becoming impaired) as a result of a failure to exercise a minimum degree of care in the supervision or guardianship of that child. Either circumstance justifies the filing of a petition to remove the child from the parent's custody.

In New York State, after one files a petition alleging child neglect (the majority of cases are for neglect, not abuse), a hearing is held, at which time the burden of proof is on the petititioner (usually the Department of Social Services). Proof of neglect often takes the form of parental admission of drug abuse. When a newborn is involved, there is the additional proof of a positive drug toxicology. We interviewed Carol Barbash, J.D., director of Legal Services for the Rockland County Department of Social Services. She handles most of the substance-abuse, child abuse, and neglect cases. Ms. Barbash has the strong conviction that in the case of a positive urine for a newborn, that is, when the neonate's urine reveals drugs, the burden of proof should be on the mother rather than on her agency. In other words, mothers should be required to explain the positive toxicology rather than the county having to prove ongoing drug use. No law in New York State requires a judge to place a pregnant addict in treatment—even if she is using drugs in her third trimester. According to federal law (*Roe* v. *Wade*) there is no child to protect. The tragedy is that even if most damage is done in the first trimester there is no way to compel the mother to seek treatment until after the child is born.

There are other problems. For example, there are growing reports sexual abuse of children, often involving violence and rape, by crack cocaine–users continue to grow. There are not enough foster homes for drug-exposed and HIV-positive and AIDS children. Our society does not allow mothers in prison to rear their children, so babies are removed from their mothers, sometimes for many years. What kind of bonding can possibly take place under these circumstances? Law guardians are usually not well versed in substance abuse and often are unsure about what is in the best interests of the child.

Is it reasonable to expect clients, especially women, to report abuse, neglect, and maltreatment of their own children if they believe that the state and local authorities will be notified? We think not. However, if the child protective authorities, child welfare authorities, and the substance abuse treatment agencies work together, children will be far better protected. It is just this kind of cooperative venture—one that would help both parent and child(ren)—that is impeded by narrowly focused laws concerning client confidentiality. How can addiction be successfully treated and the vicious cycle of abuse, maltreatment, and neglect be interrupted when they are not viewed as mutually compatible goals in the eyes of the law? Again we need to emphasize the importance of family-oriented treatment. Treatment that focuses solely on the individual often means the maintenance of child abuse and neglect! Relapse, the pseudo-client phenomenon, and the failure to treat the parents as victims of their own abuse and neglect in their own childhoods only perpetuate this awful intergenerational trauma.

Clients also have the right to decide what specific information may be released. Few addicts volunteer for treatment on their own. Ask any substance-abuse clinician, and he or she will tell you that addicts come into treatment only when the negative consequences of their addictive behavior become overwhelming. Most people entering treatment do so because of external pressure or coercion usually form the criminal justice system, employers, or family members. Somewhere the idea of *user responsibility* must be brought to bear in order for there to be a real interruption in the cycle of addictive behavior.

Treatment programs must begin to put the duality of this concept to work. If consequences bring people into treatment, then dealing with these very same consequences must become part of the actual treatment. The vast majority of addicts remain untreated. If users are to be made genuinely responsible for their behavior, treatment should not be an experience totally isolated from consequences.

Treatment settings must becomes a forum for *facing consequences,* not avoiding them. When an addict is also a parent who is busily avoiding detection and getting high, there are consequences that the children can not avoid. When a parent enters treatment, for whatever reason, what happens to these children?

We have reached an appropriate place to mention a serious problem faced by many addiction workers. We call this the problem of the *"pseudoclient,"* the client who only come to treatment because of external pressure. Without coercion (politely referred to as "therapeutic leverage") these clients would never enter treatment. One of the hallmarks of addictive behavior is *denial,* sometimes reaching almost psychotic proportions. Pseudoclients are not in denial: they know they are addicts and only wish to be left alone with their drugs. Clients in denial deserve a chance at treatment because one of the primary goals of addiction treatment is to break through denial. However, pseudoclients (the unmotivated) and real clients (mixed motivation to motivated) are not always easy to distinguish. One way to decide about who to place in the scarce treatment slots available is to determine who is willing to squarely face up to the consequences. Pseudoclients should be weeded out because they contribute disproportionately to the high turnover rate many addiction programs suffer and also make a major contribution to staff frustration and burnout.

We believe that the issue of client confidentiality versus the issue of the rights of the addict's child(ren) can be solved by linking both to the issue of client motivation. The motivated client should willingly waive confidentiality for the benefit of her/his child(ren). The following list provides practical advice about improving the present system of confidentiality.

Overcoming the Confidentiality Problem

- Addiction treatment programs should be more willing to communicate with other care-giving and service agencies.
- Treatment programs should insist that clients sign releases when the information will serve to aid their children.
- When family courts and others need to monitor client progress in treatment, particularly when issues of child placement and visitation arise, treatment staff should work together

with these agencies to establish honest treatment progress and outcome reports.

- Treatment workers (particularly those involved with addicts in outpatient programs) can not safely assume that children are well cared for. Assessments of child welfare and family resources should be part of the initial treatment assessment and plan.
- Treatment programs should follow guidelines for reporting ongoing or potential abuse and neglect of children. Treatment of addiciton should *never* be identified with failure to protect the rights and roles of children.
- Client motivation can be assessed, behaviorally, by their relative willingness to comply with the signing of releases that relate to child care (and other life-style issues). Motivation can also be assessed in terms of ongoing compliance with child care agency plans for both parent and child. Treatment staff need to become knowledgeable about these child welfare agencies and stop perceiving them as part of an adversarial relationship.
- Treatment programs must develop rational criteria for client progress. This must include urine surveillance, one of the few objective methods available. Family courts, foster care and adoption agencies, among others, need to make rulings regarding children that are based on realistic recovery criteria measured over time and reported in a timely fashion by treatment personnel.
- Treatment programs must move away from an exclusively client-based approach to a more family-based one.

Counseling staff are supposed to review the laws on confidentiality with clients so that each time a release is signed the client gives his or her informed consent. Clients need to understand that they *do* have a right to privacy and confidentiality but that they also are expected to face up to the consequences of their addictive behavior. No one can turn the clock back, but future recovery requires honestly facing up to past actions and their consequences. This is the challenge of addiction treatment. When this challenge is met, family-oriented treatment can occur. Failure to meet the challenge further isolates and endangers the children of addicts. Dr. Levy has seen this idea of "informed" consent violated time and time again by staff eager to avoid despised paper work. Hubbard (1989), in his national survey of treatment effectiveness, uncovered the fact that although clients signed treatment plans, "Many clients, however, were unaware such plans existed or did not know the nature of their contents. This finding suggests that many clients were unaware of the nature of treatment being provided to them and were not full participants in the treatment process" (69).

Too many clients use treatment agencies as a place to "drop out" on their expected roles in society. How can clients be expected to learn new modes of adapting to stress if they are allowed to pretend the past did not occur? Certainly, addicts should not be expected to just "turn it over" where their children are concerned. Programs must use confidentiality laws to help reunite families, not tear them even further apart!

Providing Help Directly to Children

Research has demonstrated that when families experience both substance abuse and child abuse and neglect, these problems must be treated simultaneously to assure the child's safety. Breaking the substance dependency is the first phase of treatment, thereby establishing an environment that allows for a functional parent/child relationship. Parenting skills can not be taught to a person who is actively using drugs. The children of these addicts suffer endlessly from insecurity, lack of a predictable parent, and impotency with regard to control of their own destiny. These children often blame themselves for being "bad" and causing their parent's addiction. They are often terrified to even acknowledge their parent's problem. If they break through their fear and denial to ask for help (whether from relatives, clergy, teachers, etc.) they risk angry parents and out-of-home placements. This continues the ironic cycle of their sense of personal responsibility for their circumstances. So they suffer, usually in silence, praying and hoping for the day when life will get better.

The current child welfare/substance abuse/child mental health prevention and treatment services are not meeting the needs of these children. It is important to recognize that in this "war," like in other wars, the battlefield wounded must be triaged. There are several kinds of "wounded" children of addicts:

1. Children living with active addict parent(s) who are not receiving treatment
2. Children living with addicted parent(s) who are undergoing treatment with varying results
3. Children who have already been removed from the home of their natural parent(s) who are addicts, and have been placed either with kinship families or in nonkinship foster care or institutional care (A distinction must be made between children who were drug-exposed in utero and those who were not. This is important for both research and clinical reasons.)

In all these circumstances the children are survivors as well as victims. They have, despite their tender years, already faced a harrowing existence. They have lived through experiences that rob them of their childhood and their own parents. They need to be exposed to age-appropriate assessments and interventions to validate them as young people who have experienced something terrible. They must be helped to feel like worthwhile human beings in their own right. Their own unique status as children of substance abuse must be give a voice.

Their memories and the powerful emotions that surround them must also be given a voice. In their brilliant chapter entitled "Ghosts in the Nursery," Fraiberg, Adelson, and Shapiro (1980) warn us about the meaning of failure with these children:

> In every nursery there are ghosts. They are the visitors from the unremembered past of the parents, the uninvited guests at the christening. The baby in these families is burdened by the oppressive past of his parents from the moment s/he enters the world. The parent, it seems, is condemned to repeat the tragedy of his/her own childhood with his/her own baby in terrible and exacting detail. . . . We see a pattern which is strikingly uniform: These are the parents who earlier, in the extremity of childhood terror, formed a pathological identification with the dangerous and assaultive enemies of the ego. Yet if we name this condition in the familiar term, "identification with the aggressor," we have not added to the sum of our knowledge of this

defense. . . . We are on sound grounds clinically and theoretically if we posit that a form of repression is present in this defense which provides motive and energy for repetition. But what is it that is repressed? From a number of cases known to us in which "identification with the aggressor" was explored clinically as a central mechanism in pathological parenting, we can report that memory for the events of childhood abuse, tyranny, and desertion was available in explicit and chilling detail. *What was not remembered was the associated affective experience.* . . . Mrs. March [the subject of a case study] could remember rejection, desertion, and incestuous experience in childhood. What she could not remember was the overwhelming anxiety, shame and worthlessness which had accompanied each of these violations of a child. When anxiety, grief, shame, self-abasement were recovered and re-experienced in therapy, Mrs. March no longer needed to inflict her own pain and her childhood sins upon her child. . . . The key to our ghost story appears to lie in the fate of affects [emotions] in childhood. Our hypothesis is that access to childhood pain becomes a powerful deterrent against repetition in parenting, while repression and isolation of a painful affect provide the psychological requirements for identification with the betrayers and the aggressors.

Fraiberg and her coauthors provide a powerful junction for adult/child mental health and addiction issues and show how the two are pathologically woven together. Children in all three categories of "triage" are in need of help from skilled child mental health and child welfare professionals who understand addictive behavior. Different intervention points in our social welfare system characterize each of the three scenarios.

Children living with active addicts are at the greatest risk and unfortunately are not usually identified until tragedy strikes. Once identified by the medical authorities or child protective services they have a chance at being removed from imminent danger. Those children with addicted parent(s) in treatment will have some chance of receiving help only if the addiction treatment program is sophisticated enough to devote staff times and resources to direct intervention with the children and the family unit. But addicted clients often refuse to involve their family in direct services. This situation will have to be reworked as a matter of agency policy or many children in crisis and need will continue to be ignored even as their parent(s) is (are) being treated. Given the high rate of relapse in addiction treatment, one can see why the case for family-oriented treatment becomes more compelling and urgent. The third group will need clinical services to be provided by the foster care agency or associated mental health/addiction service agencies.

Let us review some grim statistics that warn us about the urgency of dealing effectively with children in placement. In New York City, for the year 1977, the foster care population was 23,700. Thereafter, the population began to decline—probably because child welfare experts worked harder to keep families together. This downward trend reversed in 1985. In 1989 the figure was 38,000 and could top 50,000 within a year! Complaints of child abuse in New York City rose from 18,500 in 1979 to 60,000 in 1989. As previously mentioned, 58 percent of the children entering the system are now under the age six; this represents an increase of 11 percentage points in only three years. In 1989 about 4,800 babies will be born in New York City alone to drug-addicted mothers. The majority of these babies will end up in foster care. The people responsible for running foster care agencies must begin programs for "children in recovery" without the addicted parent available to join in the process. The program objectives essential to recovering a generation of lost children are listed below.

Children in Care without Parents

In age-appropriate groups and individual counseling and educational settings the goals are:

- To identify the reasons for living without one's natural parents
- To promote understanding of why and how their parents could abandon them or otherwise give up custody
- To validate their own worth and value as people
- To deal with fantasies and dreams of being reunited with natural parents
- To set up realistic visitation rules and procedures to ensure the physical and emotional safety of the children
- To work through the memories and affects of past negative life experiences

- To assess physical and mental functioning and provide therapeutic and remedial services where required
- To carefully screen any relatives who may seek custody to prevent a return to a negative life-style and to prevent any disruption of custody proceedings by addicted relatives
- By providing the types of services listed above, to "inoculate" the children against their own potential "rotten outcomes"

The concept of "treatment on demand" for adult addicts is becoming a popular political slogan. Children, possessed of fewer resources and lacking the ability to control their own lives, must be made the political priority. They must be provided with resources for rescue and recovery—with or without their addicted parent(s). They are not in a position to demand anything, so we as adults must make them our greatest priority and see to it that we save the next generation. The fields of addiction treatment, child welfare, and child mental health must join forces to make this goal a reality. From birth to early adulthood we must provide settings and services to assure these children a physically and mentally healthy life, a life free of the nightmare of their earlier life experiences.

Do Not Forget the Fathers

Who let the men off the hook? It should not be an acceptable idea that the addict fathers of children have all abandoned their rights and roles as parents. Even addicted lives are not necessarily reeling totally out of control. Many of the addicted male clients that we have known over two decades have been fathers. While it is true that many had run away from their responsibilities as the biological parent of a child, many others had accepted this role and had tried to be effective fathers. As one would expect, positive parenting was often severely hampered by their active addictive behavior. When both the mother and the father were addicted and living together, they would often take turns in their relative degree of dysfunction: one would care for the child(ren) while the other went off on a run or binge. In our clinical experience some fathers were more responsible than some mothers.

Our main point? Prejudicial assumptions and stereotypical-sex-role-thinking often act as a serious deterrent to identifying men who are capable of achieving recovery and becoming effective parents. It is chauvinistic to assume that family courts and addiction treatment programs, for example, should pursue mothers more aggressively than fathers. When addiction treatment becomes more family oriented, moving away from its current preoccupation with treatment of the individual, assessment of *all* family members will improve our ability to capture men in treatment. Eileen Rutter's experience in foster care have shown that addicted men sometimes respond positively to treatment and that fathers who are not addicted will take over single parenting when the mother's addiction becomes all-consuming. Like so many other things in life, addictive behavior follows multivariate patterns. Not all addicts are alike, nor are all addict parents alike. People do recover, even from addiction to crack cocaine and heroin, especially when parent skills training, remedial math and language skills training, jobs skills training, and actual job placement are made part of the treatment program. Addiction, treated in this wholistic life-style—oriented manner, can be cured. Conversations with street-level drug dealers usually reveals a life that promised riches and status and instead provided slim pickings, violence, and imprisonment. Male addicts who recognize the sadness of their lives can be turned away from the addictive lifestyle, but their best chance for recovery will come from rehabilitative approaches that deal with the root causes of addiction.

Men, too, suffer from "ghosts in the nursery." Psychotherapists who work with addicts have come to realize the importance of individual work with clients. Several projects, including the Harvard Cocaine Project and psychotherapy with methadone patients at the University of Pennsylvania School of Medicine, have demonstrated up to a 90 percent retention rate for addicts in individual therapy. This finding defies the stereotype that addicts will not come to, will not stay in, and will not benefit from individual psychotherapy. Our own clinical experience echoes the thinking of one of the major psychological theorists in the drug field, Dr. Edward Khanzian at Harvard. "Hands-on" therapists who help patients establish abstinence can then move them toward more traditional therapeutic work, addressing what Khantzian calls their "core vulnerabilities" (Khantzian & Schneider, 1985). These have to do primarily with affect (feeling) recognition and management. Most of the addicted clients Dr. Levy has treated, in agency and private practice settings, have been males. Most of them respond well to therapists who are open, take an active stance, and are both supportive and empathetic while helping them deal with self-care and resolution of dependency issues. When therapy is combined with limit setting and reality testing (urine surveillance), men can and do enter active recovery, begin to grow as people, and become better fathers in the process. Sometimes they reestablish relationships with their children after years of being absent from their children's lives.

As more women entered treatment, "special" programming for women—women-only groups, incest survivors groups, grief groups, parenting groups, and the like—were created. But what about "special" programming for men? Men are often the victims of child abuse, neglect, incest, violence, and poverty. Rarely do we hear about men's groups to deal with these issues. The time has come for addiction-treatment programs to be more sensitive to these real-world needs and to provide more professionally trained counselors to help men work these issues through in groups and—even more important—in individual counseling. For example, it has been shown that domestic abuse is the number-one factor in creating violent children. Helping fathers (and mothers) learn to handle their anger nonviolently can interrupt a cycle of violence that may go back several generations and could extend generations into the future. The majority of these men can be seen in outpatient programs while others can be helped in residential care.

We feel compelled to underscore the importance of job training and job placement. Psychotherapy and counseling are not enough. In fact, treatment plans that do not help with the real-world considerations of employment are mere "psychobabble." Studies have confirmed that the majority of addicts in government-funded treatment programs have severe handicaps to employment. The majority are high school dropouts with meager work histories, who possess few marketable skills (Deren & Randell, 1990). Unemployment rates are higher for clients in drug treatment, and even among those who work, their weekly earnings are substantially below those earned by the general population (Deren & Randell, 1983).

Schools as Mental Health Settings

We have reviewed in earlier chapters the kinds of things that go wrong in the lives of the children of substance abuse. The first task in helping them is detection. The earlier we can identify the children of addicted parents, the sooner we can intervene in meaningful and helpful ways. We have already mentioned the value of trying to discover potential problems through preventive services in prenatal and postnatal settings like hospitals. But many problems cannot be detected at this early stage in a child's life. The next place where we are most likely to pick up signs and symptoms of addicted, dysfunctional families is in our school systems. Concerned workers must remember that typically these children are silent victims. School-based programs targeted for the children of alcoholics have already been established, with some success (Morehouse, 1979; Morehouse & Richards, 1983). The children of alcoholics and drug addicts feel stigmatized and embarrassed. They are not likely to just start talking about mom or dad "getting high" in front of their teachers. We must remember that they have the same need to protect and defend their family as other children do.

Several studies have pointed to poor academic performance as a warning sign of possible trouble with addiction at home. Poor performance could be the aftermath of being born drug-exposed to drugs like cocaine or heroin, or it could be the result of poor nutrition, or it could indicate a youngster preoccupied with the fear and anxiety of living with an addicted parent. *There is no typical child of addiction,* nor are there prototypes that hold up to empirical scrutiny. As our first two chapters have revealed, the population of children of drug addicts is diverse and multivariate. The academic performance of youngsters is no sure key to problems because evidence demonstrates that most of the damage associated with addicted parenting is social and emotional in nature. Cognition certainly can be affected, but damage to self-esteem, the child's sense of personal safety, and his/her feelings of uncertainty caused by living with an addicted parent are also significant factors. For those in foster care, separation from biological parents, loss of object constancy, and uncertainty about the future are the most salient variables.

Teachers must learn to be sensitive to the kinds of depression, anxiety, hostility, and social isolation behavior that often signals a child of substance abuse. These are the children whose parents rarely appear on open school night, who rarely invite friends to their home, who often wear the same clothes everyday, who avoid direct questions about their family, who often wolf down food as if they were starving, who are very sensitive to the slightest rejection, and who are often late to school and miss lots of school days with poor or no excuses offered for these absences. The children of drug abusers feel even more shame and embarassment, due to the illegal nature of the substances involved, and are even more inclined than children of alcoholic parents, to hide parental behavior.

It is unfair and counterproductive to expect classroom teachers to have the training and expertise to make full-blown clinical assessments of these children. But teachers, because of their years working with children, are competent to pick up the more overt interactional and academic behavioral patterns that signal trouble. The children of cocaine and heroin addicts also manifest more subtle patterns of disturbance, especially "low-grade" chronic depression—a pervasive sense of sadness and dysphoria caused by emotional neglect. Many of the children of cocaine and heroin addicts may appear "hyperactive." In our clinical experience, this agitated behavior is really a "mask" for an underlying childhood depressive reaction. In fact, some psychiatrists use the term "masked depression." The primary feature of this form of depression is a behavioral overlay of anxiety, driven by underlying feeling of pervasive sadness. Teachers need help from child mental health professionals who are trained in recognizing and treating the consequences of family addiction.

Children of drug abusers do have real problems unique to living with or growing up with parents with drug-infected life-styles. However, we are concerned about an overemphasis on the addiction part of a child's life. The main feature of these children is their capacities as *survivors*. If we do not take care to avoid labeling them as *the children of drug abusers,* we will be guilty of further stigmatizing them. We admit it is a fine line: how can we point to a specific problem arena such as parental addiciton without making it the fulcrum upon which the child's entire future is defined. The data do not allow for generalizing at this point. Yet the media has already focused on the worst cases, particularly those concerning "crack babies." Media coverage has stimulated a fright and alarm reaction in schools. According to the media, crack problems began in the winter of 1984. Now, six years later, the first children born to crack-addicted parents are ready to enter the American school system. This scenario falsifies reality, for the children of heroin and nasal cocaine addicts have been with us much longer than six years. In fact, the nasal cocaine problem actually peaked in 1979. There has been no media hue and cry about the children of nasal cocaine–abusing parents. Nor was there a media outcry about children whose parents were heavy users of marijuana, PCP, or other drugs. Apart from an appropriate publicizing campaign about fetal alcohol syndrome, little has been said about other children of drug abuse. There is little clinical or empirical evidence to indicate that children born to crack cocaine addicts are profoundly different than other children, either children in general or children from dysfunctional families without drug-abusing parents. Schools have no cause for profound alarm about the children of crack-abusing parents as long as they are staffed with people trained to help *all* children with *all* kinds of problems. It is unrealistic to think that most schools are going to mount special programs just for the children of drug abusers. Therefore our advice for school teachers, drawn from our own experience and that of most of the professionals we interviewed, is quite simple: Do not treat the children of drugs abusers any differently than other children exhibiting behavior that causes adult concerns. Seek to assess them and to refer them to appropriate services as you would any other child in need. When you do create special treatment services, remember that the goal is to help the children get beyond their status as the children of substance abusers and get on with their personal growth and development.

The children of drug abusers do have some special needs, but they are not so unique nor are they so profoundly disabled that we need to single them out and make them feel even more isolated. Wherever possible, they need to be treated just like all other children. Dr. Chasnoff reports a study of 263 children in which the developmental progress of children of drug abusers was compared to a group of children whose mothers did not use drugs during pregnancy. The drug-exposed children scored within the normal range for cognitive development and were not found—as some people have inaccurately stated—to be "brain damaged." But Chasnoff did indicate that the children of drug abusers will require a structured learning environment and patient, one-on-one attention from teachers and caregivers "in order to achieve their maximum learning potential." The reason given is that drug-exposed two-year-olds scored poorest "on developmental tests that measure abilities to concentrate, interact with others in groups, and cope with an unstructured environment."

We believe that every effort must be made to mainstream the children of drug abusers in school settings. Special attention may be warranted in some cases. Chasnoff stated that "We foresee that many of these children will end up in special education or classes for the learning disabled because the standard classroom, often over-crowded, will not provide the environment they need" (*Update,* November 1989). The children of drug abusers should not be lumped into a single category. Such children need to be evaluated on a case-by-case basis. Not all children require "special education" classes because they are the children of drug abusers. They should be placed on the basis of a "bias-free" assessment, not according to a preconceived notion about how "those" children are supposed to be. We have worked with many children who, when their home life is stabilized, have made excellent school adjustments.

This brings us to the all-important issue of *cross training* (Perska & Smith, 1977). The goals and objectives of *transdisciplinary training* are:

1. The team will integrate services at the diagnostic level
2. The team will increase interdisciplinary communication
3. The team will translate diagnosis into a program plan

As we mentioned at the beginning of this chapter, professionals must move away from traditional role definitions and boundaries. By purposely blurring boundary distinctions, we can boldly move into a new service format. *Cross training* refers to the sharing of knowledge, tools, and learning. More than just teaching members of one field about the content of another is necessary. Practitioners will have to work together, often at the same time and in place, for cross training to really pay off. One technique, growing in popularity in educational settings, is *arena assessment.*

Arena assessment is a variation on the child study team known to some schools and mental health clinicians. For example, a psychologist and a classroom teacher will work together with a child: one observes while the other interivews and interacts directly with the student. The combination could involve any discipline: nurses and guidance counselors, nutritionists and speech therapists, social workers and addiction counselors. In the same arena, several disciplines can work together to assess the strengths and weakness in a child's functioning. The developing treatment plan and/or educational plan thus benefits from a cross-disciplinary perspective and tends to view the child as a whole person and as part of multiple systems (school, family, treatment, etc.). One member of the team would take primary responsibility for the treatment/education plan and ensure that linkages outside the school are successfully made.

This approach allows the single physical plant of the school to become a setting where a number of cross-trained practitioners can interact. Since children spend so much of their lives in school, it is a natural setting in which to promote social-emotional growth together with cognitive achievement. This total approach overrides the visual fragmentation of services that allows so many children to be underserved. Youths no more than adults enjoy schlepping from place to place. In this way children can be "mainstreamed" and separated out only as needed without being arbitrarily forced into just another "after school" program. Great economy and efficiency results from sharing resources in this manner. However, there will be added costs such as bringing qualified child mental health workers into the school setting. Costs could be shared by community mental health and educational budgets. Addiction workers, from community-based treatment settings, who are properly trained in family work, could also lend their skills and talents. We are not talking upon "stacking up" programs. What we are advocating is not just another visit with the school "drug counselor," but a true interdisciplinary team that is an integral part of the school.

Classroom teachers, guidance counselors, and other traditional school personnel would become part of the case conferencing and treatment/educational planning for a comprehensive approach to the children of substance abusers. This kind of cross-training enhances the knowledge base and hands-on skills of all involved and leads to real team building. More important, the child is not lost in a melange of bureaucratic agencies and paper shuffling. Each child would be assigned a primary case worker, who, while not providing all elements of care, would be responsible for coordination and continuity of care for the entire plan. The primary case worker would reach out to other agencies such as drug treatment, family court, preventive, and other social service agencies. This person would also have the all-important responsibility of working with and communicating with the child's parent(s). The parent—whether birth, foster care, or adoptive— must be involved so that home and school are working on mutually agreed-upon goals. State laws mandate that a child's special needs be met. Coordination of services from within the school setting would be a strong advance in intervening in the cycle of family addiction.

Public Law 99-457, when given some funding strength, will help to identify children, from birth to two years of age, who are at-risk for developmental disabilities. They will be eligible for assessment and comprehensive services. Once assessment is accomplished, children can begin getting the help they need prior to entering school. Schools with trained personnel can then welcome the children and mainstream them wherever possible. As we stated above, children of drug abusers should not be isolated in "special education" classes just because they are children of drug abusers. Specific disability would have to warrant such a placement. Remember, scientific study of such children has not yet enabled us to determine exactly what problems and disabilities are specifically caused by drugs per se versus other causes (mother's lack of prenatal care, poor nutrition, cigarette smoking, etc.).

Some schools are already experimenting with new programs that approximate our suggested approach. In 1987 the Los Angeles Unified School District launched a pilot program for prenatally exposed children of addicts, aged three to six. The interesting point is that these children do not otherwise qualify for special education. Several children live with parents in treatment, while others are in foster care. According to an article by Debra Viadero (*Education Week*, 25 October 1989) the twenty-three children are served by teachers, doctors, a clinical social worker, and a psychologist. All of the staff make home visits—some to provide training for the parents, others just to touch base and provide support for the families. These children are receiving the help they need in a school setting.

Another important approach is to keep pregnant teenagers in school. Schools with programs that reach out to "kids having kids" are saving two generations from rotten outcomes. Some of these high-school-aged mothers-to-be are already abusing drugs. Few can count on the boys who impregnated them to stand by them or their babies. They are almost certain to spiral into another cycle of poverty, despair, and addiction. Programs that simultaneously address the multiple problems faced by these young women can lead to genuine positive change.

As a final point in this section we wish to raise the issues of race and culture in working with the children of drug abusers. Dr. James P. Comer, Maurice Falk Professor of Child Psychiatry at the Yale University Child Study Center and associate dean of the Yale School of Medicine, wrote a powerful and moving book, *Maggie's American Dream*, (1988), in which he raises some important issues for all workers in our proposed "schools-as-mental-health" settings. He notes that "American education is structured to serve children who have had the average family experience or better. Teachers are not trained to work with children who have not had such an experience. In the selection of teachers little attention is given to their ability to work with other than mainstream children" (215). When teachers encounter youngsters, usually children of color, who bring behavior from the street or the playground into the classroom, their natural tendency is to punish this "bad" behavior rather than to work to "close the developmental gap." Comer justly claims that "children who have not been read to, helped to learn or think, express themselves, and don't show good problem-solving competence and confidence are often viewed as slow, with limited academic achievement potential." Clinicians and teachers must be more sensitive to issues of culture. Comer goes on to state that far more attention must be paid to relationship issues between the children and the staff, the children with one another, and staff with parents. Consistent with our own views, he advocates a mental health team to support the school management team in applying child-development knowledge to their endeavors. Finally, he calls for an understanding that many children lack social skills due mainly to the fact that their own parents lacked such experiences and can not impart what they themselves do not know. Compassionate listening, the sharing of sympathy combined with encouragement, is vital to these children (as they are to all children). One of our Hispanic colleagues also cautions us that just putting "rice and beans" on the menu does not make a program into one that is responsive to Latinos. Sensitivity and attitudinal skills training can help to foster a greater awareness of and rational response to racial and cultural differences.

The Art of Permanency Planning

The Adoption Assistance and Child Welfare Act (PL 96-272) established a public policy for dependent children. The intent of the law, passed in 1980, is to maintain children in their own homes by providing needed services to families to reduce the risk of placement, to reunite children in care with their own birth families, and to find adoptive homes for children who cannot be reunited with their birth families. Financial incentives were created for the states by the federal government to establish preventive and reunification programs.

But no one was thinking about the children of heroin and no one anticipated the children of crack cocaine when PL 96-272 was passed. The foster care dependency system has been overwhelmed by the consequences of homelessness, AIDS, and addiction. High staff turnover, poor pay, inadequate training of staff, a shortage of motivated law guardians, faulty selection and supervision of foster parents, excessive case loads, and myopic assignment to kinship families have all contributed to the dilemma the system now faces. As a result of all these factors, the rights of the child have been pitted directly against the protection of the family. Reduced availability of benefits for children, the continued high rate of young parents, and the advent of crack cocaine have all conspired to drive children from poor and single-parent families into placement in foster care. Once a child is placed in foster care, less attention is paid to the child's biological family, and the likelihood of families being reunited drops precipitiously. According to noted Stanford University pediatrician Dr. Edward Schor, "Not only are children in foster care unlikely to have promoted ongoing relationships with their parents, but they may be isolated from other family members. It is not unusual when siblings are placed in foster care for them to be placed in separate foster homes and to have separate case workers. Thus, the long-range planning for siblings will not be coordinated, and they may not have continuing contact with one another."

PL 96-272, was created with the intent that the best interests of the child dictate that a permanent plan for care be instituted and carried out if reunion of a fragmented family could not be effected in a reasonable time. Children are not to languish in foster care without frequent attention to legal and treatment planning needs. But the need to plan is often terribly out-of-synch with addictive behavior, whether the parent is an active addict or in recovery. What is happening is that the child welfare laws are bending over backwards for the sickest and most dyfunctional parents.

Positive Approaches to Permanency Planning

- Child welfare workers must be trained in the realities of drug addiction and its impact on families. They must be taught the realities of attempts to treat the addictions with a special view toward relapse as a frequent outcome.
- The courts must appoint diligent and thoroughgoing law guardians to represent the rights of the children. They, too, must be trained in the realities of drug addiction.
- Addicted parents must be aggressively encouraged to enter treatment and to enter into the planning process. If they fail to do so—by objective indicators such as irregular treatment attendance, dirty urines, and failure to attend permanency planning sessions—then they must be prepared to have their parental rights terminated. This will free their children for adoption.
- After surrendering their full parental rights, should they later join an addiction program, they must meet the same objective criteria—over a considerable period of time—if they are to be given supervised visiting privileges. The rights of the children must take precedence over the rights of the parents once children have been surrended.
- Children's rights advocates who are joining the fray must not develop an adversarial relationship with child welfare workers. Advocates must be prepared to visit children in their local habitats where they can see the reality of a child's life and be prepared to help families seek treatment before terminating parental rights. These children can be very manipulative and care must be taken to get the full picture before permanent decisions are made.

  The key to preventing placement outside the home and to effecting reunification must be family-centered treatment whenever possible. This must be done to prevent children from "drifting" through the foster care system.

Social worker Brian Kugel (1989) points to a related consideration for family-centered treatment:

A child welfare professional assessing one of the parents after three or six months of chemical sobriety would note that whereas the cataclysmic symptoms of dysfunction associated with chemical intoxication are absent, and visible signs of primitive loyalty to one's children may be evident and present, the subtle skills of parenting such as empathy and sound judgement are usually not visible. This should indicate that these parents are not truly functional and cannot be left in charge of a family officially labeled "reunified" without additional help.

It is at this juncture in early recovery that clients are most vulnerable to relapse. Mere abstinence is not enough. Clients must learn to cope with life, including the pressures and stress generated by parenting, by resuming the social, occupational, educational, and emotional growth abandoned prior to or during active addiction. Again, we remind the reader that children cannot be left to languish while their parents go either untreated, suffer relapse, or go away for long-term treatment. Permanency planning must be a sufficient motive and lever toward recovery or these birth parents will, in truth, have opted out of their parental role and by default renounced their own children. If loss of one's child(ren) is not adequate to motivate abstinence and a change in life-style, then one must face the consequences.

For those who choose recovery, family-centered treatment represents their best hope. The proof lies in their active participation in the planning process for their own children. This not only sets a clearer course for the child(ren) but it recognizes the reality that without consequences for one's behavior there is no change. Addictive behavior can be defined as seeking after immediate gratification while ignoring delayed negative consequences. If the negative consequence of placement and eventual loss of one's child is not enough to motivate an addicts enrollment in treatment, then society must act without hesitation to save the addict's children from the continuation of negative consequences brought about by their parent's addiction. Addictive life-styles represent a clear and present danger to the child.

Coleman and Davis (1978) conducted a national study of the role of family therapy in the field of drug abuse. They found that (1) family therapy approaches are increasing in the field; (2) the worse the addiction (i.e., frequent heroin use), the less family approaches were used; and (3) the level of expertise in family therapy is low. They conclude: "Family treatment cannot be expanded without providing the therapists with the tools to allow them to be effective.

It is hoped that these results will provide the basis for devleoping a more adequate formula for expanding family therapy training and treatment for all those dedicated to resolving the problems concomitant with drug abuse" (29).

Dr. Edward Kaufman (1984) in the introduction to his book on family case studies on the treatment of alcoholism states, "After fifteen years of struggling with the problems of substance abuse, I discovered the power of family therapy in the mid 1970s. I have found family therapy the needed ingredient to provide 'the power to change' these families." In the same book, Pauline Kaufman, director of family therapy for the Phoenix House therapeutic community and outpatient programs cautions us, "Substance-abusing families have a rare talent at circular movement. They are adept at games without end. Attempted solutions are variations of the theme 'new' solutions become new problems."

The reader is referred to the above and another text by M. Duncan Stanton and Thomas C. Todd (1982) entitled *The Family Therapy of Drug Abuse and Addiciton* for additional readings on theory, research, and practice of family therapy with drug-abusing families.

Present systems are seriously flawed. We have proposed some macrocosmic methods in this chapter. At its best, the decade of the 1980s was a period of "benign neglect" for the drug-abuse treatment field in America. At its worst, the past decade was a repudiation of the needs of poor people, minorities, women, and children. The 1990s are beginning with our nation suffering from a genuine recession. Federal, state, and local budgets are being stripped to the bone. We must all become advocates of the children of drug abusers. They have no voice of their own; without us they and we as a society are truly lost for a long time to come.

5

Treating the Children
of Drug Abusers

"Where is my mother?" he said. He looked for her. He did not see her.
He looked down. He did not see her. Did he have a mother?

—P.D. Eastman

Children of drug abusers are often scared, anxious, angry, shameful, and depressed. Many have experienced repeated abandonment, as well as physical and/or sexual abuse. Others suffer from extreme isolation and silence. The authors have not come across many such children who are happy, cheerful, and full of self-esteem. Many are actually traumatized. It is hard to know how much of their problems can be traced to genetic origin. Research is still in its infancy in terms of informing us concerning the actual damage caused by being exposed to drug(s) in utero. In many ways the children seem resilient, yet in other ways not so resilient. Ample evidence exists as to the social and emotional damage done by being drug-exposed and/or raised, to any age, in a family where drug abuse goes untreated and unchecked. As we have stated in the preceeding chapters, the children of drug addicts defy stereotyping but the damage they suffer is nevertheless manifest throughout the population. Much additional study is needed to find out what is unique about the children of drug abusers. We need to discover exactly what effect different drugs, alone and in combination, at what dose levels, at what stages of pregnancy have on the fetus, the newborn, the toddler, and the older child. We need to separate out drug effects from other independent variables such as nutrition, smoking, violence, the stress of poverty, degree of prenatal care, etc., before we can clearly and honestly say how the children of drug abusers differ from other children who have been matched for salient characteristics that might also effect behavioral, cognitive, emotional, and social development.

In the last chapter we considered broad systemic changes that we believe are long overdue. Our own work and that of other clinicians working with children and families of drug abuse has begun to reveal approaches that can help. The first step in helping is to find these children. They appear in many places if one only knows where and how to look.

Case-Finding Strategies

Children of drug abusers come from all walks of life but they are clearly overrepresented among the poorest members of our society. Virtually all of the problems encountered by the national movement to protect all of our children from abuse and neglect are to found among the children of drug abuse. Professionals experience denial of their own senses, coupled with a moral repugnance at the seamier side of life, and join the silent conspiracy to make the children "invisible." Such gatekeepers of society as teachers, physicians, nurses, clergy, therapists, and others are often trapped in a conspiracy of silence surrounding parental drug abuse: the children will not tell and the adults will not ask! For many children, such behavior on the part of many parents in their community is "normal."

Fearful of angry confrontations with manipulative and hostile parents, professionals ignore the evidence of their own senses: children who are malnourished, depressed, given to acting out, withdrawn, anxious, and the like. Such behaviors are easily explained away. Many professionals just do not dare to raise the challenge that a suspect adult is a drug abuser. We live in a very litigious era. Many caregivers are more concerned about avoiding law suits than uncovering parental addiction. Their fear is not without merit: parental rights and childrens rights are often in clear conflict. Many professionals are unsure of how far they may press, uncertain of how much support they will receive from their own superiors and agencies.

Fear of charges of racism sometimes intimidate workers. How can white professionals point the finger of suspicion at minority men and women? Fear of charges of sexism intimidate other workers. Singling out women for attention makes many male profession-als nervous. But if the fathers are mostly missing-in-action; and the only parent is the mother; and if most drug-addicted mothers are African-American and Hispanic, then let the truth be told. The parents and their children must be helped. And if the mothers and fathers will not or can not accept this help for themselves, then their children must be protected at all costs. There can be no compromis-ing these children's needs based on misguided racial or sexual poli-tics. Pediatricians and schoolteachers in Scarsdale or Grosse Pointe or Shaker Heights who ignore parental addiction are as responsible for the terrible consequences as the parents themselves. The children of poor addicts do not write books or start national movements like the children of middle-class and wealthy alcoholics. They do not make the rounds of talk shows and they do not get to promote fancy rehabilitation centers.

Let us turn our attention to the places where clinical and practical experience have shown us that the children of drug abusers are most likely to be found.

Family Shelters for Domestic Violence

During the late 1980s Dr. Levy conducted substance-abuse educa-tion and training programs for staff working in shelters for women and children who are the victims of domestic violence. According to shelter staffs, some form of alcohol or drug abuse is mentioned in the vast majority of cases. While it is clear that the men as perpetra-tors of violence are "drinking and drugging," it is more problematic to get the women themselves to admit to such behavior. Women in shelters are not routinely tested for the presence of alcohol or illicit drugs in their systems. When women seek orders from family court to protect them against brutalization by husbands and paramours they are not routinely screened for their own substance use. We do not advocate "blaming the victim," but we believe that careful screening of all adults with children who find themselves in such dire straits will afford better protection for the children. In any event, these children are the victims of at least one drug abuser and are in need of services for themselves and their families. Agency staff who seek to secure needed services for abused women and their children are in a unique position to create care that goes beyond emergency shelter. This is just one example of interagency networking that can identify and provide desperately needed services that can stem the tide of what Lisbeth Schorr (1988) calls "rotten outcomes" for the children as they grow older.

Family Shelters for the Homeless

One negative consequence of drug abuse and addiction is financial devastation that leads to a loss of housing. Addicts, in increasing numbers, are unable to make their mortgage or rent payments, and consequently lose their homes or are evicted. Some addicts are thrown out of housing by their own families whose lives they make chaotic through drug use, prostitution, theft, and violence. Many of these addicts and their children end up in family shelters for the homeless. Usually their drug abuse remains unabated and they join in drug use, crime, and neglect of their children with other addicts in the shelter.

Conversations with counselors working in city-run shelters in New York City have revealed that success in getting such parents into any form of treatment in small. Once again, the children are the helpless victims of the shifting sands of adult drug abuse. But shelter staff can identify these children and seek services for them as well as for their parents. In many cases, the children will have to be taken from the parents in order to protect them. If more family-oriented residential treatment programs were available, the multiple needs of such families could be addressed simultaneously. That is, the need for shelter, the need for drug-abuse treatment, and the need for family treatment could be combined to serve a family in distress. Unfortunately, too many addiction treatment programs see these goals as mutually exclusive. To treat homelessness merely as a "symptom" and consequence of addictive behavior, without also treating the addiction that caused it, almost guarantees the perpetuation of the problem for parent and child alike.

Welfare Housing

While it is certainly true that not all persons who receive public assistance are using or abusing drugs, welfare housing is a hotbed of drug use. In the late 1980s Dr. Levy did staff training with public health nurses who work in single-room occupancy (SRO) hotels in New York City. These dedicated and seasoned veterans, who serve the needs of some of the city's poorest inhabitants, were shocked by the effect crack cocaine was having on women and their children in the SROs. They told stories of children living in the "drug war zone" where neither child nor adult is safe from attack. Older children are often employed by drug dealers to work as lookouts. The mothers of these children find it hard to refuse the cash such employment provides because their support from the welfare system is so meager. The nurses reported that it is hard to keep up with the health needs of the mothers, whose minds and bodies are ravaged by drug abuse. Were it not for these nurses the children's health needs might go entirely unmet. Outreach to these families must be increased, for they are prime candidates for homelessness, especially when welfare checks needed to pay the rent and feed children are used instead to buy drugs.

In New York State, Andrew Cuomo, son of the Governor, has demonstrated that providing temporary housing and needed social services from a private, not-for-private base can be superior to running the show from a municipal base where a rigid bureaucratic rules, powerful labor unions, and a generation of "misguided civil libertarian suits" in city-run poverty programs conspire against efficient, cost-effective programming (Klein, 1991). Strict rules are enforced in Cuomo's shelters, including a total ban on drugs and alcohol. On-site social services are also provided.

"You have to agree to be part of the program. . . . You have to see your caseworker, get into drug treatment, or job training, or whatever is called for. You have to make sure your kids stay in school. You have to make a commitment," says Cuomo. Cuomo reports that only about 10 percent of the clients (mostly women and children) are asked to leave. The other 90 percent remain for two to eight months, until they find permanent housing and some semblance of stability in their lives.

Hospital Emergency Rooms

Hospital emergency rooms in large and middle-sized cities have been inundated with the casualties of the American drug scene. Crack and heroin, used alone or in combination, are devastating the addicts and exhausting the medical staff who must attend to them. One *New York Times* headline read "Urban Emergency Rooms: A Cocaine Nightmare" (6 August 1989). We interviewed Iris Weiss, R.N., a clinical specialist in emergency medicine for twenty-three years at Peninsula General Hospital in Far Rockaway, New York, in order to get some insight into the fate of the children of these patients. "What comes to mind, more than anything, to me is where a young woman addict tried to sell her baby to buy crack. That's how desperate it gets. We don't make a dent in the problem. . . . I really don't think we do. The staff just becomes more cynical."

Children in need of medical care are often not brought in soon enough for the presenting complaint. They have gone without treatment longer than need be, and therefore have suffered longer. Another problem is that children are often not brought in by their natural parents. Many times the natural mother's whereabouts are unknown. The person who brings the child for treatment does not have papers that show legal guardian status. This creates a problem, for child patients require the signed consent of the parent or legal guardian to receive treatment. This problem is usually solved by getting administrative consent from the administrator-on-duty. Moreover, the presenting adult often cannot provide a medical history for the child.

When the ER staff suspect child abuse or neglect, the appropriate child protective authorities are contacted. The child protective worker will come to the ER if the child cannot be sent home with a responsible adult. Otherwise, the child is admitted and the hospital social worker follows up with the child welfare authorities. The child is never sent home with the suspected party—even to the point at which police are called, if necessary.

Emergency staffs need to take an aggressive posture to help the children of drug addicts. Poor families use ERs as if they were clinics. Often the ER is the only healthcare service they use. Many younger addicts are HIV positive or have AIDS. They are malnourished and underweight. Many adult patients are repeaters. Common complaints include pelvic inflammatory disease, stomach pains, beatings, gang rape, AIDS-related pneumonia, weakness, anorexia, and vomiting of blood. The two most common presenting medical problems for addicts are acute drug intoxication and drug-induced psychoses. Ms. Weiss also noted that many of the children's parents are sixteen to eighteen years of age while the grandparents are only in their mid-to-late thirties. Case finding in emergency rooms can help to identify and aid large numbers of children of drug abusers, particularly very young children.

There are other places to look for the children of drug abusers that we will not elaborate on, but that are worthy of mention.

1. Private pediatric and adolescent medical practices
2. Child and adolescent mental health services (public and private)
3. Schools (all grades)
4. Obstetrical medical practices (and hospital maternity services)
5. Department of Social Services Agencies
   a. Aid-to-dependent children
   b. Child protective services
   c. Adult protective services
6. Family court
7. Court welfare agencies
8. Probation departments
9. Substance-abuse treatment programs for adults
10. AIDS and HIV programs

Below we offer an example of the sometimes slow and tedious process of following the clues that reveal parental addiction; in this instance, in a private-practice, child psychotherapy setting.

Case Illustration: Barry

Barry, a handsome, well-built five-year-old, was referred to Eileen Rutter, a private practitioner, for treatment through the nursery school that he attended. An especially bright little boy, Barry was hyperaggressive with the other male children in the class. He often kicked the other boys in the shins. But he was gentle with the girls. He alienated most of the female staff because after asking to be held, Barry would attempt to fondle their breasts and genitals.

Teachers noted that Barry was often sullen and quite irritable as soon as he came off the school van. He would refuse to sit down at the "circle" with the other children and would remain aloof. He frequently had to sit off by himself while class went on. Until the group times were over he would sit alone, making noises and suffering.

Sherry, Barry's mother, cancelled many appointments before finally coming in to meet Mrs. Rutter. She did not want to meet her in the nursery school because she felt the staff disliked her. She denied any use of drugs when a family history was taken. However, to a trained eye, Sherry appeared anorexic.

Sherry had two sons, born eighteen months apart. The elder, Harry, had been an easy baby, with a thin, small body. He was compliant. Barry was born after a full-term difficult pregnancy. Sherry gained seventy pounds and Barry weighed eleven pounds at birth. Sherry said that he was so big and ate so much that she would just sit him up in an infant seat and let him feed himself bottles. Mrs. Rutter asked if she ever held Barry. She said "rarely," and her tone was tinged with anger.

Part of the therapist's training is to develop self-awareness. This helps to gain mastery over those countertransferential feelings and thoughts that can interfere with therapy. Mrs. Rutter was beginning to understand why an entire nursery school staff would dislike this twenty-seven-year-old mother.

Sherry seemed eager to fill in the rest of the child's history. The marriage between Sherry and the children's father had ended two years earlier. It was a long and bitter divorce. Barry looks just like his father. Mrs. Rutter then realized that Barry's mother was displacing her anger at her former husband onto her youngest child.

Rene Spitz, a pioneer researcher on human infants, observed what happened to babies who were neglected. He found some withdrawn personalities who seemed unrelated and somewhat numb. He also found that other neglected children adapt to their environment by becoming very socialized, having a great number of relationships and indiscriminately befriending people, often with a seductive style and not really feeling close to anybody. Barry seemed to have incorporated elements of both responses.

In psychology and psychiatry, individuals with these behavioral qualities are often diagnosed as "borderline and narcissistic." The terms are reserved for description of adult behavior. Yet many children suffer from unmet needs and the younger they are, the harder it is for them to verbalize their needs in any meaningful manner. Barry was certainly reaching out for help.

Rutter began play therapy with Barry. For the first ten minutes of each session he would want to sit on her lap and "be held like a baby." She indulged him with this desired affection. But within seconds this youngster would fondle her breasts and dig under her clothes. Mrs. Rutter would only continue to hold him if he put his hands around her shoulders, neck, or hands. Barry resisted these instructions repeatedly. The physical support that he craved was denied him by entire nursery school staff because the teachers (all female) were repulsed by his sexualized behavior.

Part of the therapy included a consultation with the school staff on the etiology of sexually overstimulated children (which can result from direct sexual abuse or the witnessing of "sexually loosened" behavior). The issue of countertransference was raised. The staff felt they could not hold Barry because he frightened and disgusted them and they were unable to find the proper language to verbalize the limits he craved. One teacher assumed the primary responsibility of working with him, especially in the mornings, when he came off the school van seeming so depressed. But one by one the teaching staff learned to respond to Barry's wish to be held.

It was not as easy keeping Sherry engaged in the early phases of treatment. She cancelled most of the sessions. The sessions she did attend were painful for her. Barry did not seek attention or affection from his mother. The shift of focus to Sherry's life was a difficult transition. She was guarded. Mrs. Rutter asked her to bring in a family album.

It showed an isolated family, except for the pictures of Sherry's new boyfriend, who was disrobed in most of the pictures. Rutter still suspected cocaine use. Sherry was able to talk about her own overbearing and intrusive mother, who lived next door. She felt that her own mother rejected her and only liked the part of Sherry that was an account executive at a bank. Sherry felt that her family gave her little emotional support.

Barry was beginning to respond to play therapy. He still had to have the holding at the beginning of every session. But he tested limits of touching with less frequency. His play became centered in the dollhouse, with dozens of people coming and going. The baby dolls were ignored, despite the close proximity of the adult dolls around. When the babies were denied a wish they would strike out and not be chastised. Life would go on pretty much as before. And then the dolls would take off their clothes and touch each other for a long time.

Sherry missed her next appointment and Barry became ill at school. Mrs. Rutter spoke to Sherry on the phone and asked if she would like her to pick Barry up and drop him off at home. Sherry eagerly said yes. Mrs. Rutter found her to be in a miserable state—sore throat, fever, and gaunt as ever. The pain was so bad she could hardly speak. She asked if she could be dropped off at a local medical center for treatment.

Mrs. Rutter took this as an opportunity to meet with Sherry on a more personal level. Sherry was greatly appreciative and knew the concern was genuine. Treatment was starting to gel for both mother and child. Trust was no longer an issue. Sherry's ability to form a trusting relationship with Mrs. Rutter freed her little son to respond to the therapy, gave him a sort of permission to relate to the therapist. Sherry was then able to use her sessions to break through the concrete wall of denial about her cocaine habit. The breakthrough was Sherry's alone. She had her own insight as to how her mother avoided her, and how she had begun using cocaine and pills as a way to avoid Barry. She admitted that when she was high she would have sexual intercourse with her boyfriend. She said she thought the children were asleep, but noted that she was not always careful. Maternal neglect and abuse is exacerbated by cocaine. Sherry began to deal with her fears about attaching herself to Barry in a loving way. She felt overwhelmed by his neediness and, of course, her own.

Mrs. Rutter suggested that, along with Sherry's individual therapy sessions, she attend a parenting group held at the nursery school. It seemed an odd suggestion to Sherry in that she felt that the staff and community "hated" her. She was right. She began attending the group and sharing her problems. The group related to Sherry's plea for acceptance. They became a source of courage and strength for her as she totally abandoned her cocaine use and began to work through the family problems she had to deal with.

Barry was much more relaxed as his mother became more available to him. Mrs. Rutter began to include Sherry in the play therapy sessions. She felt that modeling the "good mother" would not induce feelings of overwhelming guilt at this point in therapy. Barry was helped to detach completely from the teaching episodes by having "complete interpretations" made to him in words that a child his age could comprehend. This helped to further alleviate any feelings of guilt or shame on his part. These were difficult sessions for both mother and son as the old tensions associated with viewing Sherry's overt sexual behavior caused Barry a flood of feelings. But it eventually brought relief as this terrifying experience was worked through. Sherry's empathy with her son's life experience grew deeper each time they were seen. Her own feelings of abandonment and rage allowed her to develop a genuine sense of compassion for Barry's plight.

The parent group brought relief from isolation for Sherry as a parent. A few of the mothers actually began to socialize with her on weekends. She developed a close connection with some of these women. Barry still found it hard to play with children his own age. Most of the nursery school children were afraid of him. Sherry reported that he did have one friend, two years older, in the neighborhood.

Therapist and patient explored how to enable a five-year-old to make friends. It turned out that Barry had free run in his neighborhood, and was allowed to cross major thoroughfares and heavily trafficked streets. He was totally without supervision. Sherry began to protect her youngest child by setting firm limits and providing closer supervision. The more he was supervised at home, the fewer problems he had with socialization at school. His feelings of omnipotence finally had some boundaries. He was really feeling safe. The hyperaggressive kicking episodes ceased.

Barry was going off to kindergarten in September. Sherry agreed with the nursery schools' recommendation for a special education class for emotionally disturbed kids. She balked at this label but came to understand that what Barry had lived through in his short life was not going to go away easily. The small ratio of staff to child would continue to enhance and build upon the success Barry was now experiencing in school and the rest of his life.

We believe that Barry's story helps to reveal several important points:

1. Children deserve help in their own right
2. Family-oriented treatment is quite powerful
3. Working with children, including quite young children, helps to build bridges to parents
4. School officials and staff must be included
5. Home visits can be invaluable
6. Perseverance and relationship building by the therapist help ferret out addictive behavior
7. Even traditionally trained therapists, when willing to move out of the office and a rigidly traditional stance, can make a real difference in the life of a child of a drug abuser (and in the life of the drug abuser as well)

8. Age-appropriate tools, like play therapy, are good diagnostic aids
9. Parenting groups are important tools in teaching skills and building parent networks

Lisbeth Schorr (1988) states:

Successful programs see the child in the context of the family and the family in the context of it's surroundings. . . . What is perhaps most striking about programs that work for the children and families in the shadows is that all of them find ways to adapt or circumvent traditional professional and bureaucratic limitations when necessary to meet the needs of those they serve. . . . Therefore, family therapy can't be up in any ivory tower but related to practical needs and services.

Some Early Projects Working with the Children of Drug Addicts

In April 1987 the New York State Division of Substance Abuse Services (DSAS, 1987) published a set of guidelines for substance-abuse treatment agencies that might be interested in working with Children of Substance Abusers (COSAs). Julio Martinez, then director of DSAS, had initiated a task force on COSAs in 1983. By 1987 the number of "COSA programs" was officially listed at only six for the entire State of New York. Of these, four were part of methadone-maintenance programs (all located in New York City), one was a drug-free residential program (also located in New York City), and one was a self-help support group located in Buffalo, New York. Dr. Levy visited the four methadone and one-drug free residential COSA programs in New York City during 1987.

It is quite clear that despite the rising tide of addiction and its destructive effect on the family, the treatment community was painfully slow in responding to the needs of children and their families. This was happening despite the fact that DSAS researchers (Deren, 1986, 1986a; Deren & Kott, 1987) estimated that more than two-thirds of clients in methadone-maintenance clinics are parents, with a total number of children exceeding 40,000! They also estimated that half of the clients in state-funded, residential, drug-free treatment programs are parents, with a total of approximately 3,000 children. Despite rhetorical pleas for a "holistic approach" to client services by DSAS, a total of six programs for children in a state with over 45,000 addicts in care (35,000 on methadone maintenance, and 10,000 in drug-free treatment) was not an impressive beginning. It was, in fact, an example of how little had changed in the orientation of the drug treatment field since the late sixties—an orientation that was client-centered, as opposed to family-centered. Our conversations with professionals from across the nation have given us no reason to believe that things were much different anywhere else in the country when it came to caring for the children of drug abusers.

Drawing from the DSAS literature (DSAS, 1987; Deren, 1984) and our field experiences, we will briefly describe several of these early programs (whose efforts are ongoing).

The Family Center Program at Odyssey House

The Odyssey House Family Center has been in existence since 1971. Housed in the MABON building on Wards Island, the early program was called the *Mothers And Babies Off Narcotics* program. It is one of the few residential, drug-free facilities in the nation to offer services to pregnant women and addicted women with children under age five. There are twenty-five beds for parents and twenty-four beds for children. The retention rate for the Family Center was 68 percent in 1989, with an average length of stay of three months. The program runs twelve to eighteen months and 35 percent of all participants actually graduate. Ninety-six percent of the clients used crack or cocaine, usually in combination with alcohol or other drugs.

The typical client in 1989 was a black women, twenty-five years old, with a 9–11th grade education, who used cocaine, most likely had one substance-abusing parent herself, possibly HIV positive, Protestant, single, with no psychiatric history, in care with one child, and a voluntary client (Ramos & Stone, 1989). During that same year twenty-two clients were inducted into the program and nine clients (and their children) graduated (that is, completed the full, twelve to eighteen months program).

According to Lorin Fischer, director of Clinical Services at the facility, the key concept is that the mother's "job" while in the program is to achieve rehabilitation while her child(ren) are in "day child care" services. The program utilizes a basic mutual self-help approach imbedded in a "community." Clients receive individual and group counseling, remedial educational services, and job training; they attend AA and NA meetings, and family therapy, peer group, and parenting-skills counseling sessions. Pregnant women are accepted and provided with both pre- and post-natal care. According to Fischer, "We try to give the women a vision. We want them to internalize a philosophy of living that allows them to think that they can be like everyone else."

Requirements for graduation include a driver's license, a high school diploma or equivalent, a full-time job, $2,000 in savings, participation in individual psychotherapy with an outside professional, and a cooperative living apartment with other Odyssey residents in the community (Odyssey House, 1988). Reentry candidates average an annual salary of $18,000 on their first job. In addition to the usual therapeutic community counseling staff, there is a pediatrician and nursing and child care staff.

The children range in age from newborns up to age six. There is a special infant nursery with a medical lounge and twenty-four-hour staff supervision. The nursery is in close proximity to the adult living quarters. A child care administrator heads a full-time staff of three. The mothers spend most of the day in treatment activities, but regular visits with the children are scheduled and there is a "parent-on-call" procedure to further extend parental responsibility. Parenting skills groups, day care, and extensive child care services, school for age-appropriate children, night coverage, and supervised mother-child interaction time daily are all elements of the parents' program. Toddlers and preschoolers are exposed to various cognitive and social programming that allow for both learning and play. School-age children attend school at local public schools. Health care for parents and children are provided at area hospitals.

One of the great "tragedies" of this unique program is its failure to take advantage of the clients and their children as sources of desperately needed information. Odyssey House has never conducted a systematic study of its women clients or their children. Much could have been learned, particularly about drug-exposed children who were actually born drug-free (most studies concern children born to women on methadone maintenance). What distinguishes the women who stayed in the program from the ones who left prematurely? How do the women and children fare after they leave Odyssey House? The program may never again have the funds that were available in the early 1970s when the research could have been done without sacrificing essential clinical services. It costs approximately $30–40,000 per family unit per year to run the programs. Some recent data drawn from the Hawaii Early Learning Profile show that the majority of children measured within normal development limits. One can only hope that data will be more systematically collected on this unique population. Still, Odyssey House remains as an example of a program and a staff that chose a difficult mission and for a significant number of addicted women and their children are making a real difference. The program has plans to open three more facilities.

In 1975 Family House was established as a demonstration project by the Eagleville Hospital and Rehabilitation Center outside of Philadelphia. From 1975 to 1981 the program served one hundred families. The program was similar to the Odyssey House program. A detailed description of the program is offered by Pearlman, West, and Dalton (1982). At the conclusion of their paper they point to the need for the careful selection of staff for such a unique program:

> Staff members in such programs need to be carefully selected. They must be flexible, sensitive, and capable of independent action yet able to work as a team, comfortable in multiple roles, with knowledge of the treatment needs not only of drug dependent women but also of children. The ability to tolerate unexpected events and periodic chaos is important. The mothers are likely to need nurturing support from the staff, especially when they begin the program. Staff members need to resist the impulse to act as substitute parents in order to strengthen family relationships. Because intense involvement with families is required, most staff cannot work with more than two or three families at any one time. . . .
>
> At no point is the program static. Staff must be prepared to periodically reevaluate the program's philosophy and procedures and client and staff needs. Instability and crisis occur in cycles, so a regular process of evaluation and change must be incorporated as an integral part of the program if it is to serve its clients and survive. Staff must

be willing to participate in this process and support each other (and have outside supports) throughout the process. (558)

This model of drug-free residential care for parents and children together needs to be replicated in other cities.

Women, Inc., and the Neil J. Houston House, in both located in Boston, are several other efforts of this kind. Even more controversial are the three prison nurseries (Taconic Correctional Facility, Bedford Hills Correctional Facility, and Rikers Island) in New York State. This experiment allows drug-addicted mothers to live in prison dormatories with their newborn child while doing time. The experiment could be expanded to include more clinical and therapeutic programming for mothers and the children like the Odyssey House Family Center in New York and Family House in Pennsylvania. It is also cost-effective.

Methadone-Maintenance COSA Programs

In New York the oldest (it began in 1975) and best established program for addicted women and their children in an outpatient setting is the Pregnant Addicts-Addicted Mothers Program (PAAM) at the New York Medical College located in East Harlem. The PAAM program is part of the Center for Comprehensive Health Practice (CCHP) which is an amalgam of five hospital-based departments: Internal Medicine, Obstetrics-Gynecology, Pediatrics, Psychiatry, and Surgery. One of the great strengths of the program is that it can draw from New York Medical College residency programs in the five departments, thereby giving it a unique and continuous source of staff. The program began with a grant from NIDA. Of the six "comprehensive care programs for pregnant addicts" that were funded by the federal government in the 1970s, only the PAAM program survived the budget cuts of the 1980s. The program now survives on a grant from the state drug agency (DSAS), medical reimbursement, and modest fees paid by non-Medicaid clients.

The PAAM program provides comprehensive treatment for pregnant addicts, their husbands, and infants. It includes obstetrical, psychosocial, and pediatric care, as well as family services organized into four units: medical, counseling, parent education, and research (Beschner & Brotman, 1977; Suffet & Brotman, 1984; Outlook, 1990). PAAM helps clients deal with issues of life-style that go beyond traditional addiction-treatment services including financial, social, nutrition, and childrearing counseling. The program is available to opiate-addicted pregnant women or women who have given birth within the past three months who were addicted during their pregnancy. Most of the clients are on a methadone-maintenance program. As David Hutson, associate director of the CCHP, has stated (Outlook, 1990): "Poor people and drug addicts need basic care. They are missing the basics of a place to live, how to get on with each other, physical health. This may involve some very specialized services, but at the heart of it is to find a group of people willing to provide the nuts and bolts, day in and day out, not worrying about whether or not this is really their professional role."

As mentioned in our discussion of Odyssey House, here too we found a staff with a "mission". The services available to the family include parent education classes, developmental assessments, and a preschool nursery. PAAM takes particular pride in the parenting curriculum that they have developed under the direction of Dr. Nina R. Lief, a pediatrician and psychiatrist, and director of the Early Childhood Development Center at the New York Medical College. Dr. Lief and her associates postulated that understanding a child's development would help parents treat their children more appropriately (Lief, 1981, 1987). Utilizing a staff of professionals and volunteers from the Junior League, they formed working groups of mothers who meet weekly for a period of three years. Listed below are the parenting themes that are taught, modeled, and discussed in these groups.

Dr. Lief conducted research on the parenting groups in which both addicted and nonaddicted parents participated (Lief, 1977, 1987). Despite some restrictions on interpretation of the data due to sample size and timespan, several broad conclusions were made (Lief, 1977):

- Through regular groups sessions, parents can increase their knowledge, skills, and enjoyment of caring for their babies. The study showed that addicted mothers, like nonaddicted

---

Pregnant Addicts-Addicted Mothers Program
Parenting Themes*

Parent's Input:

Physical Care
Patterning and Sequencing
Stimulation: Sensory and Motor
Stimulation: Communication and Language
Exploration
Social Relations

Parent's Role as a Parent:

Parental Attitudes: Interest in Achievement
and Mastery
Enjoyment of the Child as a Person
Maternal Self-Confidence

Infant's Coping:

Establishing Trust and Personal Relationships
Dealing with Separation and Individualization
Establishing Conscience Mechanisms and a Good
Self-Image

*Adapted from Lief, 1981, 1987.

---

mothers, are capable of improving their competence in parenting and of finding pleasure in the task.
- Addicted mothers were competitive with nonaddictive mothers in terms of improvement; they were also generally rated as equals in their levels of competence as parents.

Lief (1987) found that the parenting program was also quite helpful in preventing child abuse by reducing parental yelling, making the parents more tolerant of normal toddler behavior, and leading them to curb not only verbal but other forms of abuse. Lief found that there was a direct correlation between attendance at parenting meetings and improvement (lessening of abuse) in child care. Lief also found a significant correlation between parenting group attendance and less serious recurrences of neglect. Dr. Lief concludes, "While a self-selection factor may have been operating, these findings permit entertaining the hope—a plausible one—that a well-designed and well-administered parenting program has not only remedial effects, but preventive ones as well. . . . More attention to prevention through appropriate parenting may be a fundamental tool in ameliorating the problem of child abuse" (410).

Another significant finding was that "most of the addicted mothers *had spouses* who usually also participated in the parenting groups." Juliana et al. (1989) in surveying methadone-maintenance clients who are parents found 107 fathers who had sole custody of and primary responsibility for 145 children. Fathers do exist and can be reached!

In 1985 the Division of Substance Abuse (DoSA) of the Albert Einstein College of Medicine (AECOM) in New York City was awarded one of the first COSA grants by DSAS. The DoSA treats over 2400 former narcotic addicts at seven different methadone-maintenance clinics, making it the second largest substance-abuse treatment program in New York State. DoSA initially conducted a fairly extensive needs assessment project to see what problems existed and what interventions were needed for children and their parents. Three hundred and eighty one interviews were conducted; case files were also combed for information. What DoSA found is remarkable.

AECOM-DoSA Needs Assessment Findings for Children of Substance Abusers and Their Parents

- 75 percent of patients in treatment are parents.
- 5,000 children have been born to patients, and of those children about 3500 are in patient's custody and under the age eighteen.
- Approximately 20 percent of patients have children in foster care placement or cases with NYC's Child Welfare Administration.
- 23 percent of the children were suffering medical, mental

health, or social problems that required professional attention.

- The largest group of children experiencing problems were those under the age Five.
- The children in need had not been otherwise identified through mainstream health and social service systems and were under age for identification in the educational system.
- Simple services such as routine health care, day care, and child welfare preventive services were not accessed. These services were least available to children at the most critical ages.
- Most importantly, the assessment highlighted the special needs of pregnant substance-abusing women and new mothers.

The most important aspect of the assessment was the caseworker's success in getting the parents to participate, speak candidly, and help to identify children in need. The DoSA staff point out that the caseworkers who did the assessments succeeded because they had pre-existing, trust-based relationships with the patients.

Patti Juliana is a social worker who directs Children and Family Services for AECOM-DoSA. She and her colleagues (Juliana et al.,1989) state:

> We do not accept the position that mothers who have been addicted are, ipso facto, "bad mothers." They are often, however, handicapped by their own early socialization which they tend to repeat and which may have accounted in part for problems contributing to their addiction in the first place. A study of Hale House, a residential program for infants of heroin-addicted women indicated, for example, that many mothers "came from poor, one-parent families in which alcohol was abused, and children were often beaten.

In a brochure describing the Children and Family Services program, staff describe the scope of the problem as they view it:

> Substance abuse is not only the problem of the individual, but must be viewed in the context of other "systems," the family being one of the most crucial. Substance abuse by any member affects the whole family. Children raised in a substance abusing family are often the unintended victims of drug problems and are at "high risk" to de-

velop behavioral, learning or health difficulties, including alcohol and/or substance abuse. Problems which substance abuse patients face are often reflected in the family and in interactions with their children.

At the same time, patients, their partners, parents, siblings and children share a desire to "heal." Patients resistant to treatment can often be motivated through their love for their family and children and their overwhelming desire to be good parents. And research and clinical observations have consistently shown that substance abuse patients reap greater individual benefits from treatment when supported in their efforts by family members. Knowing these facts, a multidimensional range of services for patient, child, and family were defined and developed through the Division's COSA program.

The services offered by the COSA program include:

- Identification and evaluation of patients' children who are experiencing behavioral, learning, or health problems.
- Therapeutic intervention with parent and child, individually and together.
- Parent education, parent training, and parent support groups in each of the methadone clinics
- Prenatal medical and psychosocial services: identifying and working intensively with pregnant patients and parents of newborn children, assuring attention to prenatal care and AIDS-related issues; facilitating the patient's transition in their role as parents.
- Referral and advocacy for patients and their children with community-based resources including child development and family and mental health centers, child advocacy and legal services, educational and vocational programs, recreational and after-school centers, day care providers, and parent programs.
- Ongoing liaison and coordination of services with school districts and school-based substance-abuse prevention and intervention programs servicing patients' children; targeting children with identified learning, emotional, and school-related problems, and accessing special services for children within school districts.
- Preserving the integrity of patients' families—preventing fos-

ter care placement and assisting in reuniting families whose children have been placed.
• Staff training and sensitization to the special needs of patients' children and to patients in their role as parents.

The COSA staff includes the director of Children and Family Services, COSA coordinator, community/school liaison, maternity workers, and caseworkers in each division clinic. The COSA project is funded by DSAS, NYS Department of Social Services, and NIDA.

In 1988/89 the COSA project received a one-year Pregnancy Outcome Improvement Project grant from the New York State Department of Social Services. The grant provided funds for two case managers to ensure improved prenatal case, coordination of high-risk pregnancy treatment, and interdisciplinary service delivery. The managers monitor and attempt to reduce drug use during pregnancy and work with social services and other agencies to coordinate services.

During 1989 they recorded 181 pregnancies among patients: Seventy-four resulted in live births, one ended in a stillbirth, four ended with spontaneous abortions, sixty-four were terminated by elective abortions, and forty-eight were still ongoing at year's end. Forty percent (40.1 percent) were HIV positive.

At the inception of this project in 1989, thirty-two women were enrolled:

• 27 percent were involved in prenatal care and 65 percent were abusing alcohol and cocaine while enrolled in methadone treatment.
• After four months of intensive treatment provided by the Pregnancy Outcome Improvement project:
    87 percent were enrolled in prenatal care
    25 percent were abusing drugs or alcohol

The Division of Substance Abuse publishes a newsletter called *Journey.* One issue (*Journey,* 1988) contained the testimony of two children, both children of heroin addicts, one young woman and one young man, presented before the Fourth Annual Northeast Regional Methadone Conference. We believe it relates the human story behind the program description and the statistics.

Chiniqua's Story

Good morning ladies and gentlemen. My name is Chiniqua and I am seventeen years old. I want to tell you about how my mother's participation in the methadone-treatment program changed my life. She started abusing heroin when I was seven years old. She was never there for me and my sister. She was either out or always in the bed sleeping. I began to feel like she didn't want to be bothered with us. Before she got into treatment, I had all the responsibilities of the family. I managed the money. I took care of my sister and my mother as well. I did all I had to do to keep things together.

When I was eleven, my mother entered the methadone treatment program and things started getting better. She started to take on her responsibilities as a parent. It was very important to me that she went to my sixth grade graduation. If she was still a substance abuser, she would not have been there. She probably wouldn't be alive today! Since she has been in the methadone treatment program, our home life has been better. There is more understanding and more communication. Without the Albert Einstein program, none of this would have been possible. Methadone treatment not only saves lives, but it saves the kids as well, because it helps the parents cope effectively and everyone, even the whole society, benefits from that. Thank you."

John's Story

Good morning ladies and gentlemen. My name is John and I am here to discuss drug treatment programs and how they affect your families. You see, I know how it feels because my father was once a heroin addict. He used to get high every chance he had. As a result, he neglected his family. We seemed unimportant to him. It hurts to know a family member whom we all love is addicted to drugs, especially heroin.

But thanks to the methadone program he joined, my father is a better person. He no longer uses heroin or any illegal drugs. Now he spends time with us and he is very happy. It has changed our lives, not for the worst, but for the better. I feel that the methadone program is good. It helps to bring families closer together. It also decreases the number of heroin addicts in our communities. On behalf of my family and me, I would like to thank Senator Dodd and the conference for giving me this chance to speak."

Other Programs for Children and Families

One of the early federally funded hospital-based comprehensive programs was developed by Dr. Loretta Finnegan, then director of Nurseries at Philadelphia General Hospital. It, too, utilized a comprehensive approach involving a number of hospital services to meet the addicts' obstetrical, psychosocial, and addictive care needs. Dr. Finnegan is now the director of the Family Center at Jefferson Memorial Hospital and professor of Pediatrics and professor of Psychiatry and Human Behavior at Jefferson Medical College of Thomas Jefferson University in Philadelphia.

The services provided at the Family Center Program include a prenatal clinic staffed by obstetricians specially trained in the field of addiction and high-risk pregnancy; individual, group, and family therapy; detoxification and methadone maintenance; educational services including prenatal and parenting classes; and treatment of newborns for withdrawal in the newborn nursery staffed by neonatal physicians. The staff includes social workers, nurses, pharmacists, and research staff as well as obstetrical, neonatal, and psychiatric physicians (Finnegan et al., 1981). We covered a great deal of the research generated by Dr. Finnegan and her colleagues in chapter 1 of this book. Dr. Finnegan was a pioneer in establishing direct clinical services for children and addicted women as well as a continuing program of applied and basic research that has truly enriched our understanding of the children of substance abusers. Of her many published works we were most moved by her testimony to the presidential commission on the HIV epidemic (Finnegan 1987).

We are aware of a number of new drug-free programs that have recently opened in New York City. "La Casita," run by Naomi Reyes of United Bronx Parents, has established a ninety-bed residential program that will house thirty-eight homeless mothers and their children under age nine. There is a new outpatient program for women and their children run by Jacquie Cohen on the Lower East Side of Manhattan at the Betances Health Center. Harlem Hospital Center now has an obstetrical clinic run by Dr. Sterling Williams just for pregnant drug addicts that goes to great lengths to capture and hold on to patients throughout pregnancy and beyond. Also is Harlem, where the city's highest concentration of drug-exposed babies are born, the Parent and Child Enrichment Program (PACE) coordinated by Gladys Roman was launched in December 1990 with a program capacity of eighty clients. Funding for PACE comes from Medicaid and the federal Office of Substance Abuse Prevention. Ms. Roman says this is a new model. The New York City Department of Health is coordinating the participating agencies and training PACE staff. Drug counseling is provided by Reality House, prenatal care is provided by Harlem Hospital Center, and training in parenting skills comes from PACE counselors. Counseling and health care for parent and child are to be provided for one year.

Other new efforts are being tried in various locations around the nation. One example is the Steps in Recovery (S.I.R.) program in San Diego County headed by Barbara Ornelas. It was established in 1989 by San Diego County's Department of Social Services, Children's Services Bureau. The program consists of two components (*Update*, 1990): First Step parenting classes and drug/alcohol education groups. The classes are unique in that twelve mothers and their babies share the experience with the focus on the special needs of drug-exposed babies. Lecture/discussions are followed by hands-on experiences with the mothers interacting with their babies. Community services agencies provide the parent educators, sites are donated, and volunteers provide child care. The Drug Education and Recovery Groups meet for thirteen weeks. Parents are required to attend Alcoholics Anonymous and Narcotics Anonymous meetings and drug testing is done on site.

Thus, after several decades of neglect of families and children, some substance-abuse treatment programs are finally being created to serve their needs. It is encouraging to see that some of these programs are creating new models and approaches—freeing themselves from the old-line, male-dominated, high relapse approaches. Much is owed to those pioneers who started the work when no one else seemed to care.

One of the people who have helped increase our understanding of how to help all children who start life "in the shadows" is Lisbeth Schorr (1988), author of *Within Our Reach: Breaking the Cycle of Disadvantage.* She studied successful programs and drew from their experiences to summarize the attributes of interventions that work. We list them below.

Attributes of Interventions that Work*

1. Programs that are successful in reaching and helping the most disadvantaged children and families offer a broad spectrum of services.
2. Successful programs recognize that they cannot respond to people's "untidy basketfuls" of needs without regularly crossing traditional professional and bureaucratic boundaries.
3. Staff members and program structures are fundamentally flexible.
4. Programs need to see the child in the context of the family and the family in the context of its surroundings.
5. Successful programs describe their staffs as skilled and highly committed.
6. Programs serving a large number of multiproblem families see to it that services are coherent and easy to use.
7. The programs find ways to adapt or circumvent traditional professional and bureaucratic limitations when necessary to meet the needs of clients.
8. Professionals are able to redefine their roles in order to meet client needs.

We hope that each of these efforts will be carefully evaluated so that we can all learn about what works and what does not work. The addiction treatment field is still in search of a basic model/paradigm (Shaffer & Milkman, 1985) to describe addictive behavior. Evaluation studies such as the TOPS study (Hubbard, 1989) help to build effective models. These programs can also serve to build a meaningful and informative data base from which to understand:

1. Problems facing children
2. Differences and similarities with other children
3. Successful interventions with children
4. How to empower and strengthen families
5. How to get pregnant addicts to prenatal care
6. How drug exposure interacts with other variables
7. Which models to replicate and which to avoid

*Adapted from Schorr, 1988.

8. How to help children who do not live with their birthparents

A Model of Psychodynamic Family-Centered Practice for Treating the Children of Substance Abusers

Phase One: Assessment

There is a maxim in treatment circles that states "Treatment without diagnosis is malpractice!" Practitioners must try to form as clear a diagnostic impression as possible before formulating a long-term treatment plan. In a crisis or emergency a "binary" diagnosis, "treat" or "don't treat," is o.k. But differential diagnosis must be developed slowly by a careful process of getting to know the client(s) and then systematically "ruling out" inappropriate categories.

Because one is trying to form an impression of life-style and inter-active family dynamics, working strictly from an individual psychology framework is very limiting. Race and culture are an indelible part of this life-style consideration. To be more specific, we have found many of our colleagues diagnosing adults and children as suffering from "Antisocial Personality Disorder" or "Conduct Disorder." They have a tendency to perceive a sociopathic overlay with great frequency. It has been our experience that many addicts and their children come from an "antisocial" life-style when judged by white, middle-class standards. When one is a member of a poor oppressed minority, much of one's attitudes are shaped by that experience. The so-called psychopathology such people manifest is often a bias in the eyes of the clinician. The clinician must be in touch with himself/herself and hopefully relatively free of sexist, racist, classicist, AIDS and HIV–phobic and homophobic attitudes, beliefs, and feelings. Work with addicts can induce powerful feelings of countertransference including intense feelings of frustration and anger (Zimberg, 1985). Working with addict parents who may have been abusive or neglectful, or who otherwise maltreated their child(ren) can induce such feelings as a wish to protect the children, fear of the parent(s), and great anger toward the addict parent.

As in all good psychotherapeutic interventions the assessment phase should be useful for the client(s) as well as the clinicians.

Goals of Assessment Phase

- Engaging the child by building a trusting and supportive relationship. Introduce yourself and your role. Be clear about the parameters of confidentiality.
- Be sensitive to the child's tolerance or resistance. Go slowly and respect both the verbal and nonverbal clues given by the child.
- Hold to the focus of the interview. The child is involved with the clinician due to drug-abusing parent(s). Use compassionate questioning focusing on suspicions arising from drug abusing families
- Use skills of empathic atunement.

The assessment phase is essentially a fact-finding mission.

WHAT WE NEED TO LEARN FROM THE CHILDREN. To measure the child's involvement with parental addiction, try to discover the following information:

1. What is the child's awareness of parental drug use and overall alcohol and other drug-taking history?
2. What is the child's perception of his own level of engagement in the parental drug abuse?
3. What is the psychological impact on the child's level of development?
4. At what age did the child have knowledge of parental drug use?
5. Who in the child's life knew of parental drug use?
6. How "separate" is the child from parental drug abuse?
7. Has the child talked to anyone about the parental drug abuse? Who?
8. What are the emotional, cognitive, and social ramifications on self-image, sense of self, and daily functioning?
9. If of school age, is the child truant?
10. Did the child use any drugs or drink with the parent(s)?

To measure the child's attachment and basic trust, try to discover the following information:

1. What was the depth and quality of the relationship with the drug-abusing parent?
2. Can the child recall a time before parent(s) used drugs? What was the premorbid (predrug) relationship like?
3. Did the drug-abusing parent manipulate the child's perception of reality? If so, how?
4. If the child reached out for help what, if any, was the parental response?
5. What is the overall social development impact on the child? **Note:** Child may be experiencing a sense of grief and sadness due to "loss" of parental functioning. Child may be feeling a global sense of distrust about others, may exhibit anger and rage, and there is a danger of feelings of increasing isolation. Will portray self as "victim," appear helpless, and experiences a pervasive sense of lack of mastery over his/her environment.

To measure the child's fear and trauma, seek the following information:

1. What was the nature of the traumas or abuse surrounding the addiction?
   • Sexual abuse
   • Other physical abuse
   • Neglect
   • Violence perpetrated to self or others in home
   • Direct witness of parental drug abuse
   • Family breakup
2. What is the depth and breadth of the child's fear of parental abuse, neglect, or maltreatment?
3. At what age did victimization begin? With force?
4. Was sexual abuse by parents or coercion to prostitute related to getting money for drugs or drugs themselves?
5. Was violence in the home related to drug use?
6. Passive victimization: did child have to witness sexual acts in the household involving parent(s) or strangers?
7. Were young children left alone without supervision for periods of time? How long and how often?

SECRECY. A child may be stuck with the legacy of secrecy. He/she may not feel free to "tell" the clinician. Keeping secrets may be prompted by many things, including:

1. Distrust of therapist caused by lack of parental protection
2. Child may have been "sworn" to secrecy by one or more parents or other relatives
3. Feelings of guilt and shame over parental behavior
4. Feelings of guilt and shame over own behavior
5. A great sense of embarrassment about his/her family
6. Taught to lie by parent(s)
7. Fear that therapist will tell "authorities" and child will be removed from parent(s)
8. Fear of punishment by parent(s) for "telling on them"
9. Fierce sense of family loyalty

It takes time to form a trusting relationship with the child before he or she will reveal the painful facts about life with his/her parents. If you engage the parents with the child's knowledge of this, then he/she may be freer to speak about such "private family matters." Again, the clinician must present himself or herself as an open advocate for the well-being of the entire family. This sometimes feels like walking along the edge of a razor blade, particularly when the parents remain uncooperative.

Childhood Depression, Traumatized Children, and Child Abuse and Neglect

Clinicians need to be aware of three striking syndromes that will color and cloud their effort to do the fact finding: childhood depression (usually of nonpsychotic proportions), traumatized anxiety-ridden children, and abused/neglected children (often the source of the trauma). We do not usually think of children as suffering from major depression. It is important to remember that depression is a "spectrum disorder," that is, it varies from mild "blues and blahs" to major suicidal psychotic depressions. It does happen to children of drug abusers and other children who live in similar types of dysfunctional families. The age-appropriate signs and symptoms of childhood depression are listed below.

Signs of Childhood Depression

- Depressed mood: feeling sad, hopeless, discouraged, "down and out"
- Sleep disturbance, often accompanied with nightmares
- Poor self-concept: feeling worthless, devalued, unwanted
- Suicidal ideation
- Self-mutilation
- Appetite disturbance
- Irritable mood accompanied by psychomotor agitation
- Loss of interest or pleasure in most activities
- Confusion and difficulty concentrating
- Withdrawal
- Somatic complaints
- Exaggerated fears or phobias
- Despite irritability and agitation, suffers a general loss of energy and sustained fatigue

The DSM-III-R (1987) defines trauma as "a psychologically distressing event that is outside the range of usual human experiences [i.e., outside the range of such common experiences as simple bereavement, chronic illness, business losses, and marital conflict]." The DSM goes on to say that the stressor(s) would be experienced by almost anyone "with intense fear, terror and helplessness." Many of the children of drug abusers have witnessed repeated traumatic events and have themselves often been the direct victims of the trauma. Post-traumatic stress disorder (PTSD) can occur at any age, including during childhood. We quote from the DSM-III-R regarding the age-specific features of PTSD:

> Occasionally, a child may be mute or refuse to discuss the trauma, but this should not be confused with inability to remember what occurred. In younger children, distressing dreams of the event may, within several weeks, change into generalized nightmares of monsters, of rescuing others, or of threats to self and others. Young children do not have the sense that they are reliving the past; reliving trauma occurs in action, through repetitive play.
> Diminished interest in significant activities and constriction of affect both may be difficult for children to report on themselves, and should be carefully evaluated by reports from parents, teachers, and other observers. A symptom of Post-traumatic Stress Disorder in chil-

dren may be a marked change in orientation toward the future. This includes the sense of a foreshortened future, for example, a child may not expect to have a career or marriage. There may also be "omen formation," that is, belief in an ability to prophesy future untoward events.

Children may exhibit various physical symptoms, such as stomach-aches and headaches, in addition to the specific symptoms of in-creased arousal. (249)

Within the specific criteria for PTSD there are several unique to children:

B.(1) recurrent and intrusive distressing recollections of the event (in young children, repetitive play in which themes or aspects of the trauma are expressed)

C.(4) marked diminished interest in significant activities (in young children, loss of recently acquired developmental skills such as toilet training or language skills). (250)

In his book *Trauma in the Lives of Children,* Dr. Kendall Johnson (1989) states, "On the basis of . . . differing reports . . . we see that children's reactions to crisis are varied, complex and profound. However, patterns emerge that are cohesive, if not entirely predict-able. Individual response patterns are limited by the child's state of development and personal history" (49). Dr. Kendall summarizes typical posttraumatic behaviors by age categories that can be used as a guide in assessing children.

Typical Post-Traumatic Behaviors in Children

Preschool/Kindergarten Children
- Withdrawal
- Denial
- Thematic play
- Anxious attachment
- Specific fears
- Regression

Younger School-Age Children
- Performance decline
- Compensatory behavior

- Obsessive talking
- Discrepancy in mood
- Behavior changes or problems
- More elaborate reenactments
- Psychosomatic complaints

Older School-Age Children/Adolescents

- Acting-out behaviors
- Low self-esteem and self-criticism
- "Too old, too fast"
- Displaced anger

Listed below are some of the warning signs and behavioral signs of child abuse, neglect, and maltreatment. The list is not meant to be exhaustive: clinical experience will show you other things to look for with specific clients. Some signs could indicate other problems as well. Several signs appearing in combination indicate a more powerful finding.

Practitioners need to be emotionally ready and open to hearing and perceiving abuse, neglect, and maltreatment. When you report such behavior to the authorities you may fear that you are opening up a real "can of worms" or worry that the child or children will be "worse off" after you report. We can all help and protect more children. Depending on the context in which you work, reporting may be part of the therapeutic stance you need to adopt to help draw people into treatment by setting responsible limits. Clinical practitioners are not lawyers or judges or police officers. Our job is to report *suspected* cases. The child protection agency workers then carry out a more exhaustive investigation. Child abuse and neglect are not about simple black/white dichotomies: there are a great many grey areas. Keep in mind the issues we raised about confidentiality in the previous chapter. Also remember: if there are no consequences for abusive behavior, the abuser is likely to repeat it.

Many states now mandate reporting of suspected child abuse by certain professional groups and institutions. For example, as of 1988, New York State has established a new requirement for all physicians, chiropractors, dentists, registered nurses, podiatrists, optometrists, psychologists, and dental hygienists who must receive two hours of coursework or training regarding the identification and reporting of child abuse and maltreatment for the renewal of licensure. Check with your own state authorities to see if you and the institution or agency you are employed by are mandated for reporting (and training).

Signs of Child Abuse, Neglect, and Maltreatment

Warning Signs

- Parents themselves were abused or neglected.
- Family does not have friends or any emotional support system. They may move to a new location and claim no one is from their "own community."
- Marital problems. Ask about their own parents' marriages.
- Child with physical or mental health problems. Can lead a parent with no history of abusiveness to become abusive.
- Financial problems.
- Death in the family.
- Parents themselves are adolescents.
- Parents have unrealistically high expectations of child (usually in sports or academics).
- Developmentally disabled children. Parents may have unreal expectations or guilt.
- Parents expect child to be a little adult and to be a caretaker for them.
- General beliefs about violence and corporal punishment, but be aware of cultural differences. Watch for words like "spanking"—it's a term that sounds ok but may not be.
- Abusive parents rarely share actual behavior—the clinician needs to pick up "flavor" through nuances and anecdotes.
- Parent perceives and/or describes child as "bad" or "evil."
- Parents avoid routine medical checkups and/or avoid emergency care when child is ill or injured.
- Bruises, welts, or burns with specific shapes (like hanger or iron); grab marks (handmarks). Usually an accident provides a bruise or mark only on one side of the body; intentional injuries will often be bilateral
- Any injuries to genitalia are suspicious.
- Animal bites tear flesh, but human bites compress flesh (and may leave teeth marks).

- Repeat injuries are always cause for suspicion.
- Multiple or spiral fractures (caused by twisting). Falling causes breaks, spiral unlikely to be caused by accident.
- Excessive shaking can cause brain damage and physical disabilities in the very young.

Behavioral Indicators

(**Note:** These give a sign that something is wrong but do not say what is wrong.)

- Child is wary of contact, especially with his/her own parent(s). Example: crying on the school bus, on the way home.
- Child gets very apprehensive when another child cries.
- Extreme withdrawal.
- Mood changes.
- Child runs away from home (often caused by sexual abuse in teenagers). It is uncommon for older children to run away.
- Child tells you they are being abused at home. Children do not lie about sexual abuse (exception: some sociopathic adolescents). However, children may lie or exaggerate nonsexual physical abuse.
- Often during divorce proceedings one parent will say the child reported abuse by other parent. Not the same as a report directly from a child.
- Children who call themselves "bad" or in need of punishment.
- Self-mutilation (cigarette burns, cuts, etc.).
- Bed-wetting (get complete physical examination to rule out physical causes).
- Inappropriate clothing to hide injured or bruised parts of the body (example: long sleeves on a hot day).
- Suicide attempts.
- Child with very low self-esteem.
- "Failure to thrive." Child just does not look healthy or "right." May be dirty.
- Temper tantrums.
- Seductiveness in behavior (more sophisticated in older chil-

dren). Such behavior does not come naturally to children: they must learn it from someone.

- Presence of sexually transmitted diseases.
- Pregnant teenager: the younger the pregnant child, the more of a "red flag."
- Multiple sexual partners.
- In younger children, sexual knowledge they should not have. Sex is usually not that interesting to younger children. Presence of sophisticated knowledge.
- Teenagers involved in prostitution. Eighty to ninety percent of female teenage prostitutes are abused or neglected or maltreated. Percentage may be even higher for teenage male prostitutes.
- Possibility of sexual abuse by baby-sitters (i.e., a four-year-old girl molested by a twelve-year-old sitter).

You may have noticed a fair amount of overlap in the signs and symptoms of these three phenomenon: childhood depression, traumatized children, and abused/neglected/maltreated children. Dr. Loretta Finnegan (Regan et al., 1987) has pointed out that "The characteristics commonly reported in families where child abuse occur . . . are seen in the lives of drug dependent women." These characteristics include:

1. When young themselves, one or both parents have been subjected to violence.
2. One or both parents have had an unhappy, disrupted, and insecure childhood.
3. One or both parents are addicted to drugs, alcohol, or are psychotic.
4. The parents have a record of violence against each other.
5. Another child in the family has already been abused or has suffered an unexplained death.
6. Unwanted pregnancy, followed by rejection of the baby at birth or soon thereafter.
7. Failure in early bonding.
8. Both parents are under twenty, immature for their years, and socially isolated.
9. The family lives in poor housing and on a low income.
10. The family is suffering from multiple deprivations.

When you realize that the children of drug abusers are sometimes victims of a combination of all three of the problems listed above, you begin to get an idea of how stark and brutal life can be for them. By attending to these signs in the assessment phase you are opening up your clinical "listening self" to the real world of the children. You are then in a better position to help them. We will have more to say about these matters when we come to the issues of staff training and supervision later in this chapter.

Phase Two: Family-Centered Treatment

The authors believe that treatment of the parent(s) is an imperative part of the child's therapy. This does not always mean that we are doing ongoing family therapy. There are many variations on the theme. Sometimes, we never get past the assessment phase with parents. At other times, family "consultations" become an adjunct to individual work with the child. And at still other times, family sessions serve as the main vehicle for treatment. In what manner we choose to work extremely closely with the drug abusing parent(s), spouse and siblings and sometimes grandparents. If they aren't available any relative that steps forth should be evaluated. Child welfare agencies do diligent searches for existing birth family and kinship family members. The main point is that we try as hard as we can to work to unite and empower families.

Since many parents are still using drugs, history taking is at best problematic and at worst a waste of professional time. Here we explore the history of the next of kin. Often this is the other parent or a grandparent.

In many of the histories we have taken, drug and alcohol abuse extends to other family members as well. The history of drug use/abuse in families is often perceived differently by each family member. Yet, the symptom of drug abuse establishes almost indelible patterns of behavior and relating among family members. The concept of drug "abuser" symbolizes the family's maladaptation to life. Treating only the symptom, without analyzing the underlying behavior, is an injustice to the child(ren) of the addict.

Whatever the quality of the child's attachment to the drug-abusing parent(s), must be recognized as a real attachment, rich with fantasy, hope, and anguish. Engaging the drug-abusing parent(s) is quite a challenge. Yet it is the ideal treatment and ensures a better outcome for all family members.

In evaluating parents who abuse drugs we have found that the engagement period is often very difficult. When a clinician interview the abusing parent(s), countertransferential issues loom large and can interfere with the establishment of empathy and caring. Suicide is the ultimate sign of rejection that a parent can inflict on his/her child. Drug abuse and alcohol abuse is a slow journey toward suicide. Parents can also die from overdoses, street violence, AIDS and other diseases, accidents, and domestic violence. These are formidable behaviors for the clinician to confront on an emotional level. Handling personal feelings in appropriate ways is essential for the clinician to maintain effective treatment. Our clinical experience has shown us repeatedly that therapists and counselors who are active, open, supportive, and empathetic are far more likely to form good working relationships with clients. In order to engage them and draw them out, you must believe that they are not so much "self-destructive" as unskilled at taking care of themselves. Remember: often, no one ever took adequate care of the addict when he/she was a child.

The exploration of the relationship between parent(s) and child begins with the prenatal question: was this child wanted and planned for? If wanted, why? What were the fantasies of the parent(s) at the time of conception, through pregnancy, and after the actual birth. Was the parent abusing substances during the pregnancy? Factfind for specific and ongoing drug use. Request all information about prenatal care and previous attempts at rehabilitation.

Hold to focus. A good and compassionate history taking provides the beginning effort of clinician and client engagement for the purpose of helping the child and the parent(s). Explore the parents' own personal histories and that of their parents in turn. Continue to explore all areas of their life—physical, psychological, sexual, social, vocational, academic, and spiritual selves—not just the addictive behavior.

ADDICT VULNERABILITIES. Ask the parents to explain the impact of drug use on their parenting role. Inquire about their motivation for giving up drugs. Explore parent ambivalence concerning the "good" they derive from drug use. Dr. Edward Khantzian (1985) speaks of how addicts use drugs to deal with their "core vulnerabilities." He notes that drugs are used for purposes of:

- Control (of both inner and outer environments)
- Containment (of painful affects)
- Contact (with certain feeling states)
- Comfort (of a drug-induced psychological state)

For Khantzian, the addict's core vulnerabilities have to do primarily with taking care of and providing for himself/herself and special problems in pursuing their dependency needs. He states:

> They lack a sense of self-worth, comfort and nurturance from within and thus remain dependent on others and the environment to maintain a sense of well-being. Nevertheless, they are just as often counterdependent and disavow their needs. As a result, they alternate between seductive and manipulative attitudes to extract satisfaction from the environment and disdainful and aloof postures of independence and self-sufficiency that dismiss the need for others. (123)

In this framework it is easy to understand why so many heroin addicts choose methadone maintenance as their treatment of choice: methadone is an extraordinary affect modulator. The main point we wish to make is that drugs are not simply "mood-altering": they are also powerful processors of deeply experienced emotions (affects). Khantzian speaks of the addict's "dread of distress." Clients who have had problems with managing their feelings (particularly anger and rage), and who experiences chronic dysphoric and anhedonic moods, find that a powerful synthetic narcotic like methadone seems to help them stabilize their lives. Methadone works as a kind of "affective" chemotherapy. Conversely, this points to What makes methadone "work" for addicts also helps us to understand why drug-free treatment and classical therapy so often fail to work. But it also indicates the great need for individual therapy in drug-abuse treatment to help clients overcome their terrible sense of isolation.

Cocaine, in all its forms, and heroin free sexual inhibitions. Ask about sexual abuse in the family. Past research has found that alcohol and other drug abuse is a major warning sign of child abuse, neglect, and maltreatment. Even if the adults are guarded when you first probe, later on in the treatment they can come back to this topic with the knowledge that the clinician is available to listen. The same may apply to the topic of violence done to the adult addicts themselves when they were children. Often child abuse is transgenerational.

Be sensitive to all the confusion over "role" these parents often have. The purpose of the treatment intervention is to empower adult family members to do the hard work and rewarding work of parenting. Avoid being sucked into the dependency needs of the addicted parent(s). Parent interviews create the foundation for future treatment.

Often children will not engage until they have a sense that such engagement is ok with mom and/or dad. They are very careful not to "betray" or otherwise be disloyal to their parents. This was brought home to us by a thirteen-year-old girl in foster care who was suspected of being sexually abused by her father, an active drug user, but who steadfastly refused to "inform" on him. Finally, after many long and silent months, no longer able to contain her pain, she wrote her therapist, Mrs. Rutter, a long soul-wrenching letter about the incest. But even after writing the letter and acknowledging her authorship, she still could not talk about what had happened to her. But she was able to state that she did not want her father to "get into trouble."

If the child has been removed from the home, issues of visitation and reunification should be clearly addressed. It is important to be firm about drug testing and the like. You need to encourage this adult to be a better parent and to be drug free (or in appropriate chemotherapy).

HOME VISITS: BUILDING THERAPEUTIC RELATIONSHIPS. There are times when a home visit to conduct the parental interview is indicated. Home visiting enables the therapist to make his/her own assessment of the child's home environment (for historical and current understanding). A visual assessment adds to the therapist's knowledge of the child's background.

The role modeling a clinician can do in the home setting is invaluable. The parent(s) are more relaxed in their own home and can present problems they do not feel free to share in a clinic setting. For adults and children who have difficulty with expressive language, familiar surroundings create a sense of security and emotional comfort, and may lead to more openness. The clinician can obtain a "closer look" at the reality of the adults' and the child's life. One four-year-old child we worked with had only two toys: a television and a video tape player. While in the home the clinician can play with the child. This provides modeling and helps to focus attention on the child's well-being.

In the case of the schoolage child or teenager, one can see if the home is structured for school studies and homework. Does the child have a private work space, adequate light, and school supplies? The skills of daily living can be observed. On one home visit we discovered why one recovering parent could not fall asleep in her own bedroom. The place was in chaos. It was clear that "organizing and self-care" skills had to include far more than just making therapy appointments on time.

Home visits help break through the social isolation the addict experiences. A visit by one or two clinicians implies a change in the current system. Home visits can bring light into dark places. When Dr. Levy visited the PACE (Parent and Child Education) program run by Dr. Carolyn Goodman in the South Bronx he was struck by the way this program sought to help impoverished minority women who suffered from major mental disorders and substance abuse overcome their crushing social isolation. In the midst of one of the worst ghettos in America, Dr. Goodman and her staff helped the women to begin visiting each other, sharing coffee and friendship. This led to exchanging baby-sitting services. This inspirational program led Dr. Levy to introduce home visiting to the clinical regime of the Rockland County Crack/Cocaine Program run by the Town of Ramapo, Youth Counseling Service.

Head Start policy guidelines demand at least one home visit for every child to be made by the teacher and teaching assistants before the start of school. We list the rationale for this requirement here because we feel that it commends itself to clinical efforts with the children of drug abusers for similar reasons. Head Start home visits serve the following functions:

1. Meet every child in his/her own environment. This avoids the teacher appearing to the child as a stranger on the first day of school. After all, children are taught not to speak to strangers!
2. The child's anxiety about starting school is reduced.

3. The parents' anxiety about the school also decreases. Good feelings about the child's future school experience increase as parents experience the staff reaching out to and understanding their reality.
4. Teaching staff bonds with the adults and forms the basis of a cooperative working relationship.
5. Teaching staff can observe the child in his/her own home. This is an efficient way to assess family strengths and weaknesses.
6. The child observes his/her parents relating to school staff and therefore feels permission to also develop their own relationship with them.
7. Issues of culture, ethnicity, giftedness, disabling conditions, socioeconomic realities, etc., become exposed and therefore more relevant and open to exploration.
8. For families too threatened to come to school, the home visit serves to desensitize them and break through resistance to forming a working home/school relationship.
9. It is an opportunity to see how boundaries and control issues are handled at home.

We feel that home visiting with drug-abusing families of all social classes is invaluable. Of course, they are time-consuming and require flexibility on the part of the clinician. In some neighborhoods such visits include a genuine element of physical danger. If clients feel ready at this point of engagement, we next invite them to come to the clinic or office. Very often we ask family members to gather together family photograph albums and picture books to share with us. These are helpful in eliciting attitudes, beliefs, and feelings about the family unit and its individual members.

Some parents require continued home visiting to participate in treatment. The Harlem Hospital Center Visiting Nurse Program operates a 9:00–5:00 day-treatment program for addicted mothers. If a client misses a day, a staff member makes a home visit to help the client reenter the program as soon as possible. During these difficult days of recovery the babies and other children at home are at risk for abuse, neglect, and maltreatment. Thus, the home visit also ensures the well-being of the child.

In our own private psychotherapy practice we have performed

similar tasks for parents. Sometimes the doors have refused to open. More often they open widely and relapse prevention work is done on site. Here is one example from Dr. Levy's practice:

> My office called with a message that a couple I was seeing—both of whom were cocaine addicts—were having a terrible fight at home and were threatening violence. I called them and discovered that indeed one had menaced the other with a kitchen knife. They gave me permission to come to their apartment with a promise that they would "do nothing" in the meantime. They were looking for external controls: they had exhausted their own fragile defenses against frustration and rage.
>
> We talked things out together for an hour and a half. We reviewed both the overt and covert antecedents that lead to this eruption of anger. We reviewed lessons taught in my office but hard to use at home. They felt their ability to prevent such eruptions was strengthened. Naturally during the conversation several strong "urges" to get high came out on both their parts. This episode was indeed a reminder to all three of us that staying straight is hard work and like most difficult tasks requires lots of practice before it becomes a strong habit pattern and a sense of self-efficacy sets in. They were grateful for the home visit. And we were all grateful for another day without violence and drug use.

Phase Three: Working Through

THE LITTLE ONES

Case Illustration 10: Jimmy

> Jimmy, now age six, was placed in foster care at age four. His mother, Joyce, on a crack binge, had left him all alone. Neighbors reported the case to the child abuse hotline. Jimmy was placed on an "emergency" basis.
>
> He did beautifully in his new preadoptive home. All the people he came into contact with adored him. His birthmother, age twenty-eight, came to visit with her only child on just two occasions.
>
> A family history was taken. Mother seemed high during the interview but would not admit to it. Multiple efforts to

engage this woman were tried. The father's name was not listed on the birth certificate that was retrieved by the Commissioner of Social Services.

1. Home visits, both planned and unplanned, failed. Joyce was never home.
2. Joyce became undomiciled. Social work staff tracked her whereabouts from shelter to shelter.
3. Bus tickets were mailed to Joyce at the shelter in order to facilitate visiting with the social worker and Jimmy. She sold the tickets to purchase more drugs.
4. Contacts with homeless shelter staff were made to facilitate rehabilitation and a relationship with her son.

The birth-father died. Staff petitioned for the termination of parental rights on the basis of continued neglect and failure to plan. A family court judge officially surrendered the child for adoption eighteen months after he was placed in foster care.

The foster family had considered adopting Jimmy. They were loving and quite attached to him. But then the foster father developed stomach cancer six months prior to the termination of rights and he sought aggressive treatment for the disease. With great sadness, the foster parents asked the social worker to seek another adoptive placement for Jimmy.

Jimmy's believed he was in foster care because his mother was too sick to take care of him. His foster father's life-threatening illness caused him another displacement and loss due to illness. At this juncture intensive play therapy began. The goals of treatment were twofold: (1) to prepare Jimmy for adoption, and (2) to prepare a "Life Book" for Jimmy.

The "Life Book" technique uses play techniques to assess and prepare older children for adoption. It was developed by Judith Cippola, Dorothy McGown, and Mary Ann Yanullis, all of the New York Spaulding for Children Agency. This was the tool chosen to help in the "working through of Jimmy's life issues."

The process of Life Book focused on Jimmy's birth history, where he lived, and positive and negative emotions he had attached to his own memories of life thus far. Jimmy's social worker pored over his agency record and provided Jimmy with factual information about his birth mother. The issues of why he got separated from his mother were clarified for him on an age-appropriate level. He was told that his mother's "sickness" was drug addiction. Since he understood the "Just Say No" motto, the worker interpreted the illness as "Mom couldn't say no to drugs" and is still using them, so she cannot take care of him. Jimmy, with the help of his social worker, was able to clarify and remember his preschool years. The worker took Jimmy back to his first neighborhood to give his memory a concrete vision. Together they took photographs of that neighborhood.

The second part of the work focused on identifying feelings and grieving for losses. In Jimmy's treatment this was easily done through doll play and drawings. Much acting out began to surface in the classroom. The teacher was kept informed of Jimmy's feelings that had risen up from the depths of his young psyche—the past losses and his fear of being rejected by his new adoptive family.

The foster family, the teachers, the adoptive family, and the social worker were tuned into Jimmy's emotional experience. This shared "empathic atunement" is essential for Jimmy's positive self-image.

Questions came up concerning the difference in birth parents, foster parents, and adoptive parents. Fahlberg (1979) developed the list of parental roles listed below.

Parental Roles

Birth Parents:
• Gift of life
• Sex determination
• Intellectual potential
• Predisposition to diseases
• Basic personality type
• Talents

Legal Parents:
- Make major decisions
- Where you live
- Where you go to school
- Financial responsibilities
- Give consent to minors for
  - Medical
  - Drivers license
  - Marriage

Parenting Parents:
- Love
- Discipline
- Provide for daily needs like toys and clothes
- Take care of you when you are sick
- Teach values
- Religious training
- Provide life skills

In further distinguishing adoptive and foster families the language used must be concrete:

- Jimmy, when you go to your adoptive family, you will have the same last name they do.
- Your adoptive family wants you to be their son.

Since Jimmy's birth mother fueled his hopes of returning to her (early on) and his father was deceased, his feelings of anger, sadness, and loss were not delayed. They were available to him and were not projected onto other family members. The therapy also helped to bring them out. His sense of sadness was always worn on his sleeve. Jimmy did not maintain continuing unrealized fantasies of being reunited with his mother. His feelings of disengagement were more focused on his foster parents to whom he had to say goodbye. They let him know that they would still be there for him and he could call, write, or visit. The pre-adoptive visiting was held in the home of the foster parents. When Jimmy seemed ready, he moved. He made an excellent adjustment to this new permanent family.

An interesting closing note: Jimmy's teacher, an experienced first grade teacher, had no idea that Jimmy was born with a positive cocaine toxicology. She described him as a well-adjusted boy who was a slow learner. No behavior problems were noted.

We return to the case of Jonathan who we first reported on as case illustration 4 in chapter 2.

Case Illustration 4: Jonathan (continued)

Jonathan was removed from his birth parent, (his father) at age four His father, Mr. F, was encouraged to visit his child at the agency, under staff supervision, on a weekly basis. Initially Jonathan was happy to see his father and had no difficulty separating at the end of the visits. In the second year, when their attachment was deeper and more loving, separation problems arose.

Mr. F. was an only son born to a poor southern woman who raised her children alone. He was devastated by his mother's cancer and death. Although he previously had bouts of drinking and using drugs, this behavior accelerated to addictive levels in response to his loss. With all the hulabaloo and chaos around Jonathan's seizures and adjustment to foster care, Mr. F viewed his own drug problem as secondary in importance.

Mr. F. engaged in the casework process. At first he had a male worker who focused on how to parent a young child with major handicaps. Mr. F. responded with enthusiasm to his structured visits. Left to his own devices, he brought Jonathan toys and would read the newspaper while the boy ran around. Case work interventioned focused on role modeling, parenting education, and relationship issues, including Mr. F's loss of his own mother.

In the last year, Jonathan could be found sitting on his father's lap while he read a story to him. The caseworker often spoke about the birth of Jonathan. Mr. F. had said that Jonathan was unplanned but wanted. Although Mr. F. had other grown children, Jonathan was the only one at whose birth he had been present. The caseworker used this birth story to help with parent/child bonding. Mr. F would say to Jonathan at each visit "I am going to take you home with me as soon as I can." You could see the boy physically relax when the story of his birth was told aloud during many visits. Jonathan, a quiet child, did not express himself well. Yet, his hand was always extended toward both his father and the caseworker.

As mentioned, Jonathan had not been physically abused, but he had been seriously neglected. He had witnessed his father having sex when he was high. Jonathan would sometimes act out sexually. This was dealt with by his foster parents and special education teacher. He had begun to trust the adults around him.

The caseworker spent a great deal of time in the sessions reflecting the boy's behavior and introducing behavior modification techniques. Mr. F. caught on to how to do this. As Mr. F. came to understand Jonathan's deprivation, he became depressed and somewhat overwhelmed. He returned to smoking crack and drinking. The caseworker reported that Mr. F. experienced guilt over his abandonment of Jonathan as a baby and his failure to care for his own dying mother. Powerful affects like this are certain triggers for addictive behavior and an escape into drug-induced relief.

The caseworker made many visits to Mr. F's home and encouraged him to enter the drug rehabilitation program at the Veterans Administration Hospital where he had previously experienced sobriety. He entered the six-week inpatient program. Jonathan was brought to visit his father at the facility and it was made clear to the boy why his father was there. For the first time Jonathan said to his father "Dad, I want to go home with you!" His relapse was brief and he stepped up his attendance in outpatient care after his hospitalization. He attended NA and AA meetings several times each week.

At this time, Mr. F began to show Jonathan pictures of his own mother (the boy's grandmother who he never knew) and pictures of the boy's mother. Jonathan's mother is still an active addict and has no desire to see him. The caseworker noted that Mr. F. was finally doing "grief work" and not trying to "medicate" away his pain. Mr. F. asked if he could have unsupervised overnight visits. The mere mention of such visits caused Jonathan visible elation. The work of reuniting had finally begun.

Mr. F submits urine samples regularly and maintains his support systems in the rehabilitation community. He and his son have developed a warm and loving relationship.

Mr. F has voiced concern about his son's seizure disorder and has sought neurological consultations in his own neighborhood. Jonathan, whose concept of time is still primitive, knows he is going home soon. He understands the visits home are occuring on a twice monthly basis.

He and the caseworker spend time in play sessions working with two doll houses. Jonathan plays out his fears and hopes. He is still behind in language development so the worker does not flood him with words. The two-house theme is quite appropriate in Jonathan's mind. The foster parents have begun to talk to him about his returning to his birth parent. They are supportive of the plan and pray for Mr. F's continued drug-free state. The foster parents, in this case, have been ideal. They have provided a therapeutic milieu; they have loved and cared for Jonathan while preparing him to return to this father. No one can predict how well Mr. F. will continue to cope with life without drugs. There is a real fear that his history of substance abuse will repeat. However, his efforts at recovery are real and thus far sustained. Children need their parent(s) everyday; everyday Mr. F is clean and dry is another good day in his life and the life of his son.

It is important to know how to deal with disturbances in trust and attachment. Whether the child is in the home or in an alternative setting we know that many of the children of substance abusers are *neglected*. The intensity of their troubled relationships makes them uncomfortable. They sometimes act out or withdraw to cope. Other children display the following behaviors:

- Poor eye contact
- Ongoing moderate levels of anxiety
- Aggression of a physical and sexual nature
- Indiscriminate affection
- Poor social skills
- Intense levels of preoccupation
- Withdrawal, social isolation

Kliman et al. (1982) studied the mental health needs of children entering the foster care system. They report a common finding among the children of mothers with histories of substance abuse:

> Their extensive and pervasive anxiety about their mother's condition. They were often subject to feelings of depression and ambivalence toward their foster families. Some were afraid that positive responses to the foster family would signify disloyalty to their mothers. In treatment, they often expressed anxiety about their mother's condition and the possibility of relapses. This preoccupation with their mother's status at times prevented them from taking full advantage of the material and social opportunities offered them in their foster homes. Among the older children especially there was a tendency to assume a protective "parental" role towards their mothers and their younger siblings. Admirable as this quality would appear, it nevertheless interferred with their abilities to participate in and benefit from usual child-appropriate experiences. This pattern of pseudo-adult reactions tended to encourage as underlying pattern of depression or repressed hostility.
>
> Much of therapy with this group of children centered on alleviating their sense of guilt and encouraging them to talk about their mothers. Interpretations were useful in helping them gain a better perspective about their feelings and how it was affecting their reactions to the foster families. In the multiple sibling families, inter-sibling bonds were helpful in sustaining morale. Discussions about siblings often took place in treatment sessions and, while sibling bonds were encouraged, older children were also helped to seek satisfaction of their own independent needs. Interpretations of reactions of this entire group of children to their biological families were especially helpful in guidance sessions with their foster parents who were then able to view the children and their mothers with much greater empathy. (211–12)

Therapists and other involved helpers have the task of dismantling these negative behaviors and encouraging a healing process for the children in the areas of trust and attachment. "Healing" here refers to a process of creating an interpersonal wholeness. The primary disturbance in relating to people can be healed by all of us—regardless of our discipline. This healing is effected primarily by simply caring and "being there" in a consistent way that the children can feel.

Assessment of attachment potential requires looking at the areas of:

1. Reciprocity—the give and take between the child and other people
2. Ability to explore—the environment, things, and people around him/her
3. Separation response—the way the child reacts to leaving or the possibility of you or someone else leaving
4. Emotional reactivity—verbal and physical expression of positive feelings

In treating the children of drug abusers one has to form a warm and caring relationship. Consistency in the relationship is imperative, not only for purposes of treatment continuity but because loss and abandonment is so pervasive in the lives of many of these children. Beverly James, in her excellent book *Treating Tramatized Children* (1989), suggests the perspective of the therapist.

> Basically, the therapist should appear to the young person as a gentle giant who clearly, and with unshakable strength, conveys a number of very important messages:
> * I will protect you
> * I care about you
> * I will not let you hurt yourself or me
> * I am not overwhelmed by your experiences or your feelings
> * I know it is not your fault
> * I know we can face these issues together
> * I know you are going to be OK
> * I will help you to be OK

Beverly James also provides very use guidelines for conducting the clinical work that needs to be done.

Critical Aspects of Treatment*

1. The children need to acknowledge and explore their pain while in therapy, in order to integrate their experience.
2. A serialized course of treatment, using multiple clinical approaches, is often indicated. Treatment is sequenced over time and respects the vulnerabilities and readiness of the child.
3. Therapists, working alone, can rarely meet the needs of the child. A number of different caregivers need to be involved. They need to be active members of the treatment team.
4. Treatment is direct and active while also being patient. It mixes the use of material spontaneously arising from the child and material forthrightly presented by the clinician to demonstrate that the issues need not be shameful and can be dealt with directly.
5. Positive clinical messages need to be intense to be heard through the child's defenses. These messages can be delivered in fun and upbeat ways to balance the hard work being accomplished.
6. The clinical course must include attention to the physical, cognitive, emotional, and spiritual parts of the child since the damage can affect all these areas.
7. Working with traumatized children means dealing with gross, sometimes horrible situations which may have a strong personal impact on the therapist; this impact may interfere with treatment.

We have mentioned the concept of "empathic attunement" several times. It refers to listening with what Carl Rogers called the "third ear", which is really the heart. It also refers to listening and responding in a way that lets the child know that he or she is heard. We have also found that rituals, no matter how small, can be helpful. That means paying attention to the opening and closing of each session. At the end of every session, for example, one might say "We have a few minutes left before you go home, I want you to come here so I can put your drawings in a special place. Can I give you a

*Adapted from James, 1989.

hug?" The sense of being understood and respected builds trust, attachment, and self-esteem.

Children who have been neglected have difficulty in accepting the idea that their needs can be met, even by caring adults. Consistency—hanging in there with the child again and again—is part of healing. Needs cannot be met by the verbal response "I wish I had a magic wand to make your mom (dad) all better." Remember: these children have been subjected to repeated broken promises. Never promise them anything you cannot actually make good on.

As with adults who are under stress and in tense states, children cannot see all the options that may lie before them. By means of play sessions with young children or group therapy with older ones, we can break down their myopic perceptions of life in a caring manner.

Conflicting and confusing emotions are frightening to a child. Having a mother who is never there for you but whom you feel you are supposed to love anyway sets up conflict: love coexists with anger. From a nonjudgmental and teaching posture, the clinician can explain and clarify these conflicting affects and thoughts. Thus, the clinician can give the child a framework for managing his/her own conflict.

We have stated frequently in this book that it is important for the child to explore all extended family members. Such exploration is essential to establishing a sense of self. Everybody comes from someplace: the child must be provided with a personal history. Knowing the history of his other family members gives the child his/her place in the larger community of people.

Another vehicle to achieve trust and attachment is fun. The children of drug addicts have usually not had much fun in their lives. Bringing them to activities that allow humor and silliness and playfulness is vital. Abraham Maslow (1954) put "self-actualization" at the top of his hierarchy of human needs. Sometimes, in working with both children and adults, it has occurred to us that fun belongs at the top of that pyramid.

Last, in working with the "little ones," it is important to understand that what Khantzian calls the "cigar store Indian" therapist will not cut it with the children (or with most addicts, for that matter). One must have a real commitment to these children, exemplified by a willingness to get in close, to care, to laugh and cry with them, and to work things through no matter how rocky the terrain gets. Anything less just makes you another cog in the social service system bureaucracy that too often fails to serve the real needs of the youngest victims of parental drug abuse.

THE LATENCY AGE CHILD. We have found that group counseling is the best therapeutic modality to use with latency-age children. Group offers distinct advantages, particularly when used in tandem with individual therapy work. Children find it liberating to relate their experiences and vent their feelings in the presence of other children who also have addicted parents. There are many reasons why group psychotherapy (which comes in many forms) can be helpful. Listed below are the helpful aspects of group work:

Helpful Aspects of Group Therapy*

Education:	Learning how to cope
Hope:	By connecting to others in the same boat
Universality:	Not alone in the struggle
Altruism:	By helping others, discovering that one has something to give
Family Feeling:	Heal old wounds and learn about old ties
Social Skills:	Honest feedback promotes interpersonal skills
Role Modeling:	Of newer adaptive behavior shown by others
Experimentation:	Try out new ways of being
Cohesiveness:	A sense of belonging and safety
Catharsis:	Putting trauma in its proper perspective

One of the recurring themes that comes up in groups we have run is the fear of abandonment. Too many children have been left alone, neglected, while their parents went off to get high. The children often ask each other "What do you do when your mother/father is smoking crack?" Being left alone means learning how to fend for yourself, and often a younger sibling or two.

Latency-age children are supposed to enjoy the freedoms inherent

*Adapted from Yalom, 1975.

to this life stage. But the carefree latency years are just a dream for most children of drug addicts. Ellen Morehouse and Tarpley Richards (1983) in their work with latency-age children of alcoholic parents point to disturbances in role stability, environmental consistency, emotional availability, and consistency on the part of the parents. These same problems confront the children of drug addicts. The parents are lost in their drug world: getting high, crashing, copping, getting high again, ad nauseum! The child's needs are not considered. The children often interpret their parent's behaviors as an indictment: "I must be a terrible child if my mother gets high." These children, especially those removed from their parents and placed in the foster care system, believe that somehow *they* have failed their parents.

One of the most helpful aspects of group work is its educational function. When clinical staff teach children about drug use and abuse and addiction, the children begin to understand that they are not the cause of their parents' addiction and dysfunction. A universal theme running through all clinical work with children of dysfunctional families—whether hurt by alcoholism, drug addiction, mental illness, economic impoverishment—is to help the children to disassociate themselves from the powerful sense of self-blame that they carry.

The children of drug abusers are pragmatists. They want to be shown: they require proof! When parents claim to be dry and/or clean, even when they actually enter treatment, the parent/child relationship does not undergo immediate change. The child may continue to maintain the idea that he or she is "bad." Obviously, sustained parental abstinence can help. But since so many drug-abusing parents relapse, these stifling affects are reinforced again and again. Children require heavy doses of empathy and support from staff. Mommy does not become a brand new mother because she finally stops using drugs. Familial behavior patterns change very slowly, as do the child's perception of them. This is why we believe so strongly in family-oriented treatment. We try very hard, when parent and child are able, to work with them together. The apparent joys of early recovery quickly clash headlong into the difficulties. Abstinence alone does not a recovery make. For the addict, underlying personal issues and environmental pressures that promote the addictive behavior must be surfaced and worked on. For the child, he or she has their own issues. And then there is the relationship—usually fragile, tentative, and deeply disturbed. If there was a good relationship prior to the addictive live-style, we try to explore that relationship with both parent and child. Not all these children are drug-exposed in utero. For some, parental addiction started after birth.

In the groups for children of drug abusers, as in much of the individual work, consistency and rituals are highlighted. Each group begins with the same theme, session after session. We focus on the issues underlying our client's identities as children of drug abusers. These are not free-ranging groups. Children in this age group like secret clubs and codes. Rituals can be soothing and comforting to children. They also build group cohesiveness.

One need not go through life compulsively repeating, "Hi, my name is _____ and I'm the child of a drug abuser!"

There are three goals to psychotherapy as described by Lewis Wolberg (1977):

1. Removing, modifying, or retarding existing symptoms
2. Mediating disturbed patterns of behavior
3. promoting positive personality growth and development

We expose children to a group experience that helps them, not just to cope, but to understand what has happened to them and how to get beyond it. We do not tell them that they have a disease, nor do we describe the family as being diseased. We do speak of addiction as an illness. We do not tell them that they carry a genetic code for disaster. We do warn the older children and adolescents about the potential disastrous consequences of imitating parental drug-taking behavior. But we do not imply that they are necessary more at-risk than other children their own age. We ask them to learn from the painful lessons of their own families and to relate to their personal strengths and positive attributes. We speak of responsible personal decision making throughout life.

Opposition to the group leader is a common event. Group is accompanied by power struggles and tensions. However, children of drug abusers do not have a perception of parent figures as reliable, empathetic, or capable. These children often try to direct the groups or to become coleaders. We do not permit them to take over from us. We do use their sense of being "displaced" from their aspirations to be the leader as material for group discussion.

Latency-age children are guarded about their feelings. They find solace in same-sex groups. In these groups they try to convey esteem and wellness to each other. The individual child discovers he/she is not the only one who has an addicted parent. They do connect to their own peers—fellow travelers who have shared a strange common journey.

Case Illustration 11: Raheem

Raheem was living in a group home for two years. His mother denied being a drug addict. Raheem refused to discuss this issue or any aspect of his discussions with this mother. He remained mute through many group discussions. At the sixth group meeting, while another boy was talking about his mother's addiction and expressing great anger at his mother, Raheem began to nod his head in total agreement. His own painful affects were being validated by his peers. Shortly thereafter, Raheem's mother broke through her denial and began to speak of seeking treatment. Raheem became quite vocal in group in expressing his pride about his mother's attempts to fight her addiction.

Many different emotions and ideas are expressed in these groups: hope is tinged with pessimism; pride and envy vie for dominance; anger and rage are common. Regardless of the feelings expressed, the children feel validated, their sense of self confirmed. The children speak about their siblings. They often form extremely tight bonds between themselves and sibling as a way of protecting themselves from the parent. This bond also serves to forestall the massive sense of isolation caused by parental drug abuse. In sharing talk and activities, such as drawing and playing games, group members had their socialization skills enhanced. The dreaded feelings of isolation are thus successfully avoided. In this way intensive and compulsive sibling bonding is eased as well.

Individual play therapy is useful with the latency-age child, particularly for those children who have poor expressive and receptive language and for those who cannot tolerate the anxiety and stimulation that groups create. Intense one-to-one treatment can also help to resolve development issues. We find that there is no ideal modality to building a child's sense of self. Individualized treatment plans show a respect for the uniqueness of each child. We try hard to avoid any cookie-cutter approach to either describing or treating the children. We have found that individual treatment combined with some group work, strongly supported by family-oriented work, is a good working model. It is also very taxing on any one therapist: the work needs to shared by a clinical team.

Some of the play techniques that we use are adopted from the work of Cipolla, McGown, and Yanulis (Cooper, 1984).

1. *Sensory Development Techniques.* These are used to promote learning through the senses to help children become more open to the world and their own experiences. Children who have been neglected or abused have not been taught or choose not to use all of their senses to understand their environment. The child who has not learned to make distinctions among sensory experiences is confused about himself/herself, his/her body, and the outer world. This also helps children to more clearly distinguish between the real world and the fantasy worlds that they sometimes retreat into.

2. *Early Nurturing Exercises.* These demonstrate the needs of babies and help children recognize that they both require and deserve good parenting. Many children of drug abusers, we have pointed out, have learned to be extremely self-reliant. Some cannot trust the adult world and become closed off to all adults. Early nurturing exercises focus on doll play and doll "caring." Children are encouraged to use the baby oil, creams, lotions, and baby powder on themselves. It is often a beginning to let the child feel what it may be like to be loved by a nonneglectful parent.

3. *Continuity Work.* This includes using special places and rituals to emphasize constancy and continuity for the child. They have usually suffered many literal and symbolic separations from their addicted parents. These exercises enhance the continuity and value of relationships, while giving the child some control over them. The "Treasure Box" is used as a special place to keep the child's drawings, poems, and projects. The therapist can put "gifts" into the treasure box as well. Of course, the treasure box becomes filled with memories, too.

4. *The Lost Object.* This is a special toy that symbolically re-

places some of the experiences the child has missed or lost. The special object seems to enable the child to symbolically restore some of the experiences he or she missed or wants. It can represent some of the nurturing they missed. We have seen children holding, loving, and feeding a tiny stuffed animal through their thirteenth birthday.

5. *Games for Relaxing.* These help the child calm down (self-regulate) and have positive experiences with rules, boundaries, and self-control. The games are the usual board games (*Sorry,*™ checkers, cards, etc.). The New York Spalding for Children, the former Adoption Agency, also practiced this on a blanket to define the boundaries of play (similar to Montessori school techniques). If these games do not work or generate too much excitement, we have found you can always return to water play, the most soothing type of play.

All of these techniques allow the child to practice developing positive attachments in a nonthreatening atmosphere. At the same time, they can do the work of mourning what they now know they have missed.

THE ADOLESCENT. Our own clinical work with adolescents who are children of substance abusers does not differ significantly from the work we do with other adolescents who come from families with other serious problems. The guiding principles and tools that we use are as follows:

1. We treat them as young adults with respect for their individuality. We expect them to assume responsibility for their own lives.

2. We help them to understand that whatever their parents did right and wrong is in the past and separate from their own sense of self. They need to feel empowered to make their own decisions, particularly regarding their own futures. Obsessive focusing on parental flaws and blaming does not help them grow. We want them to be multidimensional people. We do not encourage them to organize their self-concept around the idea of being a "child of substance abuse."

3. We do not view addiction as a "disease" in which the children are genetically tainted by their parent(s). We share with them responsible individual decision making and point to the health and emo-

tional risks of alcohol and other drugs—which played such a destructive role in their earlier lives.

4. We work on what Erik Erikson called "identity versus role confusion." We try to strengthen the child's sense of self and his/her sense of being a unique person. We try to teach them to enjoy living in the "now" and also to begin to plan for their own futures.

5. We make use of their creations—poems, stories, essays, "rap" and other song lyrics, homework, drawings, photos, paintings, sculptures, etc. We celebrate their creations. They deserve to fully participate in their own youth culture.

6. We speak frankly with them about sexually transmitted diseases, about HIV and AIDS, about pregnancy, about dangerous drugs, about drinking and driving, about violence, about human sexual development—real-world issues for adolescents. We help them get to services like Planned Parenthood, health clinics, and whatever else they need.

7. Short of crime or threatened suicide, we mean it when we tell them the treatment setting is confidential. We help them understand that there are limits and boundaries to therapy.

8. We respect their cultural diversity and help them to develop feelings of racial and ethnic pride.

9. We work with them to develop their own strong concepts of ethics, morality, and personally defined spirituality.

The various themes we mentioned concerning work with younger children are often continued into the adolescent years. We have found that the most important aspect of the therapeutic task is to perceive each adolescent as a unique individual. Neither the literature, clinical impression, or empirical research commends placing these children into a blender and "homogenizing" them. The term "children of drug abusers" should not be used as if a single, simple stereotypical syndrome or personality is being described. We repeat: these children are a diverse population who defy stereotyping. They come from all walks of life, they have varying skill levels, varying competences, and varying deficits. And they need caring clinicians to be there for them with a variety of services.

In many ways, the children of drug abusers we have known and read about mirror the findings and impressions of two prominent child mental health professionals. Psychologist Norman Garmezy of the University of Minnesota pioneered the concept of resilience in at-risk children. In November 1990 at a conference on violence Dr. Garmezy cited a number of studies showing that most people from harsh environments do manage to find a good life for themselves. One study showed 70 percent of abused women did not end up abusing their children (contrary to what is commonly held), and another study that 74 percent of children exposed to extreme stresses did not become psychologically impaired (DeAngelis, 1991). Garmezy believes these people "represent a heartland of resilience." He further states that what is needed is some way to tap into disadvantaged children's practical intelligence, a potential gold mine of achievement.

British psychiatrist Michael Rutter "offers the hopeful message that a surprisingly large number of children become normal, successful adults despite stressful, disadvantaged, or even brutalized childhoods. Furthermore, he insists, many more children could be helped to become similarly resilient" (Pines, 1990). Dr. Rutter worked with children at Maudsley Hospital in London right after World War II. He was struck by how "varied the children's responses were" and began to study factors that protect children, including those exposed horrific early lives. Among the factors that he identified are:

- A sense of self-worth
- A sense of self-efficacy
- Establishment of good secure relationships that help develop resilience
- Adaptability, the ability to cope with changing circumstances
- Practice at social problem solving
- An inner vision of a future successful life

He points out that even when a child has a great deal going against him/her, he or she can still be OK if he or she has good experiences in one setting. Children learn problem solving primarily from watching their parents. When these role models are poor or nonexistent, children need to develop secure linkages to an adult figure who can provide the proper model. When disadvantaged children experience social success—whether as class clown, in sports, musical performance, etc.—it goes a long way in developing resiliency. When children go through a series of bureaucratic institutions that tend to stifle them, their "hope lies in doing something to alter these linkages, to see that kids who start in a bad environment don't go on having bad environments and develop a sense of impotency."

Drs. Garmenzy and Rutter collaborated on a book called *Stress, Coping, and Development in Children* (1983).

A study by David Franshel entitled "Foster Care in a Life Course Perspective" (1990) followed 585 children in foster care in five western states. He found that while 60 percent were leading stable lives seven years after leaving care another third are in danger of leading unstable lives, ranging from homelessness to criminality. Experts are saying that many states may be hurting youths in foster care by releasing them from the system at age eighteen, before they are emotionally or professionally capable of managing alone (*New York Times*, 1991). The application of appropriate treatments such as those we outline in this chapter can make the difference in these very different types of outcomes. These treatment strategies are not limited to those children of drug abusers in foster care. We must all work to prevent "rotten outcomes" and ensure life-fulfilling ones.

We have shared with you a psychodynamic model of family-centered treatment. Thus far we have emphasized the "care and feeding" of the client. We now turn our attention to the clinicians and other caregivers who work with these children.

Caring for the Caregivers

One night, as this book neared completion, Dr. Levy shared some of the content material with a graduate class at Jersey City State College that was studying the psychology of alcohol and substance abuse. The students, all mature adults, were already involved in working with children in various clinical or educational settings. The class was presented in two separate segments: first, a statement of the problem regarding the realities of living with an addicted parent(s); second, a presentation of helping interventions.

During the break following the first segment, students had these reactions:

- Two were in tears
- One pleaded for some "positive" information
- One said "how can you work with these poor souls?"
- Three were enraged at systems that do not work

- One withdrew into isolation in a corner of the room
- One was overtly angry at having to hear this material
- One wanted to know how to become a foster parent
- The others appeared downhearted

The story of the children of drug abusers is powerful and moving. It is a sad story. It engenders feelings of helplessness and hopelessness, pity, rage, empathy, despair. One thing is certain: it deeply touches all audiences. It is, after all, about children, the youngest, weakest, and most vulnerable members of our society. They tug at our heart strings and they trigger many memories of our own childhood fears and triumphs. They reach into our psyches and touch our maternal or paternal longings. They play with our feelings of omnipotence and power. We want to help them, heal them, love them, nurture them, and finally receive their love. They are the blank screen upon which we project our own fantasies, dreams, and hopes along with our own needs and unresolved issues.

We have framed the clinical work to be done by sharing the research literature, describing some early treatment efforts with children and families, and including our own clinical perspective. In terms of the impact of this work on one's professional roles and our basic humanity, it is both arduous and demanding. Therefore, we will now discuss some of the "care and feeding" of staff issues that are essential to working with the children and families we have described.

Clinical Staff Supervision

Effective leadership is essential to getting the job done for the children. Wiley and Ray (1986) have described the developmental levels needed for supervising counseling staff. Watkins (1990) has described the development of the psychotherapy supervisor. These authors emphasize not only the importance of effective supervision but how both supervisors and supervisees go through a sequence of developmental growth. The table below is taken from Watkins (1990) and describes changes in a psychotherapy supervisor's development across selected issues. They speak of stages, tasks, and crises that move both supervisor and supervisee from role shock to role recovery to role consolidation and finally to role mastery.

As indicated above, working with the children of drug abusers can be difficult, physically exhausting and emotionally draining. The children induce powerful affects in the clinician, as do the their parents. When one works with parent and child, it is hard to resist the pull of countertransference thoughts and feelings. Singer, in his reference work *Key Concepts in Psychotherapy* (1970) comments:

> Most authorities on the topic propose that countertransference represents a manifestation of a defensive orientation of the therapist in his/her relation to the patient. This defensiveness, they claim, results from anxieties the patient triggers in the therapist. . . . All of the therapist's reactions, if carefully examined, potentially further therapeutic progress because they represent subtle and what some authors call "prelogical" communicative modes capable of leading to enhanced understanding and insights.

However, when countertransferential reactions go unexamined, they may interfere with or even prevent the therapy from proceeding. The therapist working with the children of drug abusers may be repulsed, consciously or unconsciously, by any number of things. Among these are:

- Sexually seductive and provocative behavior
- Abuse, neglect, and maltreatment of a child
- HIV-positive client or client with AIDS
- Client's sexual orientation
- Client's "street" behavior
- Acceptance and then rejection by a client
- Profound dependency needs
- Posture of helplessness
- Client's apparent or real "sociopathy"
- Client's value system which differs from one's own

In one-on-one and group supervision these difficult reactions to clients may be aired and worked through. The varieties of therapist responses are usually within the normal range of thoughts and feelings raised while working with this type of population. Occasionally, these responses represent a more difficult adjustment for the therapist and may require outside professional treatment and/or a change of responsibilities. But for the most part, in our experience, these are normal people having normal responses to what are highly

TABLE 5-1.

Changes in Psychotherapy Supervisors' Development across Selected Issues

Developmental issues	Psychotherapy Supervisor Stages			
	Role shock	Role recovery/transition	Role consolidation	Role mastery
Confidence in current supervisory skill	Acutely aware of weaknesses, questions abilities, lack confidence, feel overwhelmed and unprepared	Recognize some strengths and abilities, confidence develops in restricted areas, less generalized questioning of oneself, can still easily be shaken when confronted with supervisory problems	More realistic, accurate perceptions of self and supervisees, general, firm sense of confidence in one's abilities and skills, not easily shaken when confronted with supervisory problems	Consistent, solid sense of confidence in abilities and skills, handles supervision problems effectively and appropriately
Insight about impact on supervisees	Has very limited awareness about supervisory strengths, style, and motivations, and their impact on supervisees	Developing awareness of impact on supervisees, favorable impression about impact still overshadowed by unfavorable impressions	More consistent awareness of supervisory strengths, weaknesses, style, and motivations and their impact on supervisees, favorable impressions about impact become predominant	Consistent awareness about supervisory strengths, weaknesses, and their impact, image of oneself as effective supervisor firmly established

Approach to a theoretical framework	Little if any awareness about one's own supervisory style or supervisory theory	Limited recognition of certain behaviors, ideas, and tenets that characterize one's practice of supervision, beginning reflection about a personal theory of supervision	More consistent recognition and definition of aspects that characterize one's supervisory style, a personal theory of supervision takes more solid form	Coherent, well-integrated, theoretically consistent supervisory style is evidenced, theory of supervision highly meaningful, personalized, and consistently guides practice
Sense of professional identity	No real sense of identity, no real identification with the supervisory role, looks to others for help and guidance	Crude, nascent identity core starts to take form, but is fragile and unconsolidated, less intense reliance on help and guidance of others	Considers self a "supervisor," identity core established, leans on others at difficult times, but has sufficient inner resources for self-sustenance	Well-integrated, consolidated, well-elaborated sense of identity, views self as professionally effective, facilitative supervisor, is self-reliant

Note: The structure of this table was adapted from Wiley and Ray (1986) and has been modified to apply to psychotherapy supervisors' development.

Source: C. B. Watkins, "Development of the Psychotherapy Supervisor," in *Psychotherapy: Theory, Research, Practice, Training*. 27: 553–560. Reprinted by permission.

charged abnormal situations. We all have psychic myopia, "blind spots" that blur our vision in doing clinical work. Having a supervisor who can hear you and lend empathetic support is invaluable. The supervisor can gently but firmly assist in removing some of these blind spots. We have found the use of metaphor quite helpful in supervision. Here is an example we use in helping staff deal with "borderline" clients.

The Tale of the Snake and the Tiger

The clinical supervisor (guru) tells the story of the hunter who collected snakes. His collection was both extensive and exotic. He searched the world over to complete it. Finally, there was only one more known species to be collected. This particular snake, known by its orange and black band markings, was to be found only in the deepest jungles of India.

With his faithful guide, the hunter went on his final search. After seven fruitless days he was about to give up in defeat, for the snake was nowhere to be found. Suddenly, the guide silently pointed to an orange and black banded form in the clearing that lay before them. Ever so stealthfully the hunter inched his way toward the snake. Finally it was within his grasp. He knew from years of hunting that he had to grab the snake at the end of his tail and slide his other hand quickly up behind the head. With a lightning move he did this.

Have you ever wondered what it is like to have your hand up a tiger's ass?

Experienced clinicians will tell you that borderlines often appear to be one thing and turn out to be another. They will appear to warm up to you and accept you, only to suddenly turn on you with anger and rejection. The metaphor of the snake and the tiger, a powerful teaching tool, helps the therapist to understand the difficult emotions they are experiencing (Kopp, 1969; Marlatt, 1988). In this way they "know" both intellectually and emotionally the nature of their own reaction to borderline personalities.

In 1985 George Doering, Jr., director of the Ramapo Counseling Center, and Dr. Levy conceptualized the Rockland County Crack/Cocaine Program, an outpatient treatment program for cocaine abusers (Doering & Levy, 1987, 1988, 1989). They built in one hour per week of one-to-one supervision for each counselor, as well as a once-a-week ninety-minute group meeting for the clinical supervisor and the six counselors. Mrs. Rutter has provided similar supervision to her casework staff in the foster care setting of Saint Agatha's Home of the New York Foundling Hospital. We try to support staff on both an emotional and an intellectual level. We attempt to model the kinds of things we want them to do for the clients we all serve. They, in turn, have had greater stores of inner strength and wisdom to impart to their clients. Dr. Herbert Freudenberger (1980) called burnout the "high cost of high achievement." Regular clinical supervision helps to keep the battery charged and is the most significant preventive measure against staff burnout. It is a vital link in the staff-client relationship. The best clinicians are those who are leading happy and productive lives.

Cross training is also quite a useful tool in keeping staff members sharp. Dr. Levy and Mrs. Rutter met when she invited him to share his knowledge of cocaine-treatment approaches with her team of child caseworkers. The collaboration continues.

Critical Incident Stress Debriefing

Helping those who help others sometimes takes on unexpected dimensions. Clinicians may be faced with an unexpected critical incident. Clinical staff are normal people who may have normal responses to highly traumatic, abnormal events. If they are helped to cope with the emotional trauma, future problems can be successfully prevented. We are speaking here of a blow to the psyche that breaks down one's defenses so suddenly and with such force that one cannot respond effectively. A critical incident is any event that has sufficient power to overwhelm a person's usually effective abilities to cope. Routine clinical supervision will not suffice to effectively deal with these types of reactions.

Both Mrs. Rutter and Dr. Levy have been through training in critical incident stress debriefing (CISD) run by the nation's foremost expert in the field, Dr. Jeffrey T. Mitchell, vice-president of the American Critical Incident Stress Foundation and assistant professor in the Emergency Health Sciences Department, University of Maryland. While most situations involving CISD involve trauma arising from police work, fire fighting, and emergency medical situations, mental health professionals and child welfare workers also face traumatic situations. In one situation we offered to do a debriefing after a child was murdered by a prospective adoptive parent. Unfortunately, the administrators did not act quickly enough for a debriefing to be held in timely fashion.

Here we are referring to the feelings and thoughts induced in staff by the types of realities faced by the children of drug abusers and their families. When children are abused, neglected, and maltreated; when families become violent and psychotic; when clients suffer acute episodes of depression or anxiety; when workers confront all manner of the inhumanity wrought by addiction—these can constitute critical incidents. They represent an explicit threat to neophytes and may overwhelm even the most seasoned professionals. Sometimes children are maimed, sometimes they die by the hand of another, sometimes they kill themselves. It is vital that there be personnel trained in CISD to help guide the staff directly involved through their early powerful reactions. By providing quick help, trained CISD teams can reduce the possibility of evolving problems like post-traumatic stress syndrome.

The learning involved in understanding critical incidents also prepares clinical staff to intervene with children who have been the victims of trauma. We quote from Dr. Mitchell's foreword to the book *Trauma in the Lives of Children* (Johnson, 1989):

> Parents and teachers are frequently bewildered when faced with a traumatized child or group of distressed children. They turn anxiously toward health care professionals and psychological support services, only to find that specialists are frequently not adequately trained, skilled or experienced to offer sound advice on how best to help damaged children.

Listed below are the salient points in managing critical incident stress.

Managing Critical Incident Stress*

- The professional must be encouraged not to engage in denial of his/her intense feelings.
- The most important thing a professional can do following a crisis incident is go through a personal debriefing, held as soon after the crisis as possible.
- The professional needs an opportunity to share his/her own reactions with others who are safe, who understand, and who are capable of dealing with the intensity of feelings generated by the crisis.
- The second thing the professional should do after the crisis is to find another professional who knows of the situation and its context—someone who can add perspective
- The professional needs to determine resources needed to manage the situation (human, legal, political, etc.) and make a plan for handling the emergency.
- The professional must then distance himself/herself from the situation. This can be done through recreation or other normalizing routines.
- Finally, Ongoing stress management may be indicated.

*Adapted from Johnson, 1989.

Epilogue

Woman Overcomes Bureaucratic Odds to Regain Her Children. . . .
Michelle Rogers got her children back yesterday. Mrs. Rogers, who
wanted to become a nurse but ended up homeless and on drugs, has
been struggling to reunite her family since the city placed three of
her four children in foster care two years ago. She had to overcome
her addiction to drugs and to navigate an overburdened social services bureaucracy.

—New York Times, 25 January 1991

"But it's difficult to categorize babies because there are so many
different factors affecting the infant all at once."

—Dr. Dan Griffith, developmental psychologist (NAPARE),
speaking about cocaine babies in the *New York Times*, 22,
January 1991

"My momma got into a drug treatment program and now she
comes around to see me once a week. Before that she was out there
getting high and I never even got a phone call. My social worker
says we are all going to talk together. Momma brought me a present
last week. That's the first thing she gave me in a year. She don't cry
when she looks at me now. I don't cry either."

—A nine-year-old in foster care

"In the meantime, the presence of waiting lists for public treatment
in some places obscures the larger reality: that while the need for
treatment is high, the actual demand for it is relatively low. Many
addicts undergo treatment only under compulsion. Sometimes criminal sanctions are necessary, and sometimes pressure from family and
employers can help. But if tomorrow we were able to treat all current
addicts, most of them would resist or avoid treatment."

—Dr. Herber D. Kleber, deputy director for demand reduction of
the Office of National Drug Control Policy, quoted in the
New York Times, 26 January 1990.

A Surer Way to Control Crime. . . . Drug treatment works. Researchers at the Research Triangle Institute, for example, followed
10,000 addicts and found that treatment programs caused substantial and prolonged reductions in drug abuse and criminal behavior.
The research also found that "criminal justice clients"—those
forced into treatment by courts—were as likely to benefit as voluntary admissions.

—*New York Times* editorial

"Crack Is Wack"

—Political art, Harlem, New York

> Outside there is light and fresh air
>   I can't go out there
>   anymore
> I have AIDS and I'm too sick
>   to go out there
> My Mom died of AIDS from
>   shooting drugs
> The doctors say I'm next
> I wish I could go out and
>   play with mom and the
>   other kids

—Justin, age ten, deceased

"It was so great. My dad finished his inpatient treatment program
and in three months we can live together again. He says the letter I
sent him last year made him stop being an addict. . . . I don't understand how it did that. All the letter said was 'Dad I need you—
please stop using drugs. Love, your daughter, Sally, S.W.A.K.
(sealed with a kiss).' "
—Sally is living with her dad, who is still drug-free and working to
build a better life for both of them.

The struggle to free the children of drug abusers and their parents
continues. . . . We are all Pioneers!

References

Adler, T. (1990). Cocaine babies' reactions explored. *American Psychological Association Monitor,* 21 (11), 8.

Alibrandi, L. A. (1985). The folk psychotherapy of Alcoholics Anonymous. In S. Zimerg, J. Wallace, & S. Blume (Eds.), *Practical approaches to alcoholism psychotherapy* (pp. 239–256). New York: Plenum Press.

American Psychiatric Association. (1987). *Diagnostic and Statistical Manual of Mental Disorders* (3rd ed.), rev. DSM-III-R. Washington, D.C.: Author.

Barden, J. C. (1991, January 6). After release for foster care, many turn to lives on the streets. . . . They lack simple skills to make it on their own. *New York Times.*

Barr, H. L., & Cohen, A. (1979). *The problem-drinking drug addict.* Services Research Branch Administrative Report, National Institute on Drug Abuse, DHEW. Washington, DC: U.S. Government Printing Office.

Beschner, G., & Brotman, R. (1977). *Symposium on comprehensive health care for addicted families and their children,* (National Institute on Drug Abuse, DHEW Publication No. ADM 77–480). Washington, DC: U.S. Government Printing Office.

Beschner, G., & Brotman, R. (1976). *Symposium on comprehensive health care for addicted families and their children.* National Institute on Drug Abuse, Services Research Report (DHEW, Publication No. 017-024-005908-3). Washington, DC: U.S. Government Printing Office.

Beschner, G., Reed, B. G., & Mondanaro, J. (1981). *Treatment services for drug-dependent women.* Treatment Research Monograph Series, National Institute on Drug Abuse (DHHS) Publication No. ADM 81–1177). Washington, DC: U.S. Government Printing Office.

Beschner, G., & Thompson, P. (1981). *Women and drug abuse treatment: Needs and services.* National Institute on Drug Abuse, Services Research Monograph Series (DHHS Publication No. 81–1057). Washington, DC: U.S. Government Printing Office.

Boland, M. G., & Czarniecki, L. (1991, January). Starting life with HIV. *RN,* Medical Economics Company, 54–58.

Burgouis, P. (1989). In search of Horatio Alger: Culture and ideology in the crack economy. *Contemporary Drug Problems,* 16 (4), 619–649.

Carr, J. N. (1975). Drug patterns among drug-addicted mothers: Incidence, variance in use, and effects on children. *Pediatric Annals,* July, 66–77.

Cermak, T. (1985). *A primer on adult children of alcoholics.* Pompano Beach, FL: Health Communications.

Chaisson, R. E., Bacchetti, P., Osmond, D., (1989). Cocaine use and HIV infection in intravenous drug users in San Francisco. *Journal of the American Medical Association, 261,* 561–565.

Chasnoff, I. J., Burns, W. J., Schnoll, S. H., & Burns, K. (1985). Cocaine use in pregnancy. *New England Journal of Medicine, 313,* 666–669.

Chasnoff, I. J., Bussey, M. E., Savich, P., & Stack, C. M. (1986). Perinatal cerebral infarction and maternal cocaine use. *Journal of Pediatrics, 108,* 456–459.

Chasnoff, I. J., Griffith, D. R., McGregor, S., Dirkes, K., & Burns, K. (1989). Temporal patterns of cocaine use in pregnancy: Perinatal outcome. *Journal of the American Medical Association, 261,* 1741–1744.

Chasnoff, I. J., Hatcher, R., & Burns, W. S. (1982). Polydrug- and methadone-addicted newborns: A continuum of impairment? *Pediatrics, 10,* 210–213.

Chasnoff, I. J., Schnoll, S. H., Burns, W. J., & Burns, K. (1984). Maternal non-narcotic substance abuse during pregnancy: Effects on infant development. *Neurobehavioral Toxicology and Teratology, 6,* 277–280.

Cippola, J., McGowan, D., & Yanulis, M. (1984). A manual using play techniques to assess and prepare older children for adoption, adapted from C. Cooper (*The Growing Child*). In A. Bayley and D. Batty, *In touch with children.* London: British Agency for Fostering and Adoption.

Colten, M. E. (1980). *A comparison of heroin-addicted and non-addicted mothers: Their attitudes, beliefs, and parenting experiences.* National Institute on Drug Abuse, Services Research Report (DHHS Publication No. ADM 81–1028). Washington, DC: U.S. Government Printing Office.

Comer, J. P. (1988). *Maggie's American dream: The life and times of a black family.* New York: Penguin Books.

Connaughton, J. F., Reese, D., & Finnegan, L. P. (1977). Pregnancy complicated by drug addiction. In R. Bolognese & R. Schwartz (Eds.), *Perinatal Medicine.* Baltimore: Williams & Wilkins.

Council of the New York Academy of Medicine. (1990). Drug use an urgent problem for New York City. New York: Author.

Council of Family and Child Caring Agencies (COFCCA) (1989). *Preventive services for boarder babies discharged to their biological families.* New York: COFCCA.

Crupi, M. S., Schwartz, G. C., & Weiss, C. F. (1975). *Looking ahead: The youth health center.* Washington, D.C.: Special Action Office for Drug Abuse Prevention, National Institute for Mental Health, DHEW.

Cuskey, W. R., & Wathey, B. (1982). *Female addiction.* Lexington, MA: Lexington Books.

DeAngelis, T. (1991). Living with violence: Children suffer, cope. *American Psychological Association Monitor, 22* (1), 26–27.

Deleon, G. (1984). *The therapeutic community: Study of effectiveness.* National Institute on Drug Abuse, Treatment Research Monograph Series (DHHS

Publication No. ADM 85-1286). Washington, DC: U.S. Government Printing Office.

DeLeon, G., & Rosenthal, M. (1979). Therapeutic communities. In R. L. DuPont, A. Goldstein, & J. O'Donnell (Eds.), *Handbook on drug abuse* (pp. 39–47). Washington, DC: U.S. Government Printing Office.

Densen-Gerber, J., & Rohrs, C. C. (1973). Drug addicted parents and child abuse. *Contemporary Drug Problems, 2,* 683–696.

Deren, S. (1984). *Children of substance abuser services provided by treatment programs.* Albany, NY: New York State Division of Substance Abuse Services.

Deren, S. (1986). Children of substance abusers: A review of the literature. *Journal of Substance Abuse Treatment, 3,* 77–94.

Deren, S. (1986a). *Parents in methadone treatment and their children.* Albany, NY: New York State Division of Substance Abuse Services.

Deren, S., Frank, B., & Schmeidler, J. (1988). *Children of substance abusers in New York State: Trends and estimates.* (Treatment Issue Report No. 67). Albany, NY: New York State Division of Substance Abuse Services.

Deren, S., & Kott, A. (1987). *Parents in residential drug-free treatment and their children.* Albany, NY: New York State Division of Substance Abuse Services.

Deren, S., & Randell, J. (1983). *Increasing program's utilization of vocational services* (NIDA grant proposal). New York: Narcotic and Drug Research, Inc.

Deren, S., & Randell, J. (1990). The vocational rehabilitation of substance abuse. *Journal of Applied Rehabilitation Counseling, 21* (2), 4–6.

DesJarlais, D. C., & Friedman, S. R. (1988). The psychology of preventing AIDS among intravenous drug users: A social learning conceptualization. *American Psychologist, 43,* 865–870.

DesJarlais, D. C., Friedman, S. R., Novik, D. M., Sotheran, J. L., Thomas, P., Yancovitz, S. R., Maslanosky, R., Bartelme, S., Spira, T., & Marmor, M. (1989). HIV-1 infection among intravenous drug users in Manhattan, New York City, from 1977–1987. *Journal of the American Medical Association, 261,* 1008–1012.

Dickey, S., & Hall, M. (1978, May). *The results of data analysis on 50 pregnancy and addiction studies: 1965–1977.* Paper presented at the National Drug Abuse Conference, Seattle, WA.

Division of Substance Abuse of the Albert Einstein College of Medicine of Yeshiva University. (1988, January). Children of patients speak out at methadone conference. *Journey, 7* (1), 1–2.

Doering, G. R., & Levy, S. J. (1987, 1988, 1989). *First, Second, and Third Annual Reports of the Rockland County Crack/Cocaine Program.* Town of Ramapo Youth Counseling Services, Spring Valley, New York. Submitted to the New York State Division of Substance Abuse Services. Spring Valley, NY: Author.

Dole, V. P., & Nyswander, M. E. (1965). A medical treatment for diacetylmorphine addiction. *Journal of the American Medical Association, 193,* 646–650.

Dole, V. P., & Nyswander, M. E. (1976). Methadone-maintenance treatment: A ten-year perspective. *Journal of the American Medical Association, 235,* 2117–2119.

Drug Abuse Warning Network (DAWN). (1988). Series 1, number 8. Washington, DC: National Institute on Drug Abuse.

Escamilla-Mondanaro, J. (1977). Women: Pregnancy, children, and addiction. Journal of Psychedelic Drugs, 9, 59–68.

Fagan, J., & Chin, K. (1989). Initiation into crack and cocaine: A tale of two epidemics. Contemporary Drug Problems, Winter. 16 (4), 579–617.

Fahlberg, V. (1979). Putting the pieces together: Helping children when they must move. Chelsea, England. National Resource Center for Adoption.

Fansehl, D. (1990). Foster children in a life-course perspective. New York: Columbia University Press.

Finnegan, L. P. (1976). Clinical effects of pharmacological agents on pregnancy, the fetus, and the neonate. Annals of the New York Academy of Sciences, 281, 74–89.

Finnegan, L. P. (1979). Drug dependence in pregnancy: Clinical management of mother and child. National Institute on Drug Abuse, Services Research Monograph Series (DHEW Publication No. 79-678). Washington, DC: U.S. Government Printing Office.

Finnegan, L. P. (1982). Outcome of children born to women dependent on narcotics. In B. Stimmel (Ed.), The effects of maternal alcohol and drug abuse on the newborn (pp. 55–102). New York: Haworth Press.

Finnegan, L. P. (1983). Clinical, perinatal, and developmental effects of methadone. In J. R. Cooper, F. Altman, B. S. Brown, & D. Czechowicz (Eds.), Research on the treatment of narcotic addiction: State of the art. National Institute on Drug Abuse Monograph (DHHS Publication No. ADM 83-1281, pp. 392–443). Washington, DC: U.S. Government Printing Office.

Finnegan, L. P. (1987). Testimony before the Presidential Commission on the HIV Epidemic. In Intravenous drug use and the HIV epidemic: Perinatally transmitted AIDS. Washington, DC: Mimeograph.

Finnegan, L. P., Connaughton, J. R., Kron, R. E., & Emich, J. P. (1975). Neonatal abstinence syndrome: Assessment and management. Addictive Disease: An International Journal, 2, 141–148.

Finnegan, L. P., & Fehr, K. O. (1980). The effects of opiates, sedative-hypnotics, amphetamines, cannabis, and other psychoactive drugs on the fetus and newborn. In O. J. Kalant (Ed.), Alcohol and drug problems in women, vol. 5. New York: Plenum Press.

Finnegan, L. P., Oehlberg, S. M., Regan, D., & Rudrauff, M. E. (1981). Evaluation of parenting, depression, and violence profiles in methadone-maintained women. Child Abuse and Neglect, 5, 267–273.

Finnegan, L. P., & Wapner, R. J. (1987). Narcotic addiction in pregnancy. In J. R. Neibyl (Ed.), Drug use in pregnancy. Philadelphia: Lea & Febiger.

Fontana, V. J. (1983). Report of the preliminary study of child fatalities in New York City. New York, New York: Mayor's Task Force on Child Abuse and Neglect.

Frailberg, S. (1980). Ghosts in the nursery. In S. Frailberg (Ed.), *Clinical studies in infant mental health.* New York: Basic Books.

Freudenberger, H. J. (1980). *Burnout: The high cost of high achievement.* New York: Anchor/Doubleday.

Garcia, S. A. (1989, November). Help or punish pregnant drug users? *Update, Perinatal Addiction Research and Education, 3.*

Gelardo, M. S., & Sanford, E. E. (1987). Child abuse and neglect: A review of the literature. *School Psychology Review, 16* (2), 137–155.

Green, M. (1976). Neonatal withdrawal index: A qualitative method for evaluation of narcotic abstinence in the newborn. In G. Beschner & R. Brotman (Eds.), *Symposium on comprehensive health care for addicted families and their children.* National Institute on Drug Abuse (ADAMHA 017-024-00598-3) (pp. 86–92). Washington, DC: U.S. Government Printing Office.

Green, M., & Suffet, F. (1981). The neonatal narcotic withdrawal index: A device for the improvement of care in the abstinence syndrome. *American Journal of Drug and Alcohol Abuse, 8*(2), 203–213.

Habel, L., Jaye, K., & Lee, J. (1990). Trends in reporting of maternal drug abuse and infant mortality among drug-exposed infants in New York City. *Women and Health, 16*(2), 41–58.

Hanson, B., Beschner, G., Walters, J. M., & Bovelle, E. (1985). *Life with heroin: voices from the inner city.* Lexington, MA: Lexington Books.

Howard, J., Beckwith, L., Rodning, C., & Kropenske, W. (1989). The development of young children of substance-abusing parents: Insights from 7 years of intervention and research. *Zero to Three, a Bulletin of the National Center for Clinical Infant Programs, 9*(5), 8–12.

Hubbard, R. L., Marsden, M. E., Rachal, V. J., Harwood, H. J., Cavanaugh, E. R., & Ginzburg, H. M. (1989). *Drug abuse treatment: A national study of effectiveness.* Chapel Hill: University of North Carolina Press.

Johnson, C. (1990). Testimony before the Select Committee on Children, Youth, and Families, U.S. House of Representatives. Washington, DC: Reach, Inc. Mimeograph.

Johnson, K. (1989). *Trauma in the lives of children: Crisis and stress management techniques for teachers, counselors, and student service professionals.* Claremont, CA: Hunter House.

Joshi, V. V. (1989). Pathology of AIDS in children. *Pathology Annual, 24,* part 1, 225–381.

Juliana, P., Alksne, L., Langrod, J., & Lowinson, J. (1989). *Services for children of substance abusers.* Bronx, NY: Division of Substance Abuse of the Albert Einstein College of Medicine of Yeshiva University.

Karan, L. D. (1989). AIDS prevention and chemical dependency treatment needs of women and their children. *Journal of Psychoactive Drugs, 21*(4), 395–399.

Katz, B. (1989). Natural history and clinical management of the infant born to a mother infected with human immunodeficiency virus. *Seminars in Perinatology, 13*(1), 27–34.

Kaufman, E. (Ed.). (1984). *Power to change: Family case studies in the treatment of alcoholism.* New York: Gardner Press.

Kaufman, E., & Kaufman, P. (Eds.), (1979). *Family therapy of drug and alcohol abuse.* New York: Gardner Press.

Kaestner, E., Frank, B., Marel, R., & Schmeidler, J. (1986). Substance use among females in New York State: Catching up with the males. *Journal of Alcohol and Substance Abuse, 5,* 29–49.

Kaltenbach, K., & Finnegan, L. P. (1988). The influence of the neonatal abstinence syndrome on mother-infant interactions. In E. J. Anthony & C. Chiland (Eds.), *The child in his family: Perilous development. Child raising and identity formation under stress.* New York: Wiley, Interscience.

Khantzian, E. J., & Schneider, R. J. (1985). Addiction, adaptation, and the drug of choice phenomenon: Clinical perspectives. In H. B. Milkman & H. J. Shaffer (Eds.), *The addictions* (pp. 121–130). Lexington, MA: Lexington Books.

Klein, J. (1991, January). A homeless project that works. *New York Magazine.*

Kliman, G. W., Schaeffer, M. H., & Friedman, M. J. (1982). *Preventive mental health services for children entering foster care.* White Plains, NY: Center for Preventive Psychiatry.

Kopp, S. (1972). *If you meet the Buddha on the road, kill him.* New York: Basic Books.

Kugel, B. (1989, October). *The dilemma of permanency planning.* Unpublished manuscript.

Levy, S. J. (1973). *Milieu therapy and individual differences: Some social and clinical variables.* Paper presented at the 81st annual meeting, American Psychological Association, Montreal, Canada.

Levy, S. J. (1975). Sexism in therapy. *Proceedings of the National Conference on Women, Drugs and Alcohol.* National Institute on Drug Abuse. Washington, DC: National Research and Communications.

Levy, S. J. (1982). Multiple substance abuse: Implications for treatment. *Bulletin of the Society of Psychologists in Substance Abuse, 1*(3), 110–113.

Levy, S. J., & Broudy, M. (1975). Sex role differences in the therapeutic community: Moving from sexism to androgeny. *Journal of Psychedelic Drugs, 7*(3), 291–298.

Levy, S. J., & Doyle, K. (1974). Attitudes toward women in a drug-abuse treatment program. *Journal of Drug Issues, 4,* 428–434.

Levy, S. J., & Doyle, K. (1976). Treatment of women in a methadone-maintenance treatment program. In A. Bauman (Ed.), *Women in treatment: Issues and approaches* (pp. 31–46). Arlington, VA: National Drug Abuse Center for Training and Resource Development, National Institute on Drug Abuse.

Lief, N. R. (1977). Some measures of parenting behavior for addicted and non-addicted mothers. In G. Beschner & R. Brotman (Eds.), *Symposium on com-*

prehensive health care for addicted families and their children (National Institute on Drug Abuse, DHEW, Publication No. ADM 77-480, pp. 38–47). Washington, DC: U.S. Government Printing Office.

Lief, N. R. (1981). Parenting and child services for drug-dependent women. In G. Beschner, B. Reed, & J. Mondanaro (Eds.), *Treatment services for drug-dependent women* (National Institute on Drug Abuse, USDHHS Publication No. ADM 81-1177, 1: 455–492). Washington, DC: U.S. Government Printing Office.

Lief, N. R. (1987). A program to help prevent child abuse with drug-abusing parents. *Violence, Aggression, and Terrorism, 1*(4), 403–411.

Lowinson, J. H., & Millman, R. B. (1979). Clinical aspects of methadone-maintenance treatment. In R. L. DuPont, A. Goldstein, & J. O'Donnell (Eds.), *Handbook on drug abuse* (pp. 49–56). Washington, DC: U.S. Government Printing Office.

Madden, J. D., Payne, T. F., & Miller, S. (1986). Maternal cocaine abuse and effect on the newborn. *Pediatrics, 77,* 209–211.

Mahan, S., & Hawkins, J. (1990). *Cocaine mothers and the law.* Paper presented before the American Society of Criminology annual meeting, Baltimore, MD.

Marlatt, G. A., & Fromme, K. (1988). Metaphors for addiction. In S. Peele (Ed.), *Visions of addiction* (pp. 1–24) Lexington, MA: Lexington Books.

Marlatt, G. A., & Gordon, J. R. (1985). *Relapse prevention.* New York: Guilford Press.

Maslow, A. (1954). *Motivation and personality* New York: Harper & Row.

Mayer, J., & Black, R. (1977). Child abuse and neglect in families with an alcohol- or opiate-addicted parent. *Child Abuse and Neglect, 1,* 85–98.

Mitchell, J. L., Brown, G., Williams, S., Abrams, E., & El-Salsa, W. (1981). *Pregnancy, drug addiction, and HIV: The Harlem experience.* Washington, DC: Departments of Obstetrics, Pediatrics, Infectious Disease, Harlem Hospital Center, National Institute on Drug Abuse, Services Research Branch, Institute for Human Resources Research.

Mitchell, J. T. (1983). When disaster strikes: The critical incident stress debriefing process. *Journal of Emergency Medical Services, 8*(1), 36–39.

Morehouse, E. R. (1979). Working in the schools with children of alcoholic parents. *Health and Social Work, 4*(4), 144–162.

Morehouse, E. R., & Richards, T. (1983). An examination of dysfunctional latency-age children of alcoholic parents and problems in intervention. *Children in Contemporary Society, 5*(1).

Naimerman, N., Savage, B., Haskins, B., Lear, J., & Chase, H. (1979). An assessment of the context of sex discrimination by federal recipients in the delivery of health and human developmental services, Phase 2 Report. *Report to the U.S. Department of Health, Education, and Welfare, Office for Civil Rights.* Cambridge, MA: Abt Associates.

National Committee for Prevention of Child Abuse. (1989, February). *NCPCA*

Fact Sheet. (Substance Abuse and Child Abuse, National Committee for Prevention of Child Abuse, No. 14). Washington, DC: Author.

National Council in Disability. (1990). HHS releases report on crack babies. *Focus,* *1, 8.*

New York State Division of Substance Abuse Services (1987). *Establishing services for children of substance abusers: A reference guide for treatment programs.* Albany, NY: Author.

National Institute on Drug Abuse. (1989, June). *NIDA Capsules.* Drug Abuse and Pregnancy (C-89-04).

National Institute on Drug Abuse. (1989–90). *NIDA Notes, 5.*

National Institute on Drug Abuse (1990, July). *NIDA Capsules.* Drug Abuse and AIDS (C-85-4).

O'Gorman, P. (1984). Alateen—why refer? A psychologist's viewpoint. In *Alanon faces alcoholism* (2d ed, pp. 55–62). New York: Alanon Family Group Headquarters.

Oliver-Diaz, P., & Slotwinski, J. (1984). Helping children to help themselves. *Focus on Family and Chemical Dependency,* 7(2), 36–37.

B. Ornelas. (1990, November). Steps in recovery: A program for mothers and their drug-exposed infants. *Update,* Perinatal Addiction, Research, and Education.

Outlook on Substance Abuse in New York State. (1990). Helping addicted mothers cope: PAAM Program, New York State Division of Substance Abuse Services.

Pearlman, P., West, M., & Dalton, J. (1982). Mothers and children together: Parenting in a substance-abuse program. In B. G. Reed, G. Beschner, & J. Mondanaro (Eds.), *Treatment services for drug-dependent women* (National Institute on Drug Abuse, DHHS Publication No. ADM 82-1219, pp. 532–571). Washington, DC: U.S. Government Printing Office.

Peele, S. (1989). *Diseasing of America: Addiction treatment out of control.* Lexington, MA: Lexington Books.

Perinatal Addiction Research and Education. (1989, November). *Update.*

Perinatal Addiction Research and Education. (1990, July). *Update.*

Perska, R., & Smith, J. (1977). Interdisciplinary and transdisciplinary teamwork. In R. Perske and J. Smith (Eds.), *Beyond the ordinary: Towards the development of standardized criteria.* Seattle, WA: American Association for the Education of thhe Severly/Profoundly Handicapped.

Pines, M. (1990). Resilient children: A conversation with Michael Rutter. In P. Chance & T. G. Harris (Eds.), *The best of "Psychology Today."* New York: McGraw-Hill.

Pizzo, P. A. (1989). Emerging concepts in the treatment of HIV infection in children. *Journal of the American Medical Association, 262, 1989–1992.*

Ramos, C., & Stone, W. (1989). *Odyssey House, Inc. Demographic and Statistical Report.* New York City: Odyssey House.

Regan, D. O., Ehrlich, S. M., & Finnegan, L. P. (1987). Infants of drug addicts: At risk for child abuse, neglect, and a placement in foster care. *Neurotoxicology and Teratology, 9,* 315–319.

Reinarman, C., & Levine, H. G. (1989). Crack in context: Politics and media in the making of a drug scare. *Contemporary Drug Problems, 16(4),* 535–577.

Rosenbaum, M. (1979). Difficulties in taking care of business: Women addicts as mothers. *American Journal of Drug and Alcohol Abuse, 6,* 431–446.

Russell, M., Henderson, C., & Blume, S. (1984). Children of alcoholics: A review of the literature. Buffalo, NY: New York State Division of Alcoholism and Alcohol Abuse, Research Institute on Alcoholism.

Rutherford, G. W., Oliva, G. E., Grossman, M., Green, J., Wara, D. W., Shaw, N., Eichenberg, D. F., Wofsky, C. B., Weinstein, D. H., Stroud, F., Sarsfield, E. S., & Werdegar, D. (1987). Guidelines for the control of perinatally transmitted immunodeficiency virus infection and care of infected mothers, infants, and children. *Western Journal of Medicine, 147(1),* 104–107.

Schor, E. L. (1989). Foster care. *Pediatrics in review, 10(7),* 209–215.

Schorr, L. B. (1988). *Within our reach: Breaking the cycle of Disadvantage.* New York: Anchor/Doubleday Books.

Septimus, A. (1989). Psychological aspects of caring for families of infants infected with human immunodeficiency virus. *Seminars in Perinatology, 13(1),* 49–54.

Shaffer, H. J., & Jones, S. B. (1989). *Quitting cocaine: The struggle against impulse.* Lexington, MA: Lexington Books.

Shaffer, H. J., & Milkman, H. B. (Eds.). (1985). Crisis and conflict in the addictions. In *The Addictions* (pp. ix–xviii). Lexington, MA: Lexington Books.

Singer, E. (1970). *Key concepts in psychotherapy* (2d ed.). New York: Basic Books.

Sorensen, J. L. (1990). Addiction and AIDS in the 1990s. *Psychology of Addictive Behaviors, 4(1),* 50–51.

Sowder, B. J., & Burt, M. D. (1980). *Children of heroin addicts: An assessment of health, learning, behavioral, and adjustment problems.* New York: Praeger.

Sowder, B. J., Carnes, Y. M., & Sherman, S. N. (1981). *Children of addicts in surrogate care.* Unpublished manuscript.

Spence, J. T., & Helreich, R. (1973). The Attitudes Toward Women Scale: An objective instrument to measure attitudes toward the rights and roles of women in contemporary society. In *Selected documents in psychology.* Washington, D.C.: Journal Supplement Abstract Service, American Psychological Association.

Stanton, M. D., & T. C. Todd Associates. (1982). *The family therapy of drug abuse and addiction.* New York: Guilford Press.

Starbuck, G. W., Krantzler, N., Forbes, K., & Barnes, V. (1984). Child abuse and neglect on Oahu, Hawaii: Description and analysis of four purported risk factors. *Journal of Developmental and Behavioral Pediatrics, 5(2),* 55–59.

Stimmel, B., Goldberg, J., Reisman, A., Murphy, R. J., & Teets, K. (1982). Fetal outcome in narcotic-dependent women: The importance of the type of maternal narcotic used. *American Journal of Drug and Alcohol Abuse, 9,* 383–395.

Suffet, F., & Brotman, R. (1984). A comprehensive program for pregnant addicts:

Obstetrical, neonatal, and child development outcomes. *International Journal of the Addictions, 19,* 199–219.

Watkins, C. B. (1990). Development of the psychotherapy supervisor. *Psychotherapy: Theory, Research, Practice, Training, 27,* 553–560.

White House Conference for a Drug-Free America. (1988). *Final Report* (Document No. 88-600553). Washington, DC: U.S. Government Printing Office.

Wiley, M. O., & Ray, P. B. (1986). Counseling supervision by developmental level. *Journal of Counseling Psychology, 33,* 439–445.

Woititz, J. G. (1983). *Adult children of alcoholics.* Deerfield Beach, FL: Health Communications.

Wolberg, L. (1977). *The technique of psychotherapy.* New York: Grune & Stratton.

Yablonsky, L. (1965). *Synanon: The tunnel back.* New York: Macmillan.

Yalom, I. D. (1975). *The theory and practice of group psychotherapy* (2d ed.). New York: Basic Books.

Youngstrom, N. (1990). Report calls for tripling drug treatment funding. *American Psychological Association Monitor, 21*(11), 22.

Zimberg, S. (1985). Principles of alcoholism psychotherapy. In S. Zimberg, J. Wallace, & S. Blume (Eds.), *Practical approaches to alcoholism psychotherapy* (2d ed., pp. 3–21). New York: Plenum.

Zuckerman, B., Frank, D. A., Hingson, R., Armard, H., Levenson, S. M., Kayne, H., Parker, S., Uinci, R., Aboagye, K., Fried, L. E., Cabral, H., Timperi, R., & Bauchner, H. (1989). Effects of maternal marijuana and cocaine use on fetal growth. *New England Journal of Medicine, 320,* 762–768.

Index

About the
Authors

Stephen Jay Levy is a psychologist who specializes in the treatment of addictive disorders and has served as director of several leading drug abuse programs, including the Division of Drug Abuse, New Jersey College of Medicine and Dentistry; the Alcoholism Treatment Program, Beth Israel Medical Center, New York City; the Koala Center of Nyack Hospital; and the Rockland County Crack Cocaine Program. Dr. Levy is a certified addiction specialist with the American Academy of Health Care Providers in Addictive Disorders and provides critical incident stress debriefing for emergency service personnel as a mental health consultant to the Emergency Assist Team of Rockland County. He maintains a private practice in Nanuet, New York.

Dr. Levy has served on the faculty of New York University, Hunter College, Empire State College, John Jay College of Criminal Justice, Jersey City State College, New Jersey College of Medicine and Dentistry, and the Mount Sinai School of Medicine. He has been organizing workshops and conferences on addictive behaviors for twenty-four years. In addition to writing numerous professional articles, Dr. Levy is the author of *Managing the Drugs in Your Life* (McGraw-Hill, 1983), editor of *Addictions in the Jewish Community* (Federation of Jewish Philanthropies of New York, 1986), and has recently completed *The Mentally Ill Chemical Abuser: Whose Client?* with Jacqueline Cohen, C.S.W. (Lexington Books, forthcoming).

Eileen Rutter is a board certified diplomate in clinical social work. Currently, she is an administrative supervisor of New York Foundling Hospital, the largest child welfare agency on the East Coast, for which she has developed a treatment model that serves multiply dependent families. She maintains a private practice treating children and families and consults with schools, mental health clinics, and child welfare agencies that focus on the delivery of services to families fighting substance abuse. Mrs. Rutter is also an adjunct professor of psychology at Saint Thomas Aquinas College and provides critical incident stress debriefing for emergency service personnel as a mental health consultant to the Emergency Assist Team of Rockland County. She has achieved recognition as a regional and national workshop leader and is an authoritative speaker who is well known for her expertise and rapport with workshop audiences.